ABOUT THE AUTHOR

NICHOLAS BUNNEY was born and raised on the London/Essex border before moving to study Investment and Financial Risk Management at City University, London. Having spent over a decade working in banking, an unfortunate event led to a fortunate break from work allowing some life changing introspection. What followed is the journey of self-discovery that created the content for his first self-help book, *ABCD*.

Since finishing his studies Nicholas has lived in many vibrant areas of London and the surrounding counties before finally putting down roots in leafy Hockley, Essex. He lives with his wife Candice, two beautiful children, three dogs, and lizard.

To Candice, Max, and Sienna - for making me want to be a better person and still loving me when I'm not!

NICHOLAS BUNNEY PUBLISHING

11 Nursery Drive, Hockley, Essex, SS5 4FH

First published in the Great Britain in 2023 by N J Bunney Publishing.

This Paperback Edition 2023.

ISBN: 978-1-7392855-0-0

Typeset using *Bely* by Roxane Gataud with TypeTogether and *Adrianna* by Chank Co.

Cover and Interior Design by *waynekehoe.com*

Share your ABCD journey on Instagram!

 @abcd_nicholas_bunney

1

PREFACE

'How does one go about eating an elephant? You eat it one bite at a time.'
– Desmond Tutu.[1]

16:30

It's four thirty in the afternoon, and I'm sitting at my desk, lost in so many thoughts that I feel more confused than I have in a long while. Our young puppy is looking at me, hoping for some attention, which is not forthcoming. The kids laugh and bicker audibly from the front room some 10 feet away. They are very happy and loud children who would love nothing more than for me to sneak into the room and throw them on the sofa. However, the sound blurs into the background, and my head spins. I'm numb to the present moment, dwelling on the past and anxious about the future's unknown.

My thoughts are all over the place. Having been offered a promotion at work—and accepting it—the terms have entirely changed, and I've had to reject the offer now, having told my family, colleagues, and friends. Should I stay at the company? What if I never get another shot at the promotion? What would happen if I became redundant? Feeling low, I've helped myself to a whole pack of biscuits and some ice cream, which, in turn, has added some more twists to my spiral as I scold myself for not keeping my promise to lose some of the weight I've gained recently. Maybe I should do a cleanse? Perhaps I could skip dinner? Is my fitness regime really working? Maybe I should start over? I felt like things were going well, but I just shouted at the kids—for laughing and being happy.

How am I supposed to keep all this going? Am I doing a good enough job at anything? Where do I start? What does success even look like? Am I even a good dad? Will the kids love me when they are older, or will they tell their therapists I was awful?

My phone is buzzing about 30 times on the desk while I stew. The regular WhatsApp chats filled with jokes, memes, and plans for meeting for dinner. I can feel myself subconsciously withdrawing from social interactions; I don't deserve the relaxation until I get myself sorted. Let them have fun with their extraordinary lives, and I'll join them when I've got mine sorted. Indeed, once I have everything just right, then I can get back to being a winner. Not this loser who, for some reason, is typing '30-day green tea detox results' into Google.

At that point, the door to my office slowly creaks open, and my wife, having heard my inappropriate sulk at the kids, is standing there with a telling look. The look you give a mate when they have a 'woe is me' moment or after your child tells you that they're having the worst day of their lives because their sister had 4 minutes more than them on their iPad.

'What's going on with you, grumps?' She chuckles.

I try to give the reply my dire situation deserves, one with the magnitude to galvanise my argument that my life is terrible.

'Nothing is going right. I've got to stay in this same job, I'm fat, the kids are going to grow up hating me, my mates are all going out, and I can't be bothered, and I'm almost 40, so my life might as well be over,' I say very maturely (you can hear the world's smallest violin whining in the background). 'It just feels like I've got so much going on and so many things I want to do and achieve. So many changes I want to make to feel like I'm doing a good job of life. But realistically, I'm not getting anywhere near any of them—they seem so far away from my reach.'

'Everyone has a lot on their plate, babe,' she replies, obviously not having heard how much more catastrophic my problems are. 'They can all seem pretty overwhelming when you think of it all at once. Do you know how to eat an elephant?'

'Err, what are you talking about?'

'You eat it one bite at a time. Now, get your arse out here and help with dinner. We've missed you today.'

She was right to chastise me and want to snap me out of it; I had been missing from my life while worrying about doing a good job of it. A bit like sitting in the corner spoiling Christmas Day while worrying about having to wrap the presents for next year's Christmas. We finally went together to see the kids, and I threw them onto the sofa and let their childish joy wash over me. I was back in the room, present, living.

Like so many other times—editor, please delete this part to avoid her seeing it—my wife is right about the elephant. The metaphor reminds me that I'm not special; I'm just human. Modern humans have hundreds, if not thousands, of concerns affecting them at any time, like sleeping better, being fitter, changing jobs, mourning loved ones, and navigating parenthood. These are all part of the human condition. Each of these concerns is an elephant we are trying to eat whole when we should be trying to eat it bit by bit.

My father-in-law had told my wife about this quote from Desmond Tutu in the 2010 documentary *I AM* during her own time of need. It is also a theory advocated by many of history's wisest figures, and as you'll see in this book, many of the good ideas of our ancestors have stood the test of time.

Therefore, it stands to reason that feeling overwhelmed, pressured, and uncertain about where to start are prevalent problems of the human experience.

The hardest thing to take from this incident (that led to me discovering the ABCD framework) is that it occurred AFTER I already thought I knew all the answers. I was 35 years old when I discovered my interest in self-improvement. Since 2017, I had been reading much of the content I will share in *ABCD*, though I hadn't yet realised I needed to not only know it but *apply* it.

I am a husband and father who works a regular 9-5 job like millions of other people in this country and throughout the world. I'm not a guru or psychologist or a councillor or a doctor. I'm not even an author (unless you are reading this right now, then perhaps I am!). I'm just a regular person going through what so many people go through every day.

I experienced this fast-paced, modern life full of overexposure and endless possibilities and felt a little lost. Messages everywhere seemed to be telling me that to be happy with my life, I needed to have six-pack abs, buy cryptocurrency, holiday seven times a year while maintaining a beautiful home, see all my friends regularly, take up new hobbies, and basically live my 'best life' - Oh, and call my mum once in a while!

It was just too much for anyone to do all at once–I was overwhelmed to the point of inaction.

Like many people, I had an idea of what and where I wanted to be in life. In almost any aspect of my life, I could tell you what the end goal was:

- To be a good partner.
- To be a good parent.
- To be in good physical shape.
- To sort the house out.
- To be a little better off.
- To have a happy social life.
- To find something I'm good at.
- To write a book.

The goals all felt massive when viewed at such a high level.

Even though most people have a list like this, we have no idea how to succeed at our goals. We often overestimate our control of the outcomes of plans, which can lead to letting them control us and then being disappointed when they are unsuccessful. Furthermore, we also don't know WHY these are goals. We take so much outside influence from our past, the media, our social groups, and our preconceptions of happiness that we unconsciously adopt the issues we want to solve and the goals we want to achieve. *Our values and goals are handed to us.* Even if we decide to act, the objectives are so large, that even starting the journey is daunting.

This need not be the case. In most cases, these targets are made up of many smaller parts and single actions that, when done consistently, add up to the larger goal. The achievement is the sum of its parts.

I had worked in London since I left university, catching the same train to Liverpool Street each day to the same office to do the same things with the same people. Naturally, I often thought about the bigger picture. On many occasions, I would start a gym regimen with a lofty target like *Six Pack for Holiday* or similar career goal such as *Double My Salary by 35*. Not much thought went into why I wanted these objectives and how to get there, and as seen by so many of us, the plans fell flat on their face when life and fate got in the way. I wasn't motivated or inspired enough to create the consistency required or seek the knowledge of how. Often, when something that I perceived to be more important arose, I would be distracted. Usually, the more important thing was a different goal that, driven by some social media trend etc., had become the new big thing I needed to focus on. I was flip-flopping between all the things I thought I wanted, making constant attempts and restarts, often self-sabotaging my results by moving the goalposts on myself—a jack of all trades and a master of none.

I believe this is a very common place for humans to find themselves. We're so overexposed to the modern world that we're often fed things that we supposedly *need*. We find it harder to obtain happiness or even to define what that is, and we choose the instant gratification of 'joy' from drinking alcohol, eating junk, watching endless TV, scrolling social media, or chatting to matches on dating apps. But this isn't fulfilling to us—not long-term, anyway. Once the buzz passes, we're still uncertain about where we fit in and what we want.

There are no quick fixes.

What is needed is a fair assessment of our genuine values or goals to find fewer authentic targets that we can focus on more intently as part of our principles or value systems. Then we can assess our level of control over the outcomes. If we can't control them, we can see them as *preferred* goals, where we would like to succeed but understand not to let our happiness rely on the outcomes. Therefore, it is so important to have balance and sustainability in what we aim for and our actions—we can *enjoy the journey*. From there, we can drill down into the smaller, far easier to comprehend actions we could do more regularly. Now daunting objectives are reached through completion of easily accomplished smaller steps.

For example, if you told a young, aspiring music student that you wanted them to be a Grade 8 Piano player within five years, they would find it hard to imagine reaching that lofty target. However, you can break that target down into smaller, more short-term goals. If you told that same student to learn a specific piece of music in a specific amount of time, or if you told them to play the piano 20 minutes per day, that larger goal becomes more achievable. Over time, those minor achievements culminate in playing to a Grade 8 standard.

This logic is clear when learning a particular skill. But most people have so much exposure to the world around them and their internal stories about themselves that the list of possible goals is endless and is often more existential or complex than learning to play the piano. So, what do you do?

You need to reflect on what is truly important to you. Once you do that, you can prioritise your goals and move toward them.

The fact I wasn't being authentic was becoming increasingly apparent in my life. I had a job I hated, and I felt knackered, unhealthy, and generally unhappy. My mother-in-law with terminal cancer was living with us, creating unintentional tension between my wife and me. Something had to change, and I needed to work out what I genuinely wanted for myself and my future. I needed to understand why life seemed so overwhelming. I needed to decide the difference between my priorities and all the noise. I needed to learn what happiness looked like.

So, I started to read.

Like most people looking for answers, I read books that appeared on many self-help best sellers' lists. They were a good starting point and directed my attention to the possibility that there was a way to make changes in your life. They were all full of hope, and I noticed they shared some similar themes about mindset, being present, and finding authenticity in your life. Each one sent me further down a rabbit hole, seeking more and more information. I read books on stoic philosophy, Cognitive Behavioural Therapy (CBT), addiction, happiness, efficiency, powerful habits, flow, and many other subjects. When something resonated with me, I researched it, listened to podcasts, and made endless notes as my knowledge of these subjects grew.

Soon after, my mother-in-law passed away, and I finally left my job to support my wife through that challenging time. The feeling of responsibility for my grieving wife was powerful. I'd always been told that in the event of an emergency, I had to secure my mask before those of others. It reminds me of the quote, 'You cannot serve from an empty vessel.' This was an opportunity for me to take some control over my life to be stronger for someone else. So, I dived headfirst into studying all these subjects that had taken hold of me. I decided to put on my mask.

Whilst doing so, I noticed that some common themes ran throughout most of the material I found, A – B – C - D:

Authenticity – Balance – Consistency - Discipline

It struck me that these key messages repeated, whether from an ancient philosopher, self-help guru, modern therapist, successful athlete, or motivational speaker. It appears that the wise of each generation had found the same ideas. It was straightforward to relate these lessons to almost every area of my life. Like the concept of the collective unconscious–that there are common themes and experiences that occur to mankind throughout time. It is because the themes and truths that stand the test of time are those that closely relate to the daily challenges faced by most humans through the ages.

I started applying some of what I had learned and noticed a fantastic thing. Without much work, I began feeling less overwhelmed. I had more intention and more of a grip on what was important to me and what wasn't. When I held my long list up to the scrutiny of authenticity, I realised that much of what I was worried about either wasn't of value to me or wasn't in my power to solve. This left me with much more mental energy to focus on areas more closely aligned to my own slowly emerging values and principles. There was quiet a confidence and sense of calm for the first time in many years. Of course, it wasn't perfect, but it was a damn sight better than what I'd been working with previously.

I wanted to shout all the lessons I'd learned from the rooftops. I recommended books to friends and family, hoping they would all find them equally life-changing, and we could all be smug happy enlightened legends together!

Communicating these ideas was one thing, but how would people decide how to use them? Unfortunately, I was asking people already facing many massive challenges to take on yet another. My short-lived career as a motivational speaker was over!

I soon realised that most people needed structure and narrative around these ideas and subjects. A resource that has already curated the information most common and pertinent to modern life. They wanted a process they could follow to get from where they were to where they wanted to be. A method they could apply to any number of issues they had to reasonably assess, prioritise, and plot a path toward them.

Ironically, it turned out that 'most people' included *myself*. Even though I had these ideas and themes rolling around my brain and in various notebooks, I'd still not found a way of knowing what to apply, nor did I know when and how to use them logically and simply. More work was needed to create a framework that was robust and relatable to any area of my life that would become challenging (which is all of it!).

So, after five years of trial and error in my life, many ups and downs and a valuable piece of elephant-shaped advice from my wife, I have produced what I believe is just that.

In this book, I will:

- Show why authenticity, balance, consistency, and discipline are valuable to your life.
- Give you a more useful perspective on happiness.
- Help you choose more authentic goals and values.
- Promote the balance you can rely on to enjoy your journey.
- Outline the techniques that I have used to achieve this more consistently.
- Help you use 'failures' to advance, seeing discipline as a virtue.
- Show you that these techniques can be used for most areas of life.
- Allow you to help others now that you have more capacity to do so.

The aim is not to give a shortcut or create a social media style meme that is treated as 'throwaway'. The process takes some work and introspection that is generally missing from the short, sweet pieces of advice we see from so many sources today. Many of which give us food for thought but rarely leads to the sort of changes we are hoping for. Using *ABCD* along with a little work will help you find a more considered life where you act in line with your values and principles. Important changes can then be made, where necessary, from this sold base.

Absolutely anyone can use this book. Almost all of us face issues in our lives. We all have goals we'd like to achieve. We all have challenges in the short, medium, and long term. But unfortunately, very few of us have the ability or tools to see what's important and focus on that with genuine intention.

Many of us face the sort of challenges that caused me to spiral at my desk, feeling overwhelmed. Like me we may also have access to much of the information presented in this book. I had already spent years reading and studying these ideas and themes. Lockdowns from coronavirus in the UK and the pressure of working from home and socialising far less had caused me to feel lost and unsure of where to start to get back on track. Even with my knowledge, I didn't have the process to apply when life took unexpected turns—like a global pandemic. I'd happily and rather smugly floated through a few years, thinking I had nailed it. Then in 2020, I realised I needed to make this more accessible and structured, primarily just for myself.

So, I set out to create this book and the process/ideas within it as a guide for me and others on how to improve my life and start hitting the goals I truly believed in and deal with the issues that mattered whilst letting the rest go. Life is rarely perfect, and this book doesn't claim it ever will be, but current events, including coronavirus, have brought to our attention the need to be able to decipher our priorities – life is too short to be working so hard for things that we do not need/want. Not seeing loved ones and friends for long periods and feeling like life was standing still has sharpened the need for change. After five years of research, I've compiled lessons and tools I've learned into one place. This information can be applied to many areas of life whether big or small.

Before I decided to build write *ABCD*, I didn't have had it all together, none of us do. Too many people spend their lives waiting for 'yet.' A point in their life where the conditions will be perfect for taking some action. Well, that time rarely comes, and so many of us spend our time wishing we could do what we'd love to but can't because one or more factors are not exactly right. We're waiting for *perfection.*

Knowing I am far from perfect, I decided to take some action and build the ABCD framework. It was important to bring together what I had learned in a way it could be used, firstly by me and then hopefully by others. It was as good a time as any to start.

'A man who develops himself is born twice'

– Argentine proverb.

'Empty cans make the most noise!'

– My dad telling me to stop acting like I know everything!

NICHOLAS BUNNEY

ABCD

FINDING HAPPINESS
THROUGH AWARENESS, VALUES,
PRINCIPLES, AND ACTIONS

CONTENTS

2

INTRODUCTION

'I undertook to conquer myself rather than fortune, and to alter my desires rather than change the order of the world, and to accustom myself to believe that nothing is entirely in our power except our own thoughts.'[2]
— **René Descartes.**

HAPPINESS AND FINDING FRAMEWORKS

IF WE ACCEPT THAT THE WORLD is a busy place and that we are overexposed to various points of data, how do we make sense of it all? How do we work out what our problems even are or whether they exist at all? How can we reframe our judgments to make sure we are only looking for solutions that are in our control? How do we prioritise all our hopes and dreams into realistic and authentic goals?

The answer is with a framework that helps us structure our understanding and provides us with the tools for success. One built on the awareness of why we have certain wants and problems that we feel the need to address. It's critical to identify the areas of focus in our lives that will genuinely make us happier and differentiate these areas from those we perceive to be important, but perhaps shouldn't take the priority we afford them.

But first the starting point is a philosophical one. If we take a step back and consider how we think and feel about happiness, the process becomes clearer.

WHAT DO WE MEAN BY HAPPINESS?

This question on happiness repeats in literature throughout the ages. It could be argued that in the modern era, especially in this information-heavy time we live in today, much

---

2 Descartes, R. (1637) *Discourse on the Method of Rightly Conducting One's Reason and of Seeking Truth in the Sciences.*

of the 'positive thinking' and 'goal setting' doctrines that are promoted by the self-help community are making us miserable. The many popular self-help books' suggestions that we can do anything if we set our mind to it puts all the blame for possible failures on us. In Derren Brown's brilliant book, *Happy—Why more or less everything is absolutely fine*, the magician cum philosopher uses the example of opening a coffee shop:

'We are so embroiled in the rhetoric of self-belief that to apply any qualification to the mantra "Go on! You can do anything!" seems to be actively denying people their chance of happiness. Yet when we warn, "This may not work out," we are very supportive at heart. We are asking the person to set aside, for a moment, their single-minded, emotive language of happiness (opening a coffee shop). We are reminded that their *overarching* happiness is independent of a successful café venture. We are not naysaying. We are pointing to a potentially deeper level of happiness and saying, "If this doesn't work out, as it may not, *irrespective of your enthusiasm*, there is more in life that can make you happy. Don't attach too much to this one goal."'[3]

Brown argues that if we put too much importance into what we are striving for without consideration to why and apply excessive pressure on ourselves as the sole architects of these outcomes, we feel overwhelmed and unhappy. Does this sound familiar?

Social media and other inputs on our daily lives leave us feeling like failures because we aren't *smashing our goals, living our best lives,* or *loving life*. Most content we see today is viewed through several filters (both metaphorical and technological) that can obscure the reality. It is not real-life uncut; we know this, although our minds often take information at face value. The person with several businesses, the friend who appears to be doing better than we are, the family member who has it all figured out, or the couple who is on holiday ten times a year. These are only fractions of the whole picture that are reinforced by the assumptions we make or omissions by others. We'll look more at social media later, but it's safe to say that when it is not used to enhance our life, there's a chance it adds to our perception of self-failure.

Even without these external factors, humans tend to fill our own *story* with the information we receive from the complex world around us. By this, I mean we make assumptions from our past experiences—often influenced by our parents—to fill the gaps and make sense of moments in the present. These range from simple self-preservation, like a person bitten by a dog as a child, feeling fear at the sound of a dog's bark – to much more ingrained psychological reasoning. For example, someone who's partner cheated and often took their phone with them to shower may feel residual suspicions of this reasonably normal behaviour in a new partner.

These same problems have been inherent to the human condition for millennia and that the world's greatest thinkers throughout history have sought answers to the difficulty and

---

3 Brown, D. (2016) *Happy: Why more or less everything is absolutely fine.*

upset these inauthentic tales inflict on us. Most importantly, these thinkers (from the Stoics to the modern day) tend to reach the same ideas, which are repeated through religions, scientific studies, philosophy, 12-step fellowships, and even—although crudely—in some of the self-care memes that pop up in your feed today.

Many of these issues come from a lack of consideration for and understanding of the level of control we have over our lives. We believe that we are solely responsible for the majority of what happens to us. Coupling the filtered versions of others' lives we see with this perception of control; we create a multitude of negativity for ourselves.

'I didn't get the job *because I'm useless*.'

'He left me *because I'm not good in bed*.'

'I'm not achieving my goals *because I'm a failure*.'

The fact of the matter is that we have very little control at all and often underestimate how insignificant a lot of what we do is. Of course, this is meant to be slightly jarring, but the idea is solid. In this universe, we have very little direct control. We may have some partial control over things outside of us, a bit like your role in a game of pool, but we can't affect 100% of the result if there is an external influence.

'The chief task in life is simply this: to identify and separate matters so that I can say clearly to myself which are externals not under my control and which have to do with the choices I control. Where then do I look for good and evil? Not to uncontrollable externals, but within myself to the choices that are my own...'[4]
– Epictetus.

As Stoic philosopher Epictetus says, we have control over only two things: our THOUGHTS and ACTIONS – that's it.

Sounds defeatist, right? We float on this rock in space, and we can't control any of it... great! I can already hear readers collectively throwing this book in the bin!

However, this idea holds weight if we apply it to the problems that we face. Relinquishing control is more commonly referred to as *letting go*. If we focus only on what we have influence over and accept everything else, we find a sense of calm. We begin to have fewer problems overall. Particularly if they concern the past or future, of which even our thoughts and actions are out of our control because we can only live in the present. We come to find that much of the anxiety we experience is caused by how we interpret events, rather than the events themselves. These events are also subject to some 'editing' in our heads.

---

4 Epictetus. (c108AD) *Discourses.*

As Shakespeare's hero Hamlet reminds himself when imprisoned, 'There is nothing either good or bad, but thinking makes it so.'[5] We can see some truth to this.

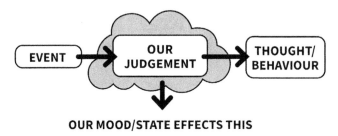

OUR MOOD/STATE EFFECTS THIS

Fig 2.1 – Our Judgement between Event and Action

We take an event, say, failing to secure a job from a recent interview, and between this event and our response—either mental or physical—there is a *gap*, a moment where our mind adds to these first impressions (see fig 2.1). It takes our past experiences, outside influences, and current mood and creates a judgement of events from which we choose our responses. For example, the interviewer didn't like you, therefore you are unlikeable. Our response is to this *thought* rather than the *event* itself.

You might become sad or lose confidence. You might be angry with yourself for being such an unlikeable person and even give up on your job search. The only fact is that you didn't get a job. If you did your best, there is nothing more to worry about. There may have been a superior candidate. You might have been considered and just lost out. You may have reminded them of a previous employee they recently let go of. None of these valid reasons for them to make their decision is a reflection on you. The actions of these interviewers are not in your control, and so they must remain external to any happiness you feel. There are 100s of reasons you might not have got the job.[6]

Many successful people attribute their successes to the more relaxed feeling that remains when we relinquish control. Speaking of the achievements he saw later in his career, *Breaking Bad* star Bryan Cranston said, 'I learned long ago to focus on things you can control and don't even pay attention to things you don't.'

You will most likely be fully aware of this. Unfortunately, we are not very good at taking advice—especially from ourselves. Yet, if a friend were to approach you with their concern around similar interview feedback, you would try to help them see that their personality likely didn't cause the issue.

Why don't we apply this reasoning to ourselves?

5 Shakespeare, W. (c1599-1601) *The Tragedy of Hamlet, Prince of Denmark.*
6 A colleague of mine once was so distracted during an interview by the need to visit the bathroom that he couldn't even remember the candidate's name!

Igor Grossman and Ethan Kross conducted a series of experiments to explore *Solomon's Paradox*, a phenomenon they named after King Solomon, who ruined his kingdom with poor decisions. They showed that people are more reasonable when reviewing problems that they're distanced from.

In one of the studies, 'Participants who were in a long-term romantic relationship were randomly assigned to reflect on a situation in which either their romantic partner cheated on them (*self-condition*), or their best friend's romantic partner cheated on their friend (*other condition*). They were then asked to reason about how their relationship or their friend's relationship, respectively, would unfold in the future and to answer questions designed to measure wise reasoning.'[7]

They discovered an asymmetry between reasonably assessing one's problems and those of others. Further studies proved that participants could remove this asymmetry by self-distancing and have more measured and wise responses to issues of their own.

Studies like these and personal experience show us that some self-distancing is required when facing a problem or challenge. Sometimes this comes in the shape of considering our control over the situation. Doing so will reveal that we don't need to be so immersed in the outcomes. Other times, the problem will be directly controlled by us, and to plan ahead, it will be essential to create this distance for ourselves. Breathing and meditation can help us produce some of this space ready for when needed. Recalling the diagram above around our responses and judgements of events, we are trying to create a *mindfulness gap*.[8]

However it is achieved, we could all benefit from slowing down our reactions. The ability to take a couple of breaths and feel them leave our bodies. Then recall the previous illustration and ask ourselves the below question to assist us in letting go and being more present with the situation. We can put our concerns into perspective.

'DO I HAVE A PROBLEM RIGHT NOW?'

In an early iteration of this book, when it was just a booklet for my own reference, there was the below decision tree (fig 2.2). I found it helpful both then and now as a first step to assess my current state, and it also proved fruitful for the rest of this book.

---

7 Grossman, I. and Kross, E. – (2014) 'Exploring Solomon's Paradox: Self Distancing Eliminates the Self-Other Asymmetry in Wise Reasoning About Close Relationships in Younger and Older Adults' – *Psychological Science*, Vol.25, Issue 8.

8 A second or two between the event/trigger and our response to it, making us more reasonable. I've practised some meditation (a good place to start is the Headspace app), and I have found it to be instrumental in creating this space; the ability to take a breath and sit with a feeling is powerful. There are many ways to do this, so it's essential to find what works for you.

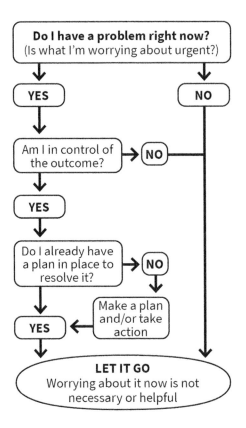

Fig 2.2 – An Important Question

These simple questions helped me realise that while we believe we are inundated with problems and overwhelmed by demands, we often needn't be anxious in the present. My first encounter with this idea came from reading *Happy*. Derren Brown's book is wonderfully insightful and played a pivotal role in the self-education and paradigm shift in my life.

One idea that has stayed with me more than most was created by a 19th Century German philosopher named Artur Schopenhauer. His idea is of a graph that plots any person's hopes, desires, and wishes on one axis (Y) – how we want the world to be. On the opposite axis is how the world actually is (X).

Schopenhauer—and, in turn, Brown—show that when we have unrealistic views on how the world should be, we to pull the graph's line towards the Y axis. However, because the true line of our life's course is not totally in our control, it will sometimes swing towards the X axis and fate (see fig 2.3).

The more we try to assert influence over elements of our life that sit outside our control, the more disturbances we create. We are fighting with the world around us and causing ourselves to be unhappy, disappointed, and frustrated.

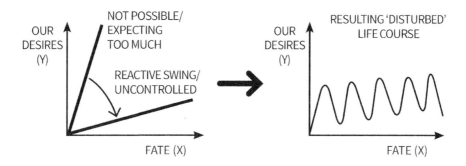

Fig 2.3 – Forcing Control Results in Disturbances

We may even actively try to make ourselves happy to move the line back in our favour with small pleasures or vices. As anyone who has ever bought a new expensive item of clothing to 'treat themselves,' can testify, the buzz is short-lived, and our true emotions soon resurface. The move between our own wishes and fate can lead to the uncomfortable and exhausting cycle of disturbances as we battle against things we cannot control (see fig 2.3).

When we relinquish control of events outside our influence, and we pay a little more attention to our thoughts (particularly by improving our responses/judgements), the course of our lives follows a straighter line between the two axes. We have a more balanced and reasonable expectation of the world and our place in it – we face less disappointments and are happier.

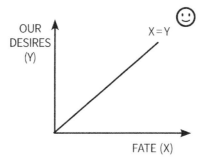

Fig 2.4[9] - X=Y

'The Diagonal,' as Schopenhauer calls it, is where X=Y (see fig 2.4). Where we feel the least disturbance and are most content. I believe it is a critical piece of thinking when considering how to apply balance in our hectic lives.

9 Brown, D. (2016) *Happy: Why more or less everything is absolutely fine.* (adapted diagram).

> *'Events and our chief aims can be in most cases compared to two forces that pull in different directions, their resultant diagonal being the course of our life.'[10]*
> – *Artur Schopenhauer.*

Brown continues this thought:

'We are told to live our lives by focusing on the future and by believing in ourselves at all costs. The result, too often, is waste and frustration. By projecting ourselves always into the hereafter we miss out on the present, on knowing ourselves and the richness of the current moment. By trying to control what we can't, we all but guarantee frustration and disappointment.

Is this the life we wish to lead?'[11]

This was the first revelation in my self-help journey and one of the cornerstones of the ABCD framework. We can react differently, ignore our old story, and be more content and happier. By letting go more often, we realise the difference between a real problem and one perceived by our irrational judgements of events and ourselves. We stop adding to first impressions and take circumstances, concerns, and goals at face value. Sometimes life is just how it is – and to be happy we must accept that.

Let's take this understanding and look at ideas of goal setting and positive thinking, we realise that if we don't succeed as we would want all of the time, then we are not failures. The world is not set up for our success, and it would be silly to think that it is. So, at any moment, whatever we would like to happen in our lives is competing with what the world has in store for us. As such, we should realise that we are fallible human beings in a world that carries on exactly how it pleases without a single concern for our hopes and dreams and be a lot more flexible with the outcomes observed in our lives.

At this point, it's essential to discuss wants and desires. Later in the book, we will see a methodology for deciding our core values, but here we can discuss the subject more broadly. When thinking about happiness, we could also take a moment to consider where our goals fit into the overall picture. Scientific studies for years have concentrated on how our happiness is affected by what we attain and achieve. Most famously, Abraham Maslow created the *Hierarchy of Needs* that shows that what a person desires changes depending on what other needs are met. While there is a definite initial response to a change in fortunes (like a lottery win), this is a short-lived joy that we become quickly accustomed to and adjust to the expectations of our standard of life.

---

10   Schopenhauer, A. (1851) *Councils and Maxims.*
11   Brown, D. (2016) *Happy: Why more or less everything is absolutely fine.*

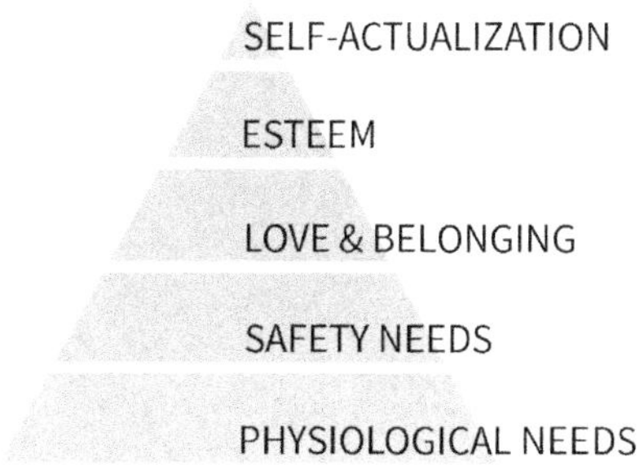

SELF-ACTUALIZATION

ESTEEM

LOVE & BELONGING

SAFETY NEEDS

PHYSIOLOGICAL NEEDS

Fig 2.5 - Maslow's Hierarchy of Needs[12]

In Abraham Maslow's 'Hierarchy of Needs Pyramid,' physiological and safety-related needs are the foundation.

These basic needs, such as food, shelter, and safety, are critical for life—other needs wain in importance in comparison. The theory is that someone's immediate concerns will be to keep their current level of needs met or to reach the level above where they are. If you don't have the basic needs to survive, your motivation to acquire them is enormous. In contrast, if physiological, safety and love needs are met, you may start to feel a need for improvements in your esteem and stature. People cannot even imagine the need for levels too far outside their current situation. A homeless person, for example, is unlikely to have any care in the world about how they can be more self-actualised if they are struggling to find their next meal.

It's also well-documented that after a person's financial level reaches a level that covers these basic needs, the less correlated happiness is with wealth. Tales of miserable million-aires and overworked executives losing relationships with family are common and packed with warnings.

In basic terms, as Greek Philosopher, Epicurus said, 'He who is not satisfied with a little is satisfied with nothing.'

Straightforward goals that affect our lives in significant and less materialistic ways are often those that bring about the most contentedness. If the authentic review of your situation allows you to take the pressure off yourself and be grateful for where you are in life, that is a brilliant outcome. Just think about how amazing it would be only to have a few smaller goals that were sustainable and enriched your life. No more striving for pointless targets because other people have/want them. No more wrestling with outcomes you can't control. That would be an improvement in most of our lives. It certainly was for me, as I lowered my expectations of goals and others around me, I could refine what I put my efforts into, and the results were fantastic.

---

12 Maslow, A. H. (1943) 'A Theory of Human Motivation' - *Psychological Review*, 50, 370-396.

The Stoics coined the term *Amor Fati*, which translates to 'Loving Fate'. The idea is that if we're indeed in control of our thoughts and aware of what we can control, then we can come to LOVE fate. We can smile and face daily struggles with good humour, even when they don't align with our desires. The reason is that we aren't in control, and as such, what has occurred has done so because the world (insert nature, fate, God, or your preference) just IS. Doing anything other than smiling and accepting this puts your happiness in the hands of something external, which is the recipe for disappointment.

I won't go as far as saying that we can all smile at the train delay that made us miss the job interview or have a little giggle when we are diagnosed with some horrible disease. However, the awareness of the ideas discussed here can act as an optimistic alternative to the frustrated state we often find ourselves in. It might be challenging to see in the moment, but with practice, it will be possible to reframe the situation into something we can learn from or see: 'When one door closes, another door opens.' It is not impossible to imagine ourselves displaying this mindset. As Ryan Holiday tells us in *The Obstacle is the Way*, many have done so in the face of colossal adversity:

'Toussaint Louverture, the former Haitian slave, turned general, so exasperated his French enemies that they once remarked: *"Cet homme fait donc l'ouverture partout"* ("This man makes an opening everywhere"). He was so fluid, so uncontainable, he was actually given the surname Louverture, meaning 'the opening.' It makes sense. Everything in his life had been an obstacle, and he turned as many of his experiences as he could into openings.'[13]

We can begin to concern ourselves only with goals we can influence, making an enjoyable journey more important than ever before. We don't hand control of our happiness to others but appreciate more of what we already have. We can set our actions so that we don't neglect the present for the future result, rendering ourselves miserable. If the thing we would like to happen does, then that's a bonus...if not, then we accept it's not in our control and take happiness from the part we played.

It's no surprise that when you take this approach, success is more likely.

The ideas we have discussed so far make up the three main Stoic Principles.

CONTROL YOUR JUDGEMENTS

Stop your thoughts causing disturbances by applying reason and not adding to first impressions of external events. This is your 'inner citadel'[14] that cannot be taken or controlled by anyone else.

---

13 Holiday, R. (2014) *The Obstacle is the Way.*
14 Metaphor often used in Stoicism to symbolise thing controlled by ourselves only as being within the walls of a secure castle

CONTROL YOUR ACTIONS

Act with virtue and in line with these reasoned judgements of the world around us. Behave like the person you are at your centre, not dictated to by external events outside our control.

ACCEPT FATE

Accept that you don't control the world and be grateful for what happens, as it is primarily out of your control. Amor Fati. Where you have some control, do your part as best as possible, regardless of the outcome. Here we are effectively *letting go*, and by relinquishing control, we remove vast amounts of stress from our lives.

I'm not professing to be a perfect Stoic, but I find these principles helpful and believe you will too. No matter how the contents of this book find you, I hope you can find different perspectives on how to approach life instead of putting excessive pressure on yourself.

This new perspective allows us to assess problems and choose authentic goals. They are meaningful to us and not selected from the lives of others. Efficiency and often even success increases when we limit our focus to the most meaningful areas of our lives.

The view of happiness as endless sunshine and rainbows is flawed.

Happiness is more akin to contentment, the removal of disturbances to our own sense of self. Instead of searching for stimulus to *make* us happy, we can *choose* to be.

Be rational in our judgements.

Be present in the moment.

Be willing to relinquish control and let go.

Be able to meet our basic needs.

Be flexible and loving with ourselves.

Be *happy*.

BUILDING A FRAMEWORK

What can we do next?

We have taken a good look at what happiness means. It's important to note here that a change of perspective is hard. An over-excited author summarising several ideas over 3/4 pages is not an instant cure to all disappointment. Also, having read the literature several times, I still regularly throw my toys out of the pram when life doesn't bow to my every command. You might not find the ideas above to be of much use, or you may want to go and do your own reading to formulate your own views. Either is perfectly fine for our framework. What's critical is acknowledging that we can sometimes have a misguided view of problems, and every ambition is an indication of what will make us happy. Many of these issues/goals are not entirely within our control. So, we must choose what we focus our precious time on and what we can let go of, so we have more time and effort to put into what matters...with a big slice of that being enjoying our lives just as they are with a little less self-criticism.

Reading this book, you will learn the ABCD framework:

AUTHENTICITY

- Assess the challenges you are facing and their importance.
- Find the goals that fit your core values and know why you want to achieve them.
- Understand the five main areas of your life and prioritise these areas.
- Realise that is it easier to work towards goals that are authentic.

BALANCE

- Approach your life with balance wherever possible accepting what you can't control.
- Set your sights on targets that can be achieved with sustainable actions.
- Be flexible in your expectations for yourself and the world around you.
- Enjoy more of your life now and spend less time fixated on future outcomes.

CONSISTENCY

- Break your value-driven goals into the next small steps you need to take.
- Learn that when we focus only on what is important to ourselves (not others or our past stories) and act with intention, we discover these small next steps are easily within our capabilities.
- Find a serene *flow state* where you have balanced your ability and the challenges faced.
- Understand that you often fail in your aims because you lack the required consistency.
- By having authentic and balanced goals, you are more likely to find this consistency.

DISCIPLINE

- See why keeping promises to yourself is the biggest confidence booster and reinforces the fact that discipline is a virtue.
- Create habits that encourage and build a high frustration tolerance, hard work is easier for things that you genuinely value.

- Understand that failures are natural and why that's a good thing; we can take stock and evaluate what is important.
- Appreciate that hard work and effort bring us more genuine contentedness than short-lived joy.
- Stop worrying about so many issues that you used to worry about and create mental space to be more present and flexible with yourself and your loved ones.

VALUES AND PRINCIPLES FRAMEWORK

- Create your own framework to define all the above, monitor your progress at the scrutiny level you can decide, and allow total flexibility to reframe or change goals as life requires.
- With the end in mind, you can break down the goals and solutions you have chosen into small next steps – the actions needed, that add up to your larger goals.

After ingesting so much valuable information and finally opening my eyes, I still had a problem. I still felt like I was a failure and completely overwhelmed by the fact that I had not transformed my life during the reflective time of the COVID-19 Lockdowns. Even though I had so much knowledge at my fingertips, I still felt as far away from my goals as I ever did. As I mentioned in my *Preface*, having ideas is only half of the battle. We need structure and tools to bring those ideas to life.

I created ABCD to provide me with that structure – I turned knowledge into action and am the happiest I've ever been. This took multiple attempts and much trial and error. Hopefully the hard work and experiences that I have had can now provide something relatable and of value to you.

Within meditation, there is a metaphor where we imagine ourselves walking down a familiar road on a typical day, and then out of nowhere, we are at the bottom of a dark hole. We consider, 'How did I get down here?' before trying to get out of the hole and back to the road. The metaphor is comparing the hole to problematic situations we face in our life. Sometimes we find ourselves behaving or struggling negatively purely because we've done it so often that we don't see it coming. Meditation aims to increase the time between certain triggers and our behaviours (the judgement gap we saw previously), to find a simple and self-compassionate path around the hole in the road.

> *'Chapter I*
> *I walk down the street.*
> *There is a deep hole in the sidewalk.*
> *I fall in.*
> *I am lost ...I am helpless.*
> *It isn't my fault.*
> *It takes me forever to find a way out.*
> **Chapter II**
> *I walk down the same street.*
> *There is a deep hole in the sidewalk.*
> *I pretend I don't see it.*
> *I fall in again.*
> *I can't believe I am in the same place.*
> *But it isn't my fault.*
> *It still takes a long time to get out.*
> **Chapter III**
> *I walk down the same street.*
> *There is a deep hole in the sidewalk.*
> *I see it is there.*
> *I still fall in ...it's a habit.*
> *My eyes are open.*
> *I know where I am.*
> *It is my fault.*
> *I get out immediately.*
> **Chapter IV**
> *I walk down the same street.*
> *There is a deep hole in the sidewalk.*
> *I walk around it.*
> *Chapter V*
> *I walk down another street.'*[15]

The lessons and techniques within the ABCD framework will contribute to the process that allows you to see the hole and walk around it. To change behaviours and outcomes that are causing you pain, increase the quality of your lives, and ultimately find the different streets on which you are happiest.

Throughout *ABCD*, I will provide areas where you can pause for thought and make some notes for yourself. This way, you can write down anything that comes to mind that you can later use within your own ABCD Framework.

---

[15] Nelson, P (1977) 'Autobiography in Five Short Chapters' - *There's a Hole in My Sidewalk: The Romance of Self-Discovery*

Pause for Thought – Please take time to make some notes:

3

SOLUTIONS - HOW CAN *ABCD* HELP?

'To get something you never had, you have to do something you never did.'[16]
– Denzel Washington.

WHAT ARE WE TRYING TO SOLVE?

As you've likely inferred thus far, we're overexposed to information. We have the extraordinary opportunity to learn at any moment—knowledge is consistently at our fingertips. Though the endless possibilities generate excitement for the modern era, it does tend clash with the human condition. It is instinctive for us to piece together a narrative of our lives and our place in the world. Throughout human evolution, these stories have afforded us the vital connection of thoughts and events to allow cognitive growth, form societies that support us, and fill gaps in findings to encourage further scientific discovery. This ability to quickly interpret information has been an incredible tool that differentiates humans from animals. It's the basis for human reasoning, but it's not necessarily compatible with this world we live in today.

Motivational speaker and stuck elevator magician, Tony Robbins[17] regularly speaks about what he calls the *Six Human Needs*:

* Certainty
* Variety
* Significance
* Love/Connection
* Growth
* Contribution[18]

---

16 University of Pennsylvania Commencement Address – Denzel Washington (2011)
17 Watch the movie Shallow Hal if this reference stumps you!
18 *TED Talk* – 'Why we do the things we do' – Tony Robbins (2006)

Humans find incredible comfort in certainty. We need assurances that we are doing the right thing, that specific outcomes are guaranteed, and that we can feel safe and secure about the future. This need is valid as, in simpler times, it meant knowing there was enough food for the next week or that home was safe for the night. But when we look for certainty in 21st-century life, we are met with so many differing data points that the hope for things to be certain is a near impossible expectation.

As discussed in the *Introduction*, this is not a new problem. For years, philosophers have advised us to let go of what we cannot control. This makes its way into our awareness through motivational sayings or memes like *life's too short* and *live for the moment*, though, some of these are misleading. They are often interpreted as instructions to do whatever we want as we please. The true message is closer to this quote from Epictetus, 'Just keep in mind: the more we value things outside our control, the less control we have.'

ALMOST NOTHING IS CERTAIN

The certainty we crave comes from control. Nothing, apart from our thoughts, judgements, actions, and responses are entirely under our control. For that reason, when we try to exert control over any other aspect of our lives, we are routinely and regularly met with disappointment. Enough disappointment is a disturbance to our mental well-being. Particularly in an era of goal setting and positive thinking, we are exposed to so many—often unrealistic—versions of a *successful* life. When we are subsequently unsuccessful in reaching these targets; we feel useless - we are failures - the only ones who don't have it all together.

There is nothing further from the truth.

We have built such high expectations that the pressure to control the beautiful, yet random world around us is crippling. We heap on rules, goals, and solutions that are utterly unsustainable in our lives. Inevitable failure in these unrealistic pursuits deters us from making more attempts. We struggle with low frustration tolerance, poor discipline and fixed mindsets telling us we aren't the sort of person who achieves X, we can't do Y, and others who have Z must be special. Our resilience is weakened.

Here is a personal example which will likely resonate with many readers:

- Seeing a picture of myself at a party, I think, 'When did I become so fat?' I become embarrassed.
- I reactively decide to lose weight. A plan is hastily drawn up to fix the anxiety I've put on myself.
- I eat healthily and visit the gym a few times.
- I generally feel pretty good about taking some sort of action.
- Once the initial shame-fuelled motivation has passed I treat myself to a takeaway.
- At my first weigh in, I find that I haven't lost any weight like I'd hoped.

- Immediately the feeling of doing something good is replaced by more anxiety and a sense of failure.
- I obviously wasn't trying hard enough, so I add more strict restriction and exercise in volumes I could never realistically maintain – perhaps even attempting a fad diet promoted online.
- Of course, this diet plan is unsustainable, and I struggle. So begins a cycle of shame and guilt with every failure.
- Results inevitably don't come as I had expected, and I become miserable.
- Eventually, I think, 'Screw this,' and defiantly claim that I am not the *type of person* who can have a six-pack. In fact, having a fit body is miserable, and the people who do are robots with no lives or rich celebrities with personal chefs.
- The goal fades into the background (for now) only to reappear as a thorn to my ego whenever a friend seamlessly eases into a healthier lifestyle, or a doctor mentions my BMI.

Sound familiar? Most of us have faced this process ourselves or been close to someone who has. It looks, even written down, extraordinarily exhausting, and we know from experience that the disturbances we feel, and the negative emotions make the whole period a very unsavoury experience.

Now.

What if, on first seeing the upsetting photo, we took a breath and looked purely at first impressions?

'I look a bit overweight in that photo.'

All the other extra commentary in our head is not relevant. Simply put, thoughts are not reality.

With less judgement, I could have responded to this picture by asking myself if wanted to change how I look. Considering WHY that might be and trying not to include anything outside of my control. I could make the reason in line with my values—not the expectations of others and any past stories about myself.

I might remember that I had a great night at the party, and it is doubtful that anyone cares about my weight, especially my close friends (and anyone who does on social media isn't important). Therefore, I laugh and let it go.

Great. No disturbances and no drama.

There's a possibility that I might find a reason to try and lose some weight. I ask myself why and admit that I'd felt out of breath dancing on the night of the party. Or more broadly, I find that I lack the stamina I used to have when playing sports. After deeper consideration, I realise that my sex life has reduced because I am self-conscious and can reasonably expect that losing a few pounds may help. Whatever the situation, I now have a reason that is authentic to me and factual. It is formed in the present by my rational mind.

With this genuine motivation, I can now take some action. This action will be more balanced, sustainable, and flexible than our earlier example. I realise when I start to feel 'pretty good' that this is the whole point of exercising – regardless of the weight loss. Likewise, I might make the small changes to my lifestyle that seem reasonable and slowly lose excess weight, allowing me to build back some confidence. Of course, I might not lose any weight at all. After all, my physical body is not totally in my control, and neither is the environment I'm attempting this in, but by having a more reasoned response, I can make behavioural changes that I can stick to – and enjoy them.

So much of what we target in life isn't aligned with our considered self and core values. We have high, unrealistic expectations that are often fuelled by irrelevant components like social media and choose overly complex or restrictive solutions that don't fit our lives. Then, as we inevitably stall in our endeavours (we are fallible as humans, let alone superhuman), we begin procrastinating and putting off actions because the perfection we seek gets further and further from our grasp. We are paralysed by our need for certainty.

This vicious cycle can be a dark place. It's stressful and upsetting and, unfortunately, synonymous with the modern human condition. Not limited to a new diet - we follow a similar path in multiple aspects of our life, even those that probably don't matter to us as much as we think. With *ABCD*'s help you will be able to answer some key questions to reduce the disappointment. We can use these questions as the basis to look at our aspirations reasonably and find courses of action. And above all, it can help us realise life is pretty good most of the time.

AUTHENTICITY

The overexposed era in which we live is the consequence of the *Information Age*. Austrian-American Economist Fritz Machlup demonstrated in 1962 that the 'knowledge industry represented 29% of the US gross national product.'[19] He believed that this signalled the beginning of the information age. Having died in 1983, he has missed the runaway acceleration that has followed:

'The world's effective capacity to exchange information through two-way telecommunication networks grew at a sustained compound annual growth rate of 30% between 1986 and 2007.'

Jump forward to 2022, and the numbers are staggering:

- '4.66 BILLION Internet Users (Jan 2021)
- 2.5 QUINTILLION Data Bytes created daily (2020)

---

[19] Machlup, F. (1962) *The Production and Distribution of Knowledge in the United States.*

- 70% of the Globe's GDP has undergone digitization (2022).'[20]

Data access and global connection brought about by the internet and our growing understanding of its capabilities are skyrocketing. This is wonderful for many reasons, from reducing intellectual poverty to connecting vulnerable communities across the globe. But as we will discuss later in the book, it clashes somewhat with some of our evolutionary adaptations. Our senses are overloaded and filling in the gaps is something our brain happily does to make sense of the world. We need to feel some certainty, and we need to feel in control. Humans have always used past experiences to form judgements in the present, but now our minds are working overtime, and our stories are becoming less and less our own.

So, we struggle to be authentic. To be considered. To be fully responsible for our own reasoned choice. As a result, we often create issues for ourselves that don't exist (or are not in our control to worry about), setting our sights on the impossible while we *shoot for the moon*, again putting our happiness in the fate of externals. This lets them control us as we face disturbance to our contentment and happiness.

Questions *ABCD* will answer:

- How can you let go of the things you can't control and be more present?
- How can you be authentic more often and, as a result, more content?
- How can you change your responses to the world around you?
- How do you find what truly matters and create some intention towards it?
- How can you choose which issues are real and address them measuredly?
- How can you ensure that the ladder you are climbing is up against the right wall?
- How do you define your main goals in areas of your lives? Your values?
- How do you differentiate between robust advice that can build upon and disingenuous clickbait and old experiences (often not even your own)?

BALANCE

Balance is a vital aspect of our lives. We seek to find a place where nothing is taken to an extreme. The earlier X=Y graph, shows a line where our desires meet the course of fate and where the balance of the two can bring us closer to happiness. Equally, on the occasions that we find ourselves in *the zone* or in a state of *flow*, we usually have hit the sweet spot between being challenged enough to focus our attention on the present without our abilities being pushed to the level where we are flying by the seat of our pants.

Good advice is often to live a more balanced life if we want to feel more content. Everything in moderation. Don't overdo it.

We hear these phrases—and they are everywhere—but we don't see much evidence of them around us. Popular culture is full of inspirational tales of those who worked their

20 'How Much Data is Created Every Day in 2022' - *https://techjury.net/blog/how-much-data-is-created-every-day/#gref*

way doggedly towards success (often omitting the ever-present luck involved). We rarely see the more cautionary side of the tale, where relationships and happiness are often lost because of their single-mindedness. That's if they are even successful, to begin with. For every success story, there are several thousand others where the protagonist pushes ahead without heeding reasoned advice and bypasses the trappings of triumph, heading instead for financial and personal ruin.

Even without hitting rock bottom, it is said that 'No one on their deathbed ever wishes they had worked more!' This is a common trope because it is true. We process information about our experience on this earth in two ways: the experiencing self and the remembering self. One primarily focuses on 'joy' and is associated with the here and now. If we live only to satisfy this side of us, we will often choose what makes us feel best in the moment (in my case, cake, Netflix or having a lay-in). The other, the remembering processor, concerns itself with how we feel now based on what we did in the past.

For example, the experience of waking up early to go for a run may not feel amazing in the moment, but looking back, there is a delayed sense of gratitude for having chosen the more challenging option. For this reason, the remembering self is often seen as that which may be greater linked to our happiness overall. Again, it is a case of balancing our lives to satisfy both; taking either option too far will see us as a lazy fat mess or an overworked restrictive mess—neither is our aim here.

It is often the people who make time for their families, their health, and their pastimes that are the most relaxing to be around. They are calmer and reassured. They have a quiet confidence about them...they are balanced. Balance is inspirational.

Our thinking often causes us further imbalance. All-or-nothing thinking is a fault in our mindset that prevents us from even starting many a journey. If we can't have perfection, we will not begin. But as Matthew McConaughey poetically recites in his delightful memoir/philosophy book *Greenlights*:

'*if only*

Means you wanted something but did not get it.

For some reason, either by your own incompetence or the world's intervention, it did not happen.

Sometimes this is just the breaks and we need to bow out gracefully.

But more often than we care to admit, we don't get what we want

Because we quit early or we didn't take the necessary risk to get it.

The more boots we put in the back side of our if onlys, the more we will get what we want.

Don't walk the *it's too late it's too soon tightrope* until you die.'[21]

So, in our framework, we must seek to choose goals that fit in and around our lives. Sustainable actions we can take towards those goals. Flexible measures of our success that accept us as fallible human beings. We aren't looking for obsessions that take us out of the present as we fixate on the future but challenges that enrich our lives whilst leaving space to enjoy them.

Questions *ABCD* will answer:

- How can you cut through the message that you should be firing on all cylinders and instead find a sustainable and flexible attitude towards the genuine targets you seek?
- How do you balance your expectations for yourself? Find medium-term goals that reflect your principles. Stop procrastinating?
- How do you enjoy your life and move towards *preferred* goals where less importance is placed on the outcomes than the process?
- How do you find a balance of your present experience whilst ensuring you look back on your lives positively?
- How do you find the next small steps you can take that allow you to experience *flow* in the task at hand with plenty of time to enjoy the scenery as you do?
- How do we ensure you aren't too busy with targets, actions, and deadlines that are unhelpful?
- How can you leave plenty of time to keep our capability high by taking care of your primary production source – *you*?

CONSISTENCY

Consistency is one of the most defining character traits of successful people. It regularly surpasses talent as a critical factor in any achievement. Those who show up time after time are most likely to see the results they are working towards. The below pyramid sums up how the proportion of people in any field reduces as consistency grows. Many people want to do something, fewer do it, and even fewer do it often enough to be great at it.

---

21 McConaughey, M. (2020) *Greenlights*.

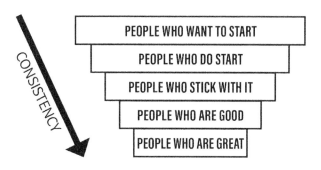

Fig 3.1 – Consistency Pyramid

Having amassed over 400,000 subscribers and recording 400 episodes of his *Modern Wisdom Podcast*, host Chris Williamson outlined the 19 key themes that run through his interviews with global experts across multiple subjects.

One of these was 'Consistency is even rarer than talent or enthusiasm,' which highlights how you are already moving towards success just by having a consistent intention. In his example, 90% of podcasts don't make it past three episodes, and of the remaining 10% that do, only 10% reach 20 episodes. So simply by recording 21 episodes of any content, you will automatically be in the world's top 1% of podcasters!

'Why? Because consistency is fu***ng well rare, that's why!'[22]

In many walks of life, the smallest amount of consistency can go a long way.

So, how do we achieve consistent behaviours?

When we apply a balanced and authentic approach to life, we see something interesting happen. We find that our actions become more consistent. Because behaving in line with our values becomes easier to sustain when we have clarity and realistic expectations.

How many of us found it practically impossible to read just a few pages of the book our schoolteachers selected for us? Bored and distracted in equal measure, the book was quickly side-lined in favour of something more interesting. We didn't choose the subject of our reading assignment. We proclaimed that Shakespeare is 'boring' and we 'just can't get into it.' Also, the reading was often bundled in with many other elements of homework that could take up hours of our evenings. Students are overwhelmed without meticulous planning, especially when revision is added to the mix.

Moving away from homework for a moment (apologies for any sore memories) and looking at other times we read in our lives. We find ourselves reading a book we can't put down about our favourite band or reading every review of the movie we plan to see that evening.

On occasion, we all find something that catches us so firmly that we read, research, and ingest endless content about it almost daily.

Both our schoolwork and these activities are *reading*.

One of them is authentically chosen by you, fitting around your life...and hours of Shakespeare at 14 years old is not.

We have solved one problem with finding consistency by following our process thus far. We're doing things we enjoy doing that will add up to results that are valuable to us—so we do them. Of course, this isn't so cut and dry, and there are many aspects to consider around consistency.

Questions *ABCD* will answer:

- What objectives you currently 'can't' do would be possible if you took consistent smaller steps towards them?
- What level of consistency can you build that allows you to keep balance and enjoy your life in one sense yet also push towards success in another?
- How do you create case studies in your life that reassure you that you are capable, and even on an off day, are good enough?
- How do you keep yourself from making unrealistic commitments that push you away from X=Y and cause disturbances in your life?
- What small daily routine could you implement to help keep your promises and develop consistency like the skill that it is?

DISCIPLINE

Discipline is too often associated with suffering. We think of an Olympian training at the pool/gym/track every hour available, neglecting their friends and social lives to rest and repeat their training until they reach the promised land of a gold medal.

Elite level CrossFit Coach and Author Ben Bergeron said, 'Discipline is doing things you don't want to do as though you love them.' In the realm of peak performance, this is absolutely true. Bergeron has many insightful ideas and strategies in his *Chasing Excellence* podcast and book, and it is well worth a listen for those seeking peak performance in any area of life.

In this framework, we don't need to go to extremes. As we'll touch on later in this book, there are psychological benefits to building discipline. From the dopamine response when we push ourselves to the confidence built from keeping promises to ourselves to the happiness we feel looking back on parts of our lives knowing we made the best decision, it is clear that self-discipline is a virtue.

'Do what others won't do today, so you can do what they can't do tomorrow' is a favourite quote of mine from CrossFit Games champion Mat Fraser (taken from an Indian Proverb). It tells us that by putting effort into what many wouldn't, we create a platform that can elevate us to levels those same people will never reach. This success is what discipline can earn us.

In Fraser's case, discipline was *eight hours* a day in the gym and training elements of his sport he hated so he would learn to be great at them—but it doesn't need to be that extreme. Though discipline is positive in our lives, what we are disciplined about and to what level is a very personal choice. It can range from being unmotivated and allowing ourselves to sit in a slump at one end of a spectrum and being an Olympian at the other. One size doesn't fit all, but when we apply a level of authenticity to our lives and allow ourselves the balance to keep life enjoyable, there is every reason to weave some discipline throughout our lives to enrich them.

In some ways, simply by reading this book, you are acknowledging that you can make some changes about your intentions. And even though the lives of others are not our concerns, by having some awareness, you already put yourself in a position to be happier and content, which many others are not.

Ultimately, even with simple acts of discipline, like how we speak to our kids or put our phones away before bed to help us sleep better, we are gaining those same psychological benefits. Suppose the reasons for actions are authentic, balanced, and consistent over a chosen period. In that case, we can change our lives by performing them regularly and having the smallest amount of discipline.

Questions *ABCD* will answer:

- How can you create goals and solutions with which you *want* to be disciplined?
- Can you reduce the stigma associated with being more disciplined?
- How do you harness these benefits, build consistency through hard work (it is less effort than you think), and build your sense of virtue – however small?
- How does discipline make you feel? How can you see the positive psychological effects of high frustration tolerance, keeping promises, and ownership of a task?
- How do you deal with failures? How can you pivot and be flexible with your goals?
- What framework can you implement to help you be disciplined and consistent once you have authentic goals?
- How do you turn the more significant values into daily habits that reflect the person you want to be?

HOW *ABCD* CAN HELP

ABCD will provide the knowledge not only to answer the questions I pose, but also some simple techniques to increase authenticity, balance, consistency, and discipline in your life.

As I mentioned, I'm not a psychologist, counsellor, life coach, influencer, or guru. Jesus, I've not even got my own life working anywhere near 100%. And crucially, I never will. Life isn't perfect, and there will never be that moment where you say to yourself, 'I think I've nailed this—no problems, no goals left to achieve and a clear horizon'...and if there ever was, we have already seen that you can easily be thrown a curveball by fate (nature/the universe/God etc.). Equally, people who move up any ladder socially, physically, financially, or otherwise, removing the issues they had a few rungs down – usually find new problems at their new level. Life is never *Inbox Zero*.[23] Here we are looking for solutions and frame-works that can apply wherever you find yourself in life.

'The wise of every generation discover the same truths.'[24]
– Shane Parrish.

I'm *not* wise—on more than one occasion, I have smashed a plate trying to open a door with my elbow, and my 10-year-old son outsmarts me regularly, but what I will write about in these pages is *wisdom* that I believe is worth bringing together into a place that can benefit others like it benefits me every day.

The advice is straightforward. Hopefully it can be of use to answer the questions we have posed in this chapter.

Now, it might all sound like nonsense, and you may feel it doesn't apply to you - that is completely fine. This is not a rigid dictate of how everyone should live their lives. The book won't contain any pre-written goals to follow, so if you were hoping for definitive answers on how to get a six-pack or become a millionaire—I'm very sorry. Those were my goals too, and only by answering the questions we have asked here did I discover that there is a much happier place to be – it is that I want to share with you. The knowledge in this book, framework, and process has allowed me to have a structure I can use to approach many of my issues and goals. It has been life-changing, and I hope it is as powerful for you too.

Use as much or little of my advice as you choose. You might solve a single problem and never use it again, or better still, realise your life is essentially tremendous and there are no problems to deal with once you look at them in the present. Wouldn't that be amazing?

---

23 *The Inbox Zero Method* developed by productivity expert Merlin Mann, where the aim is to have less and less things (starting with emails) that occupy your mind
24 *Farnam Street – Learning Community - https://fs.blog/*

Pause for Thought – Please take time to make some notes:

4

FIVE KEY AREAS OF LIFE

'To simplify complications is the first essential of Success.'
– George Earle Buckle.

IMPACTFUL CORE VALUES AND GOALS

IN CHAPTER 6 WE WILL DISCOVER some important lessons around the ABCD elements of authenticity, balance, consistency, and discipline. In *Chapter 8* I will outline some simple, yet effective techniques we can incorporate into our lives allowing us to choose values and goals that with genuinely impact our lives in a positive way.

Here, I feel it is important to highlight what I believe are the five key areas of our lives that are likely to contain many of the items we consider important to us. By considering these topics as we go deeper into the ABCD framework, we can begin to think about the core values and goals that are the most significant.

This is a very personal part of the ABCD framework. Many of you will have a clear view of the areas of your lives that would be improved and the ABCD framework will make it apparent if they are authentic. While this is the case for many readers, this book isn't only aimed at those with specific goals or issues to begin with.

A great number of us find it hard to define these significant values, either because we are overwhelmed by the world around us and don't know what to focus on (this certainly applied to me) or, perhaps, as we will discuss in *Chapter 7*, we haven't given it much thought. The ABCD framework and this book aims to help people make sense of their values and improve the areas of their life that require attention. So, this chapter will briefly explore a few areas that are significantly impactful to many of us. Their development would improve our lives and should be considered part of any review conducted.

If your number of core values that require action is easy to define and small, that is excellent. It means there is a clear focus on what to work on, and steps can be created towards it. But if you feel like some structure is needed and you are unsure of where to focus your attention, then in this chapter, I will discuss the areas that I believe cover many essential aspects of our lives; it will be hard to miss a potential value/goal if they are considered.

I regularly listen to the Ben Bergeron podcast *Chasing Excellence*, and the host repeatedly refers to the 'five factors of health.' These are the factors that Bergeron believes are crucial to the health of any person, both physically and mentally. They are listed in the introduction as 'taking ownership of how we EAT, SLEEP, TRAIN, THINK, and CONNECT with each other is how we'll optimise our health and happiness.'[25] The advice is to take some responsibility for improving these areas to better your life. Though the podcast is often more geared toward health and fitness from a sports perspective, I feel that by exploring these categories, you can find comprehensive coverage of the areas from which you can select your core values and goals.

Remembering the *Six Human Needs* from Tony Robbins and Maslow's *Hierarchy of Needs*, many of the fundamental requirements for us to build a happy life fall within these areas. Of course, there are many other areas of life, but when we begin to question what we can control or not, it often falls into one of the five areas we will discuss below.

Effectively, by taking care of these areas, we ensure we cover our basic needs, making sure we are at our best. When we are at our best, we feel more balanced and responsive to our situations – this makes us happier.

I will give some examples of what good looks like, but as I highlighted in earlier chapters, I don't know all the answers. You will find your own answers by following the ABCD framework, hopefully these suggested areas will be of use.

Let us explore these key areas and see how it would be beneficial to bring them back into focus if they are neglected.

MINDSET

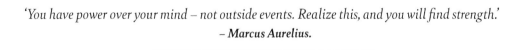

'You have power over your mind – not outside events. Realize this, and you will find strength.'
– Marcus Aurelius.

Mindset refers to how you think, mental health, emotional responses, motivation, reason, feelings, expectations, and so much more. As Marcus Aurelius tells us above, you can become stronger when you realise that you control your thoughts.

Almost everything you could want to influence or work on will have part of its success rooted in how you think. Many events and actions in life are created first in the mind and then once again in reality. How you think and feel is critical to happiness and only recently becoming more acceptable to discuss openly in our society – as this acceptance grows, humanity will be better for it.

WHY IS MINDSET IMPORTANT?

Mindset and how you think about yourself, others, and the world you live in is paramount in most of the values and goals you will choose to uphold/pursue. Many of the issues faced are made easier to bear with a different perspective (see the Stoic Principles and Judgement discussions earlier), and many of the goals you set will only come to fruition if you think about them in the right way.

All of the discussions and tools around authenticity and balance originate from adjusting how we think about things. Furthermore, the ability to keep promises to yourself and stick to a task that you value will come from the discipline of your thoughts, judgements, and expectations.

Even the values and goals you select, which sit in different areas of your life, will have mindset factors associated. Your improved perspective and mental health are critical to your happiness.

These values and goals needn't be big either. One of the next steps you can take towards some significant improvements in life is to assess how you feel on a regular basis. Doing so can give you awareness to ensure you respond in line with your values. You take ownership of your story.

WHAT COULD FALL INTO THIS AREA?

Some of the many types of values and goals you might consider that are related to your *mindset* are:

- Goals that challenge your view of the world around you and yourself.
- Letting go of old stories.
- Changing reactions to yourself and others.
- Changing how you view something/one to be happier (judgements).
- Finding time to relax.
- Goals that create a greater balance so you can be more productive.
- Mental health-focused goals.
- Becoming less stubborn or changing your expectations of yourself/others.
- Happiness-related goals.
- Changing your life situation to follow a dream or be happier.

- Enjoying the Journey.
- Work-Life Balance.
- Educational Goals / Learning new things.
- Personal Finances.
- Being more grateful.
- Therapy-related goals.
- Building Self-esteem.
- Creating Motivation.
- Becoming more Confidence.

EXAMPLES:

- Taking steps to repair a relationship where your view of an incident has caused estrangement.
- Making self-love and how you feel a core value in your life.
- A goal to switch off from work when you are at home with family.
- Routine that allows you to create more time for the things you enjoy.
- Addressing an issue in how you respond negatively to situations out of your control.
- Creating clarity around family attitudes to household spending to reduce costs and save for something.

RELATIONSHIPS

'Relationships are more important than life, but it is important for those relationships to have life in them.'
– Swami Vivekananda.

Think about the relationships in your life. How much of your happiness and how you feel is linked to how well those relationships are going? Perhaps you don't have many relationships because you don't prioritise them or because you feel you don't need them. That may be true for you, but humans are social creatures whose evolution is based upon interacting as communities and surviving together.

Our communities have shrunk with smaller family units and less co-dependence between families or generations in the same family. This doesn't mean relationships aren't still valuable. Connectedness and a sense of purpose are main drivers to strong mental health.

Even if you're not convinced, remember that we are discussing more than families, classmates, friends, and partners. We interact with many more people daily, and there will be some of these interactions that you would like to improve—the difficult colleague or uncomfortable neighbour, for example.

You can even have relationship values around how you interact with yourself (self-esteem values) and the world around you (environmental values) - these are two of the most important relationships you'll ever have.

WHY ARE RELATIONSHIPS IMPORTANT?

For most people reading this book, there will be at least one relationship you have an issue with or one goal you would have for your family. Our relationships run through all facets of life, and when we include interactions online, at work, and with our environment, it's clear that much of what we do each day falls into this category.

Even when on the journey to achieve goals and set values aside from this area, you might be surprised to see how many actions will arise that involve other people. You can't control people other than yourself, so how you interact with others and their (re)actions to your desires is critical to your success.

You may want to start a new physical activity and join a sports team. One of the steps toward this might be negotiating to leave work early with your boss or allaying your partner's possible insecurities before you can do so. Both are relationship principles, even if the actual value is to your health.

This is an essential area of our lives, and luckily, improvements in other areas and your happiness will make you a better person to have relationships with, benefitting all involved.

WHAT COULD FALL INTO THIS AREA?

Some of the many types of values and goals you might consider that are related to your *relationships* are:

- Parenting.
- Romantic relationships.
- Sexual relationships.
- Friendships.
- Self-esteem.
- Social media interactions.
- Dealing with complicated relationships (neighbours, in-laws, work relationships).
- Relationships during education.
- Finding people to confide in.
- Setting boundaries.
- Your responses to other peoples' actions outside of your control.
- Use of therapy.

- Mentoring others.
- Improving your social life or hobbies.
- Navigating conflict in a more positive way.
- Navigating divorce.
- Addressing issues with joint finances.
- Broken down relationships where a change would improve your life.
- How you interact with colleagues to get the most out of your work life.
- Managing employees.
- Challenges arising from working from home/remote social interactions.
- Charity/community/connectedness/purpose.
- Understanding your place in the world.
- Interacting with nature.
- Climate change/green/ESG values and goals.

EXAMPLES:

- Taking steps to repair a relationship where your view of an incident has caused estrangement.
- Changing *zero sum* thinking to be happy for other people's successes and stop jealousy from damaging a friendship – perhaps by limiting Social Media interactions .
- Making more effort with your partner by implementing opportunities each day to touch in with one another.
- Setting a goal to try a new hobby with others and challenge yourself to find some more opportunities to see flow.

LIFESTYLE-MOVEMENT

'The primary and most beautiful or nature's qualities is motion.'
– **Marquis de Sade.**

This is the first of two areas I refer to as *lifestyle.* Ultimately, I am suggesting that many of the values and goals you choose to prioritise will fall under the umbrella of the style you choose to live in. You may want to make sweeping changes to your life to improve your happiness or situation. Or make more specific lifestyle changes. Either way, these areas encapsulate improvements you can make towards being more authentic with how you exist and the person you want to be.

Crucially, this isn't all about health and fitness as it might first appear. We all have lifestyles. From someone changing a habit that is causing discomfort to creating more income to allow travel – these are both changes from one lifestyle to another.

The first area is movement—how you move and all elements of where you go and what you do.

WHY IS MOVEMENT IMPORTANT?

Whereas mindset impacts most values and goals and is integral to the ABCD framework, it isn't immediately apparent how your physical movement does. You could have stationary plans that require more mental commitment resulting in changes to your happiness – this is true.

However, it would be a misstep to review your life and values and not consider the many elements of movement within them. The obvious one will typically start as exercise. It hugely benefits your physical and mental well-being and longevity (even if only to achieve your other goals). You needn't stop there, though; humans move around a lot, whether in one place or around the globe and for many of you, improvements in these areas will be life changing.

Even the smallest element of another, more significant goal will require lifestyle adjustment, such as moving for a relationship. These decisions shape your life and the style in which you live it (sometimes for years).

WHAT COULD FALL INTO THIS AREA?

Some of the many types of values and goals you might consider that are related to your *movement* are:

- Fitness goals.
- Starting new hobbies.
- Sports performance-related goals.
- Values to enable enjoying later life.
- Improving family relationships through activity.
- Sex.
- Travel goals.
- Holiday anxieties.
- Socialising.
- Dancing.
- Commuting.
- Re-locating or moving.
- Confidence in yourself not born out of comparison but physical ability.

- Spending time outdoors.
- Home improvement targets.
- Volunteering/charity.
- Mental health values.
- Flow possibilities.

EXAMPLES:

- Setting a goal to improve an element of a sport to move into a more challenging team.
- Taking a walk every day to keep fit enough to play with your grandchildren.
- Finding ways each year to challenge yourself and earn donations for charity.
- Addressing values around sex to keep both partners satisfied and happy.

LIFESTYLE-DIET

'Take care of your body. It's the only place you have to live.'
– Jim Rohn.

A recent data study found that people in the UK spent 79 minutes per day eating.[26] It doesn't seem like much, but if you remove sleep and work from your daily totals, it equates to over 13% of your day - every day. This doesn't include the time socialising that can consist of food and drink (47 mins) or housework including cooking (133 mins), and it certainly doesn't include the amount of time spent THINKING about food, which some estimates place at over 2 hours a day.

Food and diet are essential both in how they maintain your life and play a prominent role in your relationships, social lives, and sometimes your anxieties and worries. Many people (this author included) have hang-ups around diet and habits that could be changed for the better.

This category, the second and most significant one related to lifestyle covers quite a large section of life. Values and goals from within it are varied and common.

WHY IS DIET IMPORTANT?

Because of the spectrum of possible values and goals in this area and the evident prevalence your diet takes in your life, it is easy to see why it is an area you could address.

---

26 Ortiz-Ospina, E. and Giattino, C. and Roser, M. (2020) 'Time Use' – *www.ourworldindata.org*

Added to this - changes you would make in this area are not all limited to how you would classically define 'diet.' I would also include most of the things you put into your body: smoking, drugs, alcohol, and so on are very common areas where people seek improvement.

Finally, because the kitchen is the hub of a home, several values and goals related to cooking, socialising, and learning make this an essential area for review.

Small changes such as making it home once a week to have dinner with your children or making packed lunches to save money for a desired musical instrument can fulfil many personal achievements that lead to greater happiness.

WHAT COULD FALL INTO THIS AREA?

Some of the many types of values and goals you might consider that are related to your *diet* are:

- Dietary goals for improved health.
- Dietary goals for enhanced performance in sport.
- Dietary goals for weight loss.
- Dietary goals for better sleep.
- Dietary goals for better focus/energy.
- Dietary goals to improve relationships with food and to keep promises to yourself.
- Adjusting to a new dietary choice/requirement.
- Reducing dietary rules to enjoy food again.
- Addressing finances around food.
- Addressing possible problematic relationships with food/drink/drugs.[27]
- Giving up smoking.
- Making more effort to cook at home.
- Making more effort to meet socially to eat and connect.
- Trying new things.
- Learning to cook.
- Family dinner time.
- Dating.

EXAMPLES:

- Setting out the small actions that could be taken each day to facilitate weight loss for an important event and beyond.
- Reducing intake of fizzy drinks as part of a goal around dental health.
- Finding a routine around dinner time to allow the family to eat together and encourage the children to cook.

---

27 Each person's approach is personal please seek professional help if you are suffering from addiction

- Targeting an improvement in knowledge around food to reduce anxiety when dating.

SLEEP

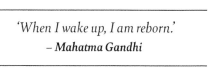

'When I wake up, I am reborn.'
– Mahatma Gandhi

Unlike the other areas discussed, sleep is less broad and all-encompassing. However, a lack of sleep drastically affects our physical capabilities to do anything. With just 24 hours of sleep deprivation, according to *Medical News Today*, we will see effects such as:

- Drowsiness.
- Irritability.
- Concentration and memory difficulties.
- Reduced coordination.
- Impaired judgment.
- Short-term memory problems.
- Raised levels of stress hormones, such as cortisol and adrenaline.
- Increased blood sugar levels.
- Higher risk of accidents.
- Muscle tension.[28]

So extended periods of insufficient sleep will make progress in any number of goals and adherence to even the most important values close to impossible. Please don't ignore it.

WHY IS SLEEP IMPORTANT?

When unsatisfied with your lives, particularly concerning work, you tend to overindulge in your leisure time. That might be through *living for the weekends* or staying up late at night to switch off from the day's stresses.

The problem is that when you are tired, your ability to cope reduces, your stress increases, and your judgement can become impaired. Also, the hormone production and regenerative processes during sleep are incomplete, so you are running on empty.

Thankfully, when you review your situation using the ABCD framework, you will hopefully free up some time and enjoyment of the journey and realise that when well rested, you can wake up able to take on far more. Of course, you will not be able to change your situation instantly, but with minor improvements, you can see enough change to make you appreciate your days enough and be content with a good night's sleep.

WHAT COULD FALL INTO THIS AREA?

Some of the many types of values and goals you might consider that are related to your *sleep* are:

- Stress reduction goals.
- Improving ability to be present and let go.
- Learning progressive muscle relaxation to aid sleep.
- Increasing energy/focus.
- Sleep hygiene goals.
- Improving sleep quality.
- Letting go of dreams.
- Stopping poor sleep affecting relationships during early parenthood.
- Finding healthy sleep patterns when working night shifts.
- Sports recovery goals.

EXAMPLES:

- Implementing changes to a bedtime routine to allow an earlier wake-up time for a new job.
- Changing diet to allow a better night's sleep at a time when tired due to family commitments.
- Sub-goals of recovery from illness/recovery that includes taking extra sleep throughout the day.
- Creating a plan to get sufficient sleep when working anti-social working hours or shifts.

A slight uptick in performance and mood brought about by good sleep will add momentum to any other value or goal. It's worth thinking about adding something like a bedtime routine and/or morning routine to the sub-goals of a larger target.

SUMMARY

As with so much in life, the ABCD framework is fluid and interconnected. We prioritise what is important to us so we can focus on taking the small next steps towards making it a reality. The process helps us to remain on a sustainable journey that we enjoy. However, improvement in any crucial area of our lives will also lead to a knock-on effect in other areas. We needn't worry if the core values we pick don't originate from the areas we have discussed in this chapter. They are just suggestions that cover a broad spectrum of the lives many of us live. They are a starting point.

Considering the ABCD factors, we can draw a balance between the light, loving contentment of our AB side and then challenge ourselves and create flow opportunities with the CD side. The wonderful thing is that this will spill into other areas, so the interconnectivity remains. We're trying to improve the overall quality of our experience by enhancing the authentically chosen areas of most consequence.

I wish I could tell you that I had it licked. That when you do a review like the one here in *ABCD*, that life becomes easy. The reality is, it doesn't, and to expect it is to go against what we learned about happiness at the start of this book.

By making minor improvements in these critical areas, I can say from experience that you can see life-changing results. By reducing cognitive dissonance, you create space in your mind to enjoy the journey and be productive when it counts. A satisfied calm will permeate and benefit most other areas of your life.

Authenticity allows balance, balance allows consistency, consistency allows discipline, and discipline allows authenticity. Every element of the ABCD framework is connected. Success in one area benefits another; work in one place can bring life to another.

With this understanding and some target areas in mind, it will become clear how impactful the work I am proposing is.

Pause for Thought – Please take time to make some notes:

5

SOME MORE ABOUT ME
(AND THE WORLD AROUND US)

'Some people are lost in their fires, while others are forged by them.'[29]
– Unknown.

LIFE IS NOT STRAIGHTFORWARD!

IT MIGHT BE HELPFUL HERE to touch back in with my story. It's important to note that I didn't just read a few books and suddenly have all my problems vanish. I touched on the idea in the *Preface* that lack of information isn't the problem most of us face. My problem was that I had TOO MUCH information and external markers I could negatively compare my life to.

I started to read more literature on the subjects contained in this book in 2016, just after my 35th birthday, when I had decided to take a break from alcohol.[30] There was a bit of clarity for the first time in a long while, and I decided to research and learn more about the topics that stuck with me. Each time I'd read a new book, I would find some references or subjects I could relate to, and I would go a little further down the rabbit hole, adding to my knowledge as I went. It was very enlightening, but ultimately, life is complicated, and without a robust process, I still found myself in trouble.

My wife's mother died in early 2017. She had lived with us for two years, and after suffering an undignified injury from a negligent surgeon and fighting legal battles for years, she passed away from a short battle with cancer at the age of 69. This had been her 6th cancer battle in 30 years, and though my wife was so solid during each of the others, this felt

---

29 *I am Sober App* – Daily Motivations – Though I've not covered it in this book; people's relationship with alcohol varies and I have struggled with mine. This application is very good when you are logging your time Alcohol Free as I have

30 Many readers are just about to put the book down in disgust—bear with me, this doesn't end with me telling you to give up the booze!

different: quick, unrelenting, and final. Our world felt like it had fallen apart; we had an open legal battle, complicated estate, work stresses, and were grieving. We aren't the first people to deal with any of these things, yet it felt very lonely at the time. We questioned how we'd ever get through it. But, like many of you will have experienced in your own life, humans are extraordinarily resilient.

This period went how it does for many people in the same situation. Grief causes pressure and stress that can often lead to adopting inauthentic coping strategies. I displayed character traits nowhere near those of the person I wanted to be. My struggles with binge eating, alcohol, and control (especially that of my wife's emotions) came flooding in with full force. To borrow Portia Nelson's analogy, I would blindly walk down the same road over and over, then wake up down a massive hole wondering how I'd gotten myself in that state. Whether it be overeating, displays of anger, or selfishly closing out people who needed me most—I reverted to old stories from my past. The parts of everyone's lives that form their perception of the world around them—their stories—are not always how they would like to behave in the present. As I was finding, even with the knowledge of what a more reasonable and considered life could look like...I lacked something of substance to anchor to, and my old behaviours kicked in to protect me from the uncertain time I was facing. This caused those around me and myself damage.

The Greek historian and author Herodotus is quoted as saying, 'The worst pain a man can suffer is to have insight into much and power over nothing.'[31]

This couldn't have been more true - I was miserable and upset, made worse by the fact that I *thought* I knew how to get out of the rut but still couldn't. I believe this isn't uncommon for many of us. We often apply tremendous pressure on ourselves and harshly self-judge when we fail to meet our own high expectations. This judgement is sometimes attributed to our *Inner Parent/Parent Ego* – we repeat observed behaviour of authority figures from when we were young. These, often faulty behaviours, are then incorporated into our own stories as acceptable responses to life (we'll revisit this later).

When the dust later settled and I looked back on the years that followed, I had serious questions about how I had handled those challenges.

- How was it that I had made the effort to learn so much about myself yet when I needed this knowledge it failed me?
- Why was it that I could create goals and solutions for myself and my family but fail to make steady progress towards them?
- What is the difference between my approach and the approach used by those who appeared to be flourishing?

---

31 Herodotus (c484-425 BCE)

These questions all led me to the same conclusion: I had been overwhelmed by need to solve the large problems in my life when I could have broken them down into the small next step necessary to get my family and I out of our difficult times. But how could I have gone about this? I needed structure.

If you don't put what you value into a framework or system, if you don't authentically assess and balance the plans you make, if you don't have consistency in your behaviours and apply them with discipline when things are going well—then when they are not, and you are tested—you won't stand a chance.

These thoughts resonated with me. People around the world would have easy access to many of the messages I had found. They are plastered over social media in the form of memes and inspirational videos on a near daily basis. But just reading them and giving them a *like* doesn't align them with your core values.

Starting with the questions posed in the *Introduction*, I began to write and create study cards that started to offer some structure around what I had been studying. I could use them as reference and some helpful techniques began to take shape which form the basis of the tools I will provide later in this book. I carried them everywhere and read them regularly (in fact I still do) they became a guidebook to my own behaviours. They were named after the Artur Schopenhauer idea—*X=Y* (see fig 5.1).

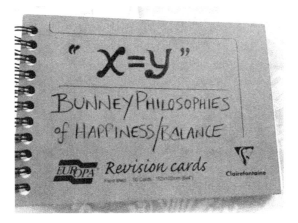

Fig 5.1 – My first attempt at 'Self-Help'

Only when the coronavirus pandemic, with its uncertainty, fear, frustration, and endless lockdowns, had smashed my resolve once again did I realise that a further step was needed. As we spoke about in the *Preface*, the missing piece was discovered by a simple yet brilliant comment from a wife trying to support her slightly pathetic husband.

Without those life events and the continued reading of the subjects, I would not have reached this point. Those small actions, unknown to me, were the small bites of that larger elephant. Without focusing on changing my life overall, I was concentrating on more minor elements that I could manage easily. These, in turn, had the positive effect on my life that had seemed out of reach before. Before I knew it, I had built a strategy not only for the situation I had found myself in, but a strategy that was useful in ALL situations – for ALL people.

That scruffy little booklet was the first step towards building the ABCD framework you are reading in these pages.

SOCIAL MEDIA

'Social media connects billions of people around the globe. In doing so, it disconnects us from reality and creates false ideals that many struggle to achieve.'[32]
– Adam Friscia.

In our quest to simplify our authentic story, it is important to discuss a topic that has added confusion to the challenge we face.

Despite opening this section with a fairly damning quote, I must start by acknowledging that technological advances made in most of our lifetimes are astonishing. As humans, we live in a much more prosperous and healthy society than our ancestors did because of these advances. Life expectancy has reached highs that could never have been predicted before the 'Scientific-technical revolution' (1940-1970); Life expectancy in the UK in 1940 was 62.34, an increase of around 20 years, which grew over the preceding 175 years. In 2020 that number was 81.15[33] years, a similar jump taking less than half the time.

The advances come thick and fast. So fast that even at a relatively young 40 years old, my early memories of technology that blew me away now seem severely antiquated in comparison to what have now.

The ability to share valuable information and technologies has transformed humanity. In an age where it is easy to forget the utility of the technological advances we have made[34], there is no denying that many of them have been positive. Knowledge is power and its widespread availability due to the internet is a major factor in lowering global suffering and poverty. Plus, the connectivity between groups thousands of miles apart means we are more likely to find the support of like-minded people, reducing stigmatism of once ostracised groups. The fact my children are not fazed by the idea of a same sex couple

---

32 'Opinion commentary – Social Media connects us to one another, creates reality disconnect' – Adam Friscia (2021) – *www.theslateonline.com*
33 O'Neil, A. (2022) 'Life Expectancy (from birth) in the United Kingdom from 1765 to 2020' - *https://www.statista.com/*
34 I'm not sure the benefit of seeing the same dance 500 times on Tik Tok, but my daughter evidently does!

and are brilliantly colour blind are both consequences of this more connected global community, and long may it continue.

Connectivity is essential to human happiness. This need for connectivity comes from our social group's primal need to be respected and valued. Social media and the internet's global reach can provide us with this, at the touch of a button, like never before in history.

This is not to say it is all rainbows and butterflies; this information comes at a cost. Despite efforts made by large social media platforms, online content is largely unregulated. This leads to vast amounts of information on any subject, much of which is conflicting and not backed by scientific evidence. Modern society expects results fast. The large volumes of information and technology that are such a benefit to us also lead to increases in impatience. Why wait to check if something is factual or for more information on a subject when you can instantly have all you need to know in a single tweet? So as more prominent old-school media try to keep up in a saturated marketplace, we see a race to the bottom with a preference for quantity over quality.

Adding the financial incentives of being seen, liked, viewed, and retweeted to the mix and any guarantee of consistent factuality is lost. The marketplace allows people to use social media platforms to take advantage of our confusion and impatience to manipulate us and feed us (at best) innocently ill-conceived content and (at worst) blatant lies to capture our attention for marketing revenue.[35]

Much of the advice we see is genuine and useful, but some most certainly isn't. Unfortunately, telling the difference between the two is a difficult task. Without a clear idea of our own values, we tend to find ourselves adopting a lot of what we ingest as fact. This means part of our own values and stories are built on what we observe externally in others, rather than what we observe internally of ourselves.

There is, of course, valuable content on social media – I'll be using it to promote this book (@abcd_nicholas_bunney).

Though for the purpose of discovering our genuine values, the reliability of sources and content make some of it problematic. Authenticity, which allows us to assess what we hold close to us, cannot be found looking at other people's lives, nor should it be sought from advertising designed to keep you hungry for more and feeling inadequate. Balance, which is so crucial to satisfaction in life, is not promoted by extreme actions sold to us as quick fixes, nor can we be genuinely balanced if we are overloaded with the things we 'should' be doing to *live our best lives*. Especially if the lives are those presented by social media influencers with ulterior motives, through filtered representations of their lives.

---

35 I'm not here to take on social media, I use it like most people, but these firms spend serious money to keep you engaged. Billions are invested in behavioural studies to extend screen time and sell adverts. Facebook spent $24.655bn on research and development in 2021, and former director Tim Kendall stated the goal for the firm was 'Updating the app with increased addictiveness for a consistent boost in engagement.' Much of this research and development goes into keeping people scrolling for longer. We're fully aware of this practice, and the unfortunate side effect is that we are vastly overexposed to low-quality information.

It is completely fine not to have a six-pack if you don't want one. You shouldn't feel guilty for not being a property owner by 30 if that's not important to you—and even if it is, success is measured by your chosen metrics—not anyone else's.

Epictetus, the famous Stoic Philosopher, once questioned: 'If a person gave your body to some passer-by, you'd be furious. Yet you hand over your mind to anyone who comes along, so they may abuse you, leaving it disturbed and troubled – Have you no shame in that?'[36]

We're very protective of our physical being but are much less fussy regarding how we spend our mental power, time, and what we concern ourselves with. We must treat our minds and actions with similar care and ensure they are entirely our own.

This confusing landscape leaves many of us (myself included) unhappy, lacking the ability to relax and be present and feeling overwhelmed by our overexposure to so many streams of information. It's no wonder we struggle to live authentic lives with so many goals to target presented to us by the media we consume. Fear of failure that follows is the primal one that others do not like us (the fear of being expelled from our tribe) or that we are not good enough compared to other people's (edited) versions of a perfect life. Comparison can make us deeply unhappy and is precisely what is happening in today's society. As US president Theodore Roosevelt summed up long before our time:

'Comparison is the thief of joy.'

I'll finish this section with a recent anecdote from a lunchtime stroll.

I am lucky enough to work near the Thames River in London. There is something very relaxing about walking by the river, and I try to do so during my lunch whenever possible. In one recent walk, I was walking around the Tower of London, where they are planting thousands of flowers to bloom into a display in the summer. It's fascinating when you spend a bit of time looking at it. The myriad of different walls and buildings within the walls makes you wonder what they would have been used for when the castle was occupied. I walked up some steps to Tower Bridge and headed south over the Thames when I heard a commotion from across the road. A girl in her early twenties had been live streaming herself cycling across the bridge, presumably for social media. However, on a busy traffic-laden bridge, whilst driving one-handed and not paying attention to the road, she had driven rather comically into a barrier and fallen from her bike. Of course, I am not happy that a cyclist might have hurt themselves, but the situation made me consider the actual situation. The girl (who thankfully was more embarrassed than hurt) had risked her life to get the perfect video of herself driving under a historic landmark – *why*?

At that moment, it was far more important to advertise the visit to the bridge on social media than to enjoy the bridge for what it is. The opinions of others are more important

---

36 Epictetus. (c125 CE) *Enchiridion of Epictetus.*

than the present moment. In this case, even to the point of blindly driving through traffic one-handed. The present moment was lost.

Nobel prize-winning Psychologist and Economist Daniel Kahneman presents a thought experiment in his seminal work *Thinking, Fast and Slow* that addresses the idea of what is important when choosing our experiences:

'At the end of a vacation, all the pictures and videos will be destroyed. Furthermore, you will swallow a potion that will wipe out all your memories of the vacation.

How would this prospect affect your vacation plans? How much would you be willing to pay for it, relative to a normally memorable vacation?'[37]

The question takes aim at how we place so much importance on the ending of a story and our memories of it. You will remember that the 'Remembering Self' is more concerned with overall happiness than the 'Experiencing Self'—the two processors of our experiences that feed into our happiness. When referencing a study on the above question, Kahneman remarks, 'Statistical analysis established that the intentions for future vacations were entirely determined by the final valuation – even when the score did not accurately represent the quality of the experience.'[38] In other words, we place much of the value of our experiences on how they ended and the associated memories.

Recent explosions in social media use have pushed this phenomenon even further. People seem not to enjoy life in the present at all. If the ending of an experience or the memory of it is the most valuable part – then the social currency of others' opinion of your memories (via comments on social media) increases the skew even further. This feeds heavily on our human need to feel connected.

We have already discussed the idea of the present moment and will cover it further in this book. But as I continued my walk along one of the U.K.s most iconic locations, I couldn't help taking mental note of the behaviours of the people I passed. Some take simple photo snapshots for later memories, but most walk with their heads deep in their phones, auto-pilot engaged. There were even a few people recreating TikTok dances with 'like friendly' backdrops. The question I kept returning to, much like that of Kahneman is: 'If these people couldn't share this experience with others, would they even choose to have them?'

I suspect that in the case of the one-handed cyclist and many others, the answer would be—NO.

To be happy, we need to be content in the present moment. For us to have a purpose, we need to point ourselves towards endeavours that are authentic to us intentionally. For all its fun and positives, social media can play an active part in preventing this from happening.

---

37   Kahneman, D. (2011) *Thinking, Fast and Slow*.
38   Kahneman, D. (2011) *Thinking, Fast and Slow*.

When we embark on a journey, either short such as a tourist activity or long like a property renovation, are we doing it for us? Or are we doing it for the pleasure we feel from other people seeing, liking, and commenting on the result? We can all admit that it feels great when you post on social media and receive positive feedback, even from strangers. Unfortunately, it also feels terrible to be criticised by those same strangers. We have developed impatience and are quickly bored while also overloading ourselves with daily exposure to thousands of ideas. We cannot find an authentic and balanced journey for ourselves that can challenge us and add some purpose to our lives. Between viewing everyone else's beautiful lives, wondering what we *should* be doing and keeping up with the Joneses as part of our daily activity, there isn't enough time to filter through the data and still find values and goals that mean something to us.

Thankfully there is a simple solution.

Using *ABCD* you will be able to take back the authorship of your own story. You will assess what is truly important to you (and you only) and build a balanced and consistent path towards achieving it. You will have a structured approach that can be applied across your life in a myriad of different areas – turning large goals to small simple actions. It's the important structure that I had been missing and now has transformed my life for the better. I know what is important to me and this helps me to navigate our wonderfully complex world with a quiet confidence and less anxiety than ever before.

I truly hope that *ABCD* does the same for you.[39]

---

39 Or at least plan your next holiday authentically and avoid cycling into a wall!

6

LESSONS

'Live as though you were to die tomorrow. Learn as if you were to live forever.'
– Mahatma Gandhi.

COMMON THEMES

I REVISITED THE MATERIAL that resonated with me the most—this time taking a more active approach; singling out ideas that would best serve me in my life. I stopped reading and started *learning*. Researching with the intention of creating a framework lit a fire underneath me. I'd been so passive in my understanding of what was possible, and I was embarrassed that I'd not done this sooner. People make their own decisions and lead their own lives which is what makes us all so wonderfully different. I needn't have felt ashamed that I hadn't taken some ownership of my struggles; many people never do, and that is a tragedy, so whenever we start to *take action*, it is a massive step we can be proud of. I was turning knowledge into strength by identifying my core values and living in line with them.

Initially, I was curious to understand the often-quoted dictum 'Let Go' as I was overthinking my life too much; Starting there I re-read my first ever self-help book with the purpose of using the information - I found I could apply many of the lessons. I started to spot descriptions of behaviours I could identify with and possible solutions. From there, I cast a net to capture similar content or expand on even the most minor ideas within the literature I had already consumed. I subscribed to newsletters and podcasts, read studies referenced in the literature and even bought dummy guides on subjects I didn't understand. If that approach sounds like something you may enjoy, then the *References* chapter at the end of this book will help you kick-start your research and light a fire of your own.

If not, I have you covered. The one thing that jumped out at me more and more was that most of the ideas I found could be applied to many areas of my life. That suggested to me, as my life is relatively normal, that the ideas could be helpful to a broader audience. My challenges were not individual to me. Many of us are going through the same. These common areas of life were regularly referenced in the texts (we covered the main ones in *Chapter 4*), and applicable to these areas were the same lessons repeatedly.

As we saw in the *Preface*, the name of this book contains the acronym ABCD for a reason. The common themes I discovered time and again were:

AUTHENTICITY
BALANCE
CONSISTENCY
DISCIPLINE

I soon realised that once we understand the nature of happiness covered earlier in the book, it is impossible to live a *good* life without some attention given to these factors. Indeed, striving for goals that are not authentic to us in an imbalanced way lacking in consistency or discipline is unlikely to bring us any satisfaction at all. Though many of us are doing just that. These elements must be carefully considered. Unfortunately, many people, including myself, do not, and they walk blindly through many areas of life, overwhelmed, disappointed, and unhappy. We don't intentionally take ownership of our stories; we choose unsustainable paths that reflect our lack of self-understanding. We lack values and principles that guide us through decision-making and challenges.

In this chapter, I will try to bring together some of the best ideas and lessons I have found in each of these areas to hopefully answer some of the questions we asked in *Chapter 3*. Using these in later chapters, we can build a straightforward framework around *ABCD* and the important areas of our own lives so we can start acting like the people we want to be once and for all. Bringing some happiness and pride to our lives.

AUTHENTICITY

Authenticity is the first theme that appears regularly and is heavily linked to our happiness. We're talking about how we decide best to live, act, think, and exist. Ideas around control, our judgements, and the stories we tell ourselves have been common in a great deal of self-help literature for generations.

Here are the stand-out ideas that I discovered:

CONTROL, JUDGEMENTS, AND HAPPINESS

Our first step in authenticity, before we can assess ourselves honestly and choose the true best path in any area of life, comes from awareness. Human life is full of *wants*, things we aspire to or desire for ourselves. In many cases, we believe that attaining these wants will bring us happiness; in some cases, they might. In many other cases, however, we find ourselves achieving goals but still lacking something. In even more cases, the want stays out of our reach permanently, causing great stress – even if the goal may not have even been genuine.

These topics are all addressed with the understanding of *control*. Many great minds have pondered the idea of a person's control over their own life. Most famously, in ancient Greece, a group of philosophers who used to wander the marketplaces starting conversations with the public about life clearly defined what they believed were the parameters to our control, and therefore our *happiness*.

Famous stoics from Marcus Aurelius to Theodore Roosevelt to Derren Brown believe in the three building blocks or tenets of Stoicism that you will remember from earlier:

- Control your judgements
- Control your actions
- Accept fate

They tell us that within our control are our thoughts and actions – THAT'S IT—nothing more and nothing less. Not the past, future, or other people's actions; only these two factors that relate most closely to us.

We may feel that we control a great deal of the world around us, but the truth is that we don't. Equally, our significance in the universe is inconsequential. As John Maxwell said, 'You cannot overestimate the unimportance of practically everything!'

Now, life isn't all doom and gloom. It is fantastic news for us, especially in authentically assessing what we should be putting our efforts into. The Stoics remind us that we have a unique skill that distinguishes us from animals. We have our own *reasoned choice*, helping us assess situations and choose the best course of action instead of acting on instinct. As we saw earlier, the mental gap in which we apply this reasoning can be short (particularly if tired, hungry, or stressed), causing us to react rather than respond. Our job here is to use knowledge of the Stoic tenets and practices that take care of our basic needs so that we can grow this gap.

'Between stimulus and response is a space – in that space is our power to choose our response. In our response lies our growth and freedom.'
– Viktor Frankl.

We tend to populate this space with judgements, which originate from our past experiences, some of which that are not useful in the present. Cognitive Behavioural Therapy (CBT) is a well-established psycho-social intervention that aims to reduce anxiety and depression by challenging our thoughts and attitudes and the associated behaviours. There are many connections between this relatively new therapy (Initially practised by Aaron Beck in the 1980s) and Stoicism; most of all, they believe we can change faults in our thinking. CBT is used to apply reason to our judgements, which are with us from life experiences and our childhood.

CBT practitioners and Priory Clinic therapists Rob Wilson and Rhena Branch are the authors of *CBT for Dummies*, one of the first books I read when I started therapy to face the issues I was having in my life. In the chapter 'You Feel the Way You Think,' the authors clearly and simply show how our judgements of events and the historic meaning we attach to these events can cause us much anxiety that we can learn to change.

'The meaning you attach to any sort of event influences the emotional responses you have to that event. Positive events normally lead to positive feelings of happiness and excitement, whereas negative events typically lead to negative feelings like sadness and anxiety.

However, the meanings you attach to certain types of negative events will not be wholly accurate, realistic, or helpful. Sometimes, your thinking may lead you to assign extreme meanings to events, leaving you feeling disturbed...

...CBT involves identifying thoughts, beliefs, and meanings that are activated when you are feeling emotionally disturbed. If you assign less extreme, more helpful, more *accurate* meanings to negative events, you are likely to experience less extreme, less disturbing emotional and behavioural responses.'[40]

Think about it – we often, say that people with a short fuse are *reactive* and that this is a negative trait. Whereas being *considered* and *reasonable* are admirable qualities reflective of someone with a longer fuse who has the ability to respond to events calmly.

Consider this scenario:

You are driving to work, and a car cuts you up without signalling and is swerving on the road. Many people's immediate response to this would be to become angry, and even after some time, they would still claim, 'Some arsehole cut me up today; people are unbelievable.'

Your brain has taken an event and created a judgement (driver = arsehole), and the behaviour that followed was to be angry/shout/swear.

Suppose we were to add an additional piece of information to that scenario, either retrospectively (you find out later after you're already angry) or in real-time. In the passenger seat of that recklessly driven car is a small child who is seriously injured. The driver, the child's father, is desperately trying to find medical help to save his son's life. With this information, the judgement of the situation changes completely. We're now concerned, curious, and even saddened by the events. Our anger immediately subsides.

---

40   Wilson, R. and Branch, R. (2006) *Cognitive Behavioural Therapy for Dummies.*

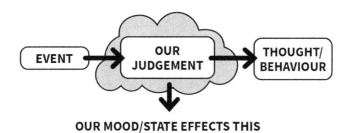

OUR MOOD/STATE EFFECTS THIS

Fig 6.1

We're human and, as such, can change our judgements based on new evidence or with rational thinking. To do this, we must try to nurture and grow the gap between events and actions where these judgements occur (as seen in the *Introduction* and fig 6.1). The first step towards this is the awareness we are developing in this book. It's frequently true that we behave in a certain way only to regret doing so. Being more considered and reasonable is a better approach; taking a breath, using a third-person perspective, and other tactics can be used to assess the situation, ensuring we act more authentically – how we would want to act.

> *'If your distress has some external cause, it is not the thing itself that troubles you, but your own judgement of it – and you can erase this immediately.'[41]*
> *– Marcus Aurelius.*

This quote from Marcus Aurelius' diaries was written when he was Roman Emperor in the 2nd Century. What makes these diary entries fascinating is that they are not intended to be read by the public. Having been thrust into power following the adoption of his uncle by Hadrian, Marcus was never raised to be a future Emperor. He was unlucky enough to reign during some of the Empire's bloodiest and most brutal wars. Many of the 'meditations,' as they are now known, were written while away at war and read like personal *pep talks* to help him navigate the stresses of his life, and nearly 2000 years later, they still feel surprisingly relevant. Even with war raging on and the pressures of heading the largest empire in the world, Marcus often questions his judgements of situations and the control he has over them.

When we consider these ideas of control, we soon realise that we rarely have a problem in the present, or that we can adjust our thinking to be less concerned with things outside of our control. In turn, we are less disappointed when the world around us doesn't act how we had hoped.

There are, of course, areas of life outside of this where we have not all but *some* part to play in the outcome. Desires in these areas are 'Preferred Indifferents' (you would like an

---

41 Hammond, M. (2006) *The Meditations of Marcus Aurelius.*

outcome but can't wholly impact it). You can, however, grow your influence on them by focusing on the part you play.

Stephen Covey has an interesting theory around a person's circle of influence growing as they act with more integrity and reason. In essence, by acting with more authenticity regarding the things they can control, their control over their lives, and ultimately their happiness increases.

Firstly, we are asked to imagine the wide range of concerns we have in our lives. This contains anything we are interested in, regardless of our influence over it. This is our 'Circle of Concern.'

Fig 6.2 – Circle of Concern

Secondly, we picture our 'Circle of Influence,' a subset of things we care about that we also control the outcomes of.

Fig 6.3 – Circle of Influence

Lastly, Covey demonstrates how by focusing only on our 'Circle of Influence,' we can increase its overall size within our wider concerns.

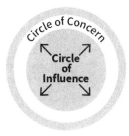

Fig 6.4 – Circle of Influence Grows

Covey tells us that much can be discovered from our proactivity and our level of self-aware-ness, and this can dictate our mindset within our life.

'Proactive people focus their efforts on the Circle of Influence. They work on the things they can do something about. The nature of their energy is positive, enlarging and mag-nifying their Circle of Influence to increase.

Reactive people, on the other hand, focus their efforts on the Circle of Concern. They focus on the weakness of other people, the problems in the environment, and circumstances over which they have no control. Their focus results in blaming and accusing attitudes, reactive language, and increased feelings of victimization. The negative energy generated by that focus, combined with neglect in areas they could do something about, causes their Circle of Influence to shrink.'[42]

I am not prescribing to give up on areas of our lives. Instead, we can have significant influ-ence and success in life in general, but only if we cease to concentrate on the things we can't control. This way, we can reduce our anxiety over areas that won't necessarily change and grow our influence more generally throughout our lives.

The Stoics were often highly influential people and held high power office (relinquishing control isn't equal to taking no actions at all), but they understood their control of situa-tions and they knew that it could be taken away from them by fate. This is a key factor in the discussion around control. We don't only apply the idea to achievements, but also to what we already have and may lose.

Many Stoics recommend the practice of imagining yourself *without* your possessions and current life, even as far as picturing that you had lost a loved one or your own life (Meditations on Mortality, as Seneca describes, help you to accept the fleeting nature of life). Visualisation of this sort is not a harmful practice; it helps us appreciate what we have now and cherish every moment it is with us.

These theories reduce the power of the *wants* in our life. We're often blindly driven to gain and achieve more, which can leave us consistently disappointed, especially if these wants

42 Covey, S. R. (1989) *The 7 Habits of Highly Effective People.* (including adapted diagrams – Fig 6.2-6.4)

lie outside of our control. It is important to remember this at the outset of our process to discover our core values and goals. Doing so grounds us and makes us more authentic and content instantly. Derren Brown remarks:

'If we are to live more felicitous (happy, joyous, fortunate) lives, we should not bother greatly with the common approach, namely gathering for ourselves the popular trappings of success. Such an aim is difficult to implement and impossible to entirely fulfil. Instead, we should train ourselves – as and when we remember – to feel satisfied with what comes more easily. That way, we are far more likely to reach a point of relatively undisturbed happy contentment. If happiness lies in the relationships between what we *desire* and what we *have*, we are being encouraged to consider the first part of the equation rather than obsess over the second.'[43]

Gratitude is one way to achieve this that is more popular than picturing yourself destitute or widowed (I wonder why!). Exactly how you practice this is a personal choice out of the scope of our advice here. Still, many good morning routines include appreciation for where we are in life to remind us that life is often an underappreciated gift. Positivity of this kind can improve our mood and therefore our judgements.

Relinquishing control often leads to us being largely more content with our lives. In turn, as we experience far fewer disturbances from our expectations of others and the world, we are HAPPIER. You may be thinking, 'Content? That's boring. I want to be ecstatic!' but the great thinkers we are drawing from tend to disagree.

You will remember our old friend Artur Schopenhauer. The premise of the 'X=Y' theory is linked to the idea of relinquishing control. The world/fate will behave exactly how they always were, and a lot of the time, this will be against the general outcomes you would wish for. The graph shows us that sometimes, life goes your way and other times, it doesn't; the course of our life will often travel a line in between (where X=Y).

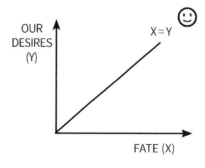

Fig 6.5 – X=Y

43 Brown, D. (2016) *Happy: Why more or less everything is absolutely fine.*

My therapist drew my attention to the idea *Good is Good Enough*, which gives us a similar message. The idea is that real happiness is found in being content and concerning yourself with only what truly matters (which is often less than we imagine). We often feel relatively content and happy overall, which is interpreted as *boring*. Whether it is the world around us or our own experiences, something in us wants to feel tangible joy to translate that into happiness. Boredom leads to us seeking thrills to give us some excitement. However, many of the things we chase are external to us (and in some people's cases can be vices like alcohol, drugs etc.), so we can't have them forever. When they pass, we feel more unhappy than we would have done otherwise. Being content is sustainable and balanced—endless joy is not.

The unsustainability of constantly seeking pleasure can be demonstrated by the cycle of joy and hangover associated to the dopamine response around alcohol.

As with many addictions, there is a spectrum where anyone engaging in that activity sits. As we perform the activity more regularly, we develop a tolerance toward the effects. This is shown clearly in the book *This Naked Mind* by Annie Grace. Though the book primarily deals with addiction to alcohol, the science referenced holds to any addictive substance or activity. When we engage in our chosen vice, our production of the neurotransmitter dopamine spikes as a motivator/reward, and in between these spikes, we feel low. With alcohol use, this is called a *hangover*, which many of you will be familiar with. Grace argues that rather than there being addicts and those who are not, we all experience these hangovers to some level, and they are a sign of withdrawal, which ultimately linger until the next time we have a drink. Over time, the amount of alcohol required to feel 'normal' grows, and we effectively spiral lower until we depend on alcohol to get a baseline feeling of normality (See fig 6.6).

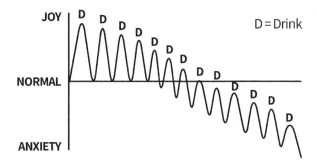

Fig 6.6[44]- Dopamine Cycle of Addiction

Grace continues in the book to reference a study at McGill University, where Rats who were given the ability to manually stimulate the reward centre of their brains (nucleus accumbens) with a lever would neglect their young, forego sex, and stop eating to the point

---

44 Grace, A. (2018) *This Naked Mind: Control Alcohol.* (adapted diagram)

of starvation— instead electing to press the lever thousands of times repeatedly. This of course simplifies the study somewhat, but the idea is scalable. We often find ourselves being selfish both to our basic needs and the needs/feelings of others when focused on anything too strongly.[45]

This phenomenon of mood cycling lower is not limited to addictions, I've spent many perfectly fine weekdays after an exciting weekend feeling low, chomping at the bit for more excitement to come. In doing so, I forget that feeling content and happy with life (even on a dull Wednesday) means I'm likely to be content more regularly (being happy with a little = being happy with a lot).

In summary, we are saying that trying to take the course of life in a particular direction where you are not responsible for all outcomes means that you are placing your happiness outside of your circle of control—your inner citadel.

Some of these are things you can (and regularly do) let go of with ease—small things like when you catch yourself caring a little too much about someone else's behaviour. We reasonably stop ourselves and think, 'Why do I care? It's got nothing to do with me'. However, this train of thought should also be applied to many other areas of life if we want to be happy.

How much can we truly influence our income, for example?

Many people set targets championing their desire to be a millionaire by a certain age. It might even appear to an audience on many social media feeds that this is an achievement you can achieve with certainty if you work hard enough.

I believed that if I did all the *right* things, I would excel in my career, make constant progress, and earn ever-increasing salaries. However, as our discussion suggests, I am only in control of my efforts. I had graduated with a 1st class honours degree from a good university, never taken a break or gap year, and been the perfect employee. Despite this approach, and though I had loyally worked for the same company for 12 years – my goals were not being realised. I was still the lowest-paid and most junior member of my team, and various mergers and acquisitions had meant the same management no longer owned the company – much of my hard work had been worthless.

Initially, I had beaten myself up for not achieving more of my goals – I was the only one to blame. This caused me incredible amounts of guilt and shame as I watched others around me excel as I stood still. But it became clear as I entered my self-help journey that all I could do was my best. I couldn't control decisions made by the management or the financial circumstances the firm found itself in. Unfortunately, I had done my part, which was not enough to reach the expected level.

---

45   Grace, A. (2018) *This Naked Mind: Control Alcohol.*

Rather than take this realisation negatively, I used it to let go of control. I stopped expecting so much of others – particularly the jealousy associated with others' success – and my stress was reduced. If I had done my best, then that was enough for me. With that mindset, I could focus solely on my thoughts and actions; I chose to be happy and only worry about my own part in my career. This relaxed and comfortable version of myself was a far cry from the stressed mess I had become.

You can't control it all, no matter how hard you try. So be careful how much power you hand over to the outcomes of your desires.

Ultimately, here we are seeing part of why authenticity is essential to our happiness. We can remove some of the disturbances we feel as humans by genuinely concerning ourselves with only what we can control. We can control our judgements of events and each other (and even ourselves) so that we are less disappointed with how life can sometimes be. We can choose actions as responses to events or how we live life in general to fit a set of values and principles that genuinely reflect what matters to us. Then and only then can we start to see life-changing progress toward these goals as we act intentionally towards them.

If we don't keep our concerns closely aligned with things that we can take responsibility for and control, then we concern ourselves with things out of our control. We root our happiness or emotional state in *external* factors—often other people's opinions, desires, or actions. By the very nature of control, we allow these things/people to control us. It is a miserable and uncertain life to have your emotional state linked to these externals, changing at the whim of others. We *must* avoid this at all costs; otherwise, our story becomes someone else's.

The brilliant British Psychologist Windy Dryden sums it up brilliantly in his seminal work 'The 10 Steps to Positive Living,' where he says:

'To summarize, take responsibility for that which is in your sphere of influence. Taking responsibility for your thoughts, feelings and actions will encourage you to change your unhealthy thinking patterns linked to your self-defeating emotions and behaviours.'[46]

We will use the ABCD framework to identify what we control and make our desired values and goals authentic to us.

OUR TRUE STORY AND VALUES

We have already referenced Tony Robbin's *Six Human Needs* in this book. The list is simple yet impactful when you consider almost every want, need, and emotion you find yourself having. It is of great comfort to know that most of what we feel we are struggling with alone is part of the human experience.

One of the elements on this list is 'Certainty':

---

46 Dryden, W. (1994) *10 Steps to Positive Living.*

'Certainty is the need to avoid pain and ideally find some comfort. That is why this is the most basic need we all have – a survival mechanism. We have to have certainty to even function in our daily lives. Have you ever been in a situation where you felt uncertain about something that was really important, like your health or the health of a loved one? How about uncertainty about your job or whether you're going to make enough money to make ends meet? When our certainty is threatened, it is difficult to think clearly. When we are uncertain about something that matters, nothing else functions.'[47]

When we think of our *self*, we cannot do so without considering the *storyline* we have running in our heads. We rarely think of anything else when picturing ourselves, reflecting, reminiscing, and any form of introspection.

It is this need for certainty that we satisfy with this story. Human existence is very complicated, and the environments we are exposed to contain endless nuances and infinite possible outcomes. We give ourselves a certain level of comfort and prevent mental exhaustion by filling the gaps in our knowledge, understanding and experience with assumptions we have collected along the way. Because we have historical references to many situations we repeatedly see in life, we can fill in the gaps and save ourselves a great deal of daily anxiety.

In psychology, this is called our 'narrative identity,' where humans give themselves a sense of identity, purpose, and self by evolving a narrative that integrates our life experiences to help us reconstruct a past, perceive our present, and predict our future. The German Psychologist Erik Erikson theorised that we have stages in our development where others heavily influence us and affect how we think and behave in future phases of our development. Most notably, in Toddlerhood, Early Childhood, and Middle Childhood (1-10 years old), we are facing the existential questions:

- Is it okay to be me?
- Is it okay for me to do, move, and act?
- Can I make it in the world of people and things?

Erikson also poses that we develop the answers to psychosocial crisis at each stage from our significant relations:

- Trust vs Mistrust-Mother
- Autonomy vs Shame and Doubt-Parents
- Initiative vs Guilt – Family[48]

---

47 'Why You Are The Way You Are' – *www.tonyrobbins.com*

48 Erikson, E. (1959) 'Identity and the Life Cycle' – *Psychological Issues*, Vol 1, No.1.

Similar theories exist from some of the greatest thinkers of modern times, with Freud (Erikson was a student of Freud's daughter) and Jong acknowledging the impact of our upbringing on how we develop through stages in our lives and perceive the world around us.

We are not the sole author of our childhood stories. It is a collection of world views and assumptions we have built up over the years of our life. Quite a lot is experienced in our formative years as we observe parents' and caregivers' behaviour. They shape how we see the world around us, how we think that world should be, and how we think the world sees us. These stories can also be heavily influenced by cultural references we see around us. Throughout our lives, we add to this story with every passing incident. We're subconsciously drawn to judgements that align with the storyline perpetuating throughout our lives. This perpetual reinforcement of our outlook comes, in large part, from 'Confirmation Bias.' This is where we have a subconscious bias towards explanations that are already known to us. If we have been exposed to a cheating spouse (either as a child or in our own relationships), we may feel infidelity is the most likely reason for a partner's perceived suspect behaviour. They have gone quiet, always looking at their phone, out late with work. The writing will likely be on the wall long before any actual facts have been gathered.

The media even further amplify this phenomenon. Algorithms choosing content for our feeds are selected based on the content we have previously liked/shared. This creates an *echo chamber* effect that feeds our views and preferences back to us until it is almost all we see. The effect is dangerous–look at the rise in hateful behaviour and polarisation of populations as the conversation moves away from the real world to the online one (Brexit, Trump, Masks, Vaccines, etc.). Funnily enough, when you meet people in real life, most people are genuine, warm, friendly, and open to normal, rational discussion on any number of topics. In reality, we all just want to get along.

Our story is an evolutionary development and serves a vital purpose in our survival. Seeing the behaviour of other humans and the natural world and then making future choices based on assumptions from what we have seen; this ability would have saved the lives of many of our ancestors. But as the world around us has become a (mostly) safer place and the number of different situations we find ourselves in expands across more social scenarios, we have to be a little more considerate of a simple fact.

Our stories can be wrong.

The partner who is working late may be busy with work. They may be quiet because they are stressed or unwell. If they opened up to you about these anxieties and asked for help, the suspicion passed down to us from broken homes would most likely dissolve into worry for their wellbeing. Now, of course, they also may be having an affair! I am not saying everything we believe is wrong, only that making assumptions based on historical, sometimes faulty, views of how the world exists *can* lead us down the wrong path. Sometimes our stories are inaccurate.

Oliver Sacks puts it beautifully in *Hallucinations*:

'We now know that memories are not fixed or frozen, like Proust's jars of preserves in a larder, but are transformed, disassembled, reassembled, and recategorized with every act of recollection.'[49]

Holding our longstanding views up to critical reasoning is most important in the realm of authenticity. Particularly relating to how we view ourselves. Our judgements of ourselves are often the harshest opinions that we have. You've heard the phrase, 'I am my own toughest critic.' Well, this fits quite nicely with another common phrase: 'I am my own worst enemy.' We're so firmly tethered to our opinion of ourselves—*who we are*—that it can lead to us making choices in our life that serve only to placate a view that might not even be true. Our internal narrative may no longer suit the person we want to be.

One area of psychology closely related to CBT is Transactional Analysis, which suggests that every person has three possible 'ego states' we draw from during social interactions and thought processes. The PAC Model, formulated by Eric Berne in the 1950s, illustrates that we learn all the life skills and positive character traits needed for our life in our first 17 years. Those of us free from psychological conditions understand empathy, compassion, morals, boundaries etc., from this age onwards. Berne named the 'state' that we are in when we show reasoned behaviours like these the 'Adult Ego State.' This theory becomes important in our search for authenticity if we spend extended periods out of this state (see fig 6.7).

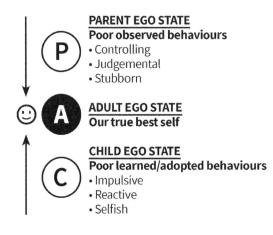

PARENT EGO STATE
Poor observed behaviours
• Controlling
• Judgemental
• Stubborn

ADULT EGO STATE
Our true best self

CHILD EGO STATE
Poor learned/adopted behaviours
• Impulsive
• Reactive
• Selfish

Fig 6.7 – The PAC Model

When we act out negative personality traits such as selfishness, reactiveness, and need for control, we are copying behaviours we learned to comfort us as children, the 'Child Ego State.' When we behave in a judgemental, shaming, inflexible or restrictive way, we often copy behaviours that we saw from parents and other authoritative figures. We held on to

---

49 Sacks, O. (2012) *Hallucinations*.

them and now use them reactively in the present. This is the 'Parent Ego State.' This area of therapy is fascinating, and although exploring it thoroughly is out of scope for this book, the idea that a lot of our behaviours and opinions are from childhood can explain why there is a need to reassess what views we genuinely hold dear and believe—as an adult.[50]

This section has covered much evidence that points to the same place. We're deciding how to live our lives, referring to a jigsaw puzzle of inputs pieced from external sources. This sense of self is vitally important to us; it forms our philosophy in life that influences many of the choices we make and views we hold. But does it stand up to scrutiny? Are we being authentic to who we are and want to be, or are we at the mercy of other people's views and episodes from our past? Are we honouring ourselves?

Just as we can use our very human skill of reason to change our judgements of external events to be happier, we can also change the judgements we make about our own lives so that we are more authentic and live in line with our *core values.*

This is called living a 'Considered Life.' We take back authorship of our story to ensure that it is right for us.

Put another way. You are not your thoughts—some of the assumptions about yourself you hold can change if you want them to.

It's common for us to start toward a goal or set ourselves a challenge, and much like the analogy of the hole in the road, we find ourselves acting contrary to what we had set out to do. Our automatic behaviours combine with a deep-seated opinion of who we are, and we are down the hole before we notice we are heading for it. When we are aware of who we are in the present and what we really want, we tend to behave with more intention and focus on being the type of person we *want* to be, not the person we *think* we are. Just as children in school are taught to have a growth mindset to change 'I can't do maths' into 'I can't do maths YET,' we can also see ourselves being more considered, choosing actions that genuinely suit us, and living a more fulfilling life.

As we build up our awareness and understanding of these ideas, we are more likely to start cultivating the habits of the person we want to be. This is gold dust for the decisions we can make regarding what we spend our time on and how we live our lives.

So far, we have spoken mostly about failing at upholding values and achieving goals we set for ourselves due to our expectations, judgements, and control. There is another side to this coin, which is equally, if not more, heart-breaking. We will all be aware of someone who appears to have it all yet seems miserable. Someone who took every action society, or their family told them SHOULD be important to them, from school to college to university to a profession, and so on. It is often said that if you love what you do, you'll never work a day in your life, and unfortunately for many, the opposite is also just as true. Even

---

50 Interpreted from - Berne, E. (1957 and 1958) 'Ego states in psychotherapy' and 'Transactional analysis: A new and effective method of group therapy' – *American Journal of Psychotherapy*, 11(2) and 12(4).

with success we can be miserable – if what we worked so hard toward wasn't authentically chosen by us from the beginning.

Nothing is worse than getting to the top of a ladder to realise it is against the wrong wall.

To continue my earlier example, what became apparent as I became more relaxed and confident in myself – I realised that I didn't really like the job I had been doing for over a decade! Taking away the external aspects of salary, job title, and status, I was left with a pretty boring job on a trading desk, surrounded by toxic people, answering to people I didn't respect.

I chose to take a life-changing action. Probably the first authentic decision I had made in my 'career.' I left my job and retrained in a different profession. A profession that had more of the qualities I would enjoy, hours that allowed me to spend time with my family more, and more chance of progression. Though it has been tough, this change not only gave me a career I enjoy, but also allowed my life to move philosophically to where it is today.

I am happy.[51]

Through the ABCD framework, I offer you an alternative where you can examine, as I did, the things that you assign importance to and ensure that they fit with your core values—your true story.

Earlier, we mentioned the idea of a circle of influence/control. One of the proponents of this theory is the bestselling author and educator Stephen R. Covey. He is known globally for his book *The 7 Habits of Highly Effective People*. Here, he sets out a road map for people to follow when trying to be more effective and efficient. Millions of copies have been sold worldwide, and I found his work referenced in various places I visited whilst looking for inspiration. Early in the book, Covey establishes that many of us require a paradigm shift in how we think before we can effectively move towards anything of value:

'It's a principle that all things are created twice (once in our head then again in the real world), but not all first creations are by our conscious design. In our personal lives, if we do not develop our own self-awareness and become responsible or our own first creations, we empower other people and circumstances outside our Circle of Influence to shape much of our lives by default. We reactively live the scripts handed to us by family, associates, other people's agendas, the pressures of circumstance – scripts from our earlier years, from our training, our conditioning.

These scripts come from people, not principles. And they rise out of deep vulnerabilities, our deep dependency on others and our needs for acceptance and love, for belonging, for a sense of importance and worth, for a feeling that we matter.

---

51 Not only did this authentic action feel empowering, but since then I have discovered the contents of this book, a sport I love, new close friends, and many other facets to a happier existence – authenticity gave me freedom.

Whether we are aware of it or not, whether we are in control of it or not, there is a first creation to every part of our lives. We are either the second creation of our own proactive design, or we are the second creation of other people's agendas, of circumstances or of past habits.'[52]

Even if the required analysis seems too onerous, we can all benefit from some introspection. Especially when choosing what we spend our time on, as we will never replenish this precious resource.

The values and goals we choose to focus on are our *core values*. The areas that are important to us that deserve our attention, the outcomes that move our life, no matter how little, towards the version of ourselves we want to be. The best version of ourselves.

DO WE HAVE A PROBLEM RIGHT NOW/IS THIS GOAL IN LINE WITH MY VALUES?

Suppose we are intentionally acting authentically when addressing issues. In that case, we can ask ourselves the question we posed in the *Introduction*: 'Do I have a problem right now?' This time we can draw upon the ideas we have seen above and make a more authentic and reasoned choice about what matters to us. Making rational decisions about what we should focus on and prioritise. With any luck, the number of issues that we can affect or that concern us will reduce along with the stresses we face. Likewise, this question can be reframed as: 'What genuine goals align with my values?'

We stop clutching aimlessly at the wants and needs we think we require because we're told we do. We can take a breath and decide to address a few areas in our lives that will make the most significant difference to us personally. These can be big or small, but they are much more likely to be authentic to you, within your control, and more representative of your happiness. The beauty of this authenticity is that because you have picked these areas in this way, you are far more likely to be willing to work consistently towards them.

The Stoics (yes, them again) had a word for this state: *Euthymia*. This means believing in yourself and trusting you are on the right path.

We can experience this too. We develop confidence in our decisions and are more steadfast in our reasoning because we genuinely follow our *own path*. The best way to do this is to apply our human reason and authenticity to ensure that our internal values align with our external behaviours. In this way, we behave like the person we want to be and gain contentment and confidence in our behaviours.

Dr Rangan Chatterjee has a theory in his book *Happy Mind, Happy Life* that our happiness can be seen as a three-legged stool, where each leg is a crucial element of our happiness. These are contentment, control, and alignment. In our discussion around authenticity, I feel

---

52 Covey, S. R. (1989) *The 7 Habits of Highly Effective People.*

the idea of alignment Chatterjee presents further shows us the importance of authorship of our own story and the importance of self-awareness.

'ALIGNMENT Feeling aligned means that the person you want to be, and the person you are actually being out there in the world are one and the same.'[53]

Understanding an authentic version of our story, choosing genuine problems to solve and targets to strive for based on that story and then acting in line with these values is paramount to our happiness.

Finally, on the subject of authenticity, we can use the following simple technique to assess our goals and targets. We often find ourselves desiring things in life, and on occasion, you will find yourself making decisions without first evaluating WHY?

In the ABCD framework, we will ask ourselves this question. With a simple technique whereby when you select the goals you would like to achieve (or value you would like to hold), you mindfully ask, 'Why?'

The answer may be shallow or simple, so ask yourself again, 'Why?'

It sounds so simple, but it is truly revealing to honestly question your motives. It may even feel a little uncomfortable as you repeat this line of questioning up to five times. Ideally, you will replace older values and goals with more positive, genuine ones - saving yourself many negative emotions that come hand in hand with having your ladder up against the wrong wall.

'The Privilege of a lifetime is to become who you truly are.'
– Carl Jung.

SUMMARY

I have shown that the first cornerstone of our ABCD framework requires you to assess what you truly value and to understand your vision of the world and your place in it:

- **LET GO**—Understand that you only have control over your thoughts and actions. Keep these concerns within your priorities and let go of what you don't control to relieve stress and disappointment. Be more present.
- **MIND THE GAP**—Apply reason to your judgements. Acknowledge that, often, the judgement, not the event itself, creates your poor feelings and behaviours. You can control these judgements and reduce the issues you face.
- **CONSIDERED LIFE**—Humans use stories to fill in the gaps and create automatic responses to situations based on experience. But often, these assumptions are given

---

53 Chatterjee, Dr R. (2022) *Happy Mind, Happy Life.*

to you by others directly or indirectly and can be false. Take an honest look at what's important to you and who you are right now in the present.

- **VALUES & PRINCIPLES**—The things you think are essential to you may not be. They are adopted into your story or absorbed subconsciously from media. Look more considerately and find the areas of your life that you truly want to change/ grow. You will see an approach that aligns who you are with what you want.
- **AUTHENTIC AIMS**—Now you see what to work on. You can see that many of your issues are not problems at all, given what you now know to be true. The targets and goals you had coveted only to fail repeatedly, are seen for what they really are... inauthentic to your considered self (or out of your control in reality). Start making new goals (and questioning WHY) that will change your life; even if you are only partially responsible for them, you understand that doing your part to your best ability is enough.

These simple yet effective ideas, backed up by various sources, go a long way towards answering the questions we posed in *Chapter 3* of this book. They show that we can severely reduce the stresses and the overwhelming number of challenges we are setting ourselves. We can spend more time on our actual lives because we know that deep down, only a few areas need attention, and they are genuine to us. If we make this approach sustainable and enjoyable, then there's no reason it can't fit easily into our everyday life. For this reason, the ABCD framework will provide tools for us to be more BALANCED.

Pause for Thought – Please take time to make some notes:

BALANCE

Balance is the only sustainable approach to life. This should be obvious to us, yet we become increasingly overwhelmed and impatient with the desire for instant gratification and our overexposure to the world's endless possibilities. As a result, the adage of 'Slow and steady wins the race' is replaced with something far harder to sustain. Authenticity and balance go hand in hand. They form half of the ABCD framework primarily concerned with our happiness and how we can ensure we enjoy our journey, regardless of the result. Balance prevents us from burning out from striving for something whilst neglecting other important areas of our lives.

WHY BALANCE IS GOOD

If authenticity is being true to yourself, then balance is being *honest* with yourself.

We can balance the actions we take and the life we live, and we'll cover this later in this section, but the first step in accepting balance into the ABCD framework takes place in the *mind*. We've already seen that understanding what we control and letting go of what we don't is a solid idea. But it remains just that unless we believe it; an idea.

As Schopenhauer (and later Derren Brown) demonstrates, we can see our aims along one axis of a graph (Y) and fate on the other (X). The idea represented is that most people spend large parts of their lives expectantly forcing the graph line toward the Y-axis. In other words, they try to control every element of the world around them so that it suits their wants and needs. When we have this outlook, we are perpetually disappointed. Events that happen that don't fit into our plans are unthinkable and make us quite disturbed.

We may think that the vile comments written about online articles are those of the insane. These people can't be very happy if they can get so angry about something that doesn't affect them. But somewhere within all of us is a tendency to do just that, only most of us do this in a far more subtle way. By getting anxious, angry, or upset at all manner of things we can't control. These emotions make us unhappy far more often than we need to be. In reality, the graph we plot in our life will be somewhere between X and Y – something more like X=Y (Seen earlier and in fig 6.8).

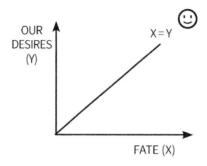

Fig 6.8 — X=Y

Understanding this idea around control, which we covered in the section on authenticity, is an excellent start to combating unhappiness. Furthermore, the idea of balance can be applied to a multitude of different areas—being bored versus being anxious, social life versus family life, chocolate vs salad...

It is harmful to have too much of anything, even if it's perceived as 'good,' and this is mainly because any extreme is unsustainable. That's why it is an extreme. People who spend too much time in these mental or physical extremes tend to fall foul of mental health issues. As we mentioned, it is far more favourable to be content longer term than jumping for joy one minute and miserable the next.

One of the most critical balancing acts is:

CORE VALUES/GOALS versus THE REALITY OF LIFE.

Letting go of some control of our expectations allows us to strike a balance between these two opposing forces. When we do, we choose far more realistic objectives and fairly assess our ability to obtain them.

Humans are fallible; every one of us. No one alive has ever been or will be perfect. No matter what stories we are told when we are young or whom we look to for inspiration now—we all have faults and differences. Flexibility with ourselves and others is critical to our happiness. In the same way that the person in the pub every day may find themself with an alcohol use disorder, the person who expects 100% achievement of their goals will find themselves living a very stressful and disappointing existence[54]. This is amplified further if our emotional reactions are also imbalanced.

In *CBT for Dummies*, Rob Wilson and Rhena Branch provide a simple yet informative guide to their field. Having had some CBT as part of my own therapy, it was clear that so many people could benefit from its message. One crucial factor is how we speak to ourselves; it is meaningful because it feeds our internal storyline. If we tell ourselves we are useless, we

---

[54] In fact the need for control is central in many addictions and mental health issues.

will believe it. Another factor is that many of us have pretty biased ways of thinking that can often feed unhealthy negative emotions we are having.

Unhealthy Negative Emotions, the authors explain, are inflexible, painful, extreme, and unrealistic. They trap us and make the solutions feel too far from our reach:

ANXIETY

DEPRESSION

ANGER

SHAME

HURT

JEALOUSY

GUILT

They are BIG words for BIG feelings that can overwhelm anyone who experiences them[55]. Many of us find ourselves in these states, especially when we feel things aren't going our way or that we have somehow failed. CBT suggests that biased thoughts create an unbalanced mindset.[56]

Here are some examples and suggestions to reframe them:

ALL OR NOTHING THINKING

One failure or obstacle means overall failure. 'I've eaten a chocolate bar, so my diet is ruined; I might as well have a takeaway and start the diet again Monday.' This is not correct. Use both/and language to speak in a more balanced way. 'I can BOTH enjoy some chocolate AND remain on course in my diet.'

ADDING TO FIRST IMPRESSIONS

Creating a meaning of an event with only basic facts. 'My colleague has had their bonus meeting today, and I haven't been told about mine yet—that means it's bad news—I'm probably getting fired.' Mostly, you only have the first piece of information, and it is not reasonable to guess the second part purely to feed the negativity you are feeling.

---

55 In my experience using therapy to unpack these feelings and our 'story' can be beneficial to anyone who is lucky enough to undertake it – that being said some of these emotions can be symptomatic of more serious mental health conditions – if you believe you are suffering from such a condition some resources can be found *https://www.nhs.uk/mental-health/* (UK only) or contact the Samaritans (*https://www.samaritans.org/*) if you are in need of someone to speak to

56 Wilson, R. and Branch, R. (2006) 'Chapter 2 – Spotting Errors in Your Thinking' (Ed) - *Cognitive Behavioural Therapy for Dummies.*

CATASTROPHISING

Imagining the worst. 'Mum isn't answering the phone; Something bad must have happened.' No, she is most likely to be busy, and you can call tomorrow.

FORTUNE TELLING

You are predicting the future and creating anxiety. Think of the number of times you have caused yourself disturbance because you 'knew' what was going to happen, only for it not to go as you imagined. This is one of the critical aspects of letting go of control. *You can't control the future, so you can't predict it.* Certainly not by referring to an unreliable source like your past story, which plays right into your anxiety's hands.

OTHERS

Overgeneralisation, Globally Rating, Discounting the Positives...

Seeing this thinking for what it is, we make fairer assessments of our situation. We can take a breath, regroup, and see our thoughts like clouds passing through an otherwise sunny sky—noting they exist but knowing we can let them pass and still be in the sunshine. We can lengthen the gap between thoughts, judgements, and behaviours.

When we practice this, we find that the unhealthy negative emotions become smaller, *healthy* negative emotions:

Realistic Concern

Sadness

Annoyance

Regret (in place of shame)

Disappointment

Concern

Regret (in place of guilt)

These are flexible, balanced, and resolvable. We can and will experience all of these and it is good to, as they help us understand ourselves and our values. Professor of Counselling at the University of London, Windy Dryden, gives some guidance on how some acceptance can be achieved as one of the steps that can be taken to happiness. This step is to 'Allow yourself to experience healthy negative emotions,' in which he states that being able to do so is a 'hallmark of mental health' and displays the following traits:

- A flexible philosophy of desire.
- An anti-awfulizing philosophy coupled with an acceptance of reality.
- A philosophy of high frustration tolerance.
- A philosophy of self and other acceptance.[57]

Effectively, those who can consider how they think will experience more balanced emotional states. This mental balance keeps us on a more stable footing to enjoy our lives no matter our challenges.

This is relevant in our ABCD framework because as we look at sustainability and a balanced approach to our actions, a balanced approach to our thoughts is equally important. A healthy mind is balanced and accepts that it can't have its way in every moment. We must be aware of our thoughts when working towards our targets and solutions and keep ourselves in check, appreciating that they are only thoughts and not reality. Neither perfection nor extreme action is required to get the most out of life, so please don't let your mind tell you otherwise.

When working out our approach towards our core values and goals, we still need flexibility with the outcome and mental compassion with our efforts. We can BOTH authentically evaluate our lives AND find purpose to improve ourselves. Lowering our expectations in line with reality is a vital step in realising this.

Epicurus said, 'Desire what you already have, and you will have all you need.'

This doesn't align with the modern trend of hyper-productive lifestyles where we *sleep when we're dead*, *smash life* and *don't stop till we hit our goals*. We see a myriad of examples of people pushing this extreme approach as the only way to be successful. We must avoid falling into this trap. Even if those promoting these ideas truly don't have any balance and do live with this intensity (which is unlikely)—I'd argue there is still something philosophically missing deep down within them.

Our best approach is to be in a state of balance as often as possible both in our view of what we expect to happen and our part in it—balanced in how we perceive ourselves along this journey. This means balancing one goal with another, and all values with any other values we hold. We are not siloed off into different areas of our life – they all interact constantly. Even the ABCD framework is a balancing act between areas most concerned with happiness, flexibility, and going easy on yourself (AB) and those concerned with consistency, work ethic, and discipline (CD). Both sides need to be somewhat present to find a middle ground where we work towards the things that matter. - yet leaving enough space in our minds and lives to actually enjoy them.

We will see a technique later to help us visualise where the balance across all important areas of our life suits us best.

57 Dryden, W. (1994) *10 Steps to Positive Living.*

Here we have seen why balancing our thoughts is critical in assessing how we are doing and plotting a course through our lives. The other central element of balance is that of our actions and what we choose to do once we know our values/goals. It is so crucial at this stage to choose your actions wisely. We've done some of the hard work by picking authentic goals, meaning we care about them deep down—this makes being consistent with them far more straightforward—they are ours. But this consistency is impossible if we set ourselves too big a task. Remember, however genuine, many of the things we decide to work on are still only partially in our control. The promotion, the physique, the personal milestone – they all have a massive chunk of luck and fate (and external input) that factor into the outcome.

In a tennis match, players can only do their best with the part they play. Once the ball is over the net, it's out of their control. We can see our role in our lives in the same light and do our best to relinquish control of the outcome. This way, we don't pin our hopes and emotions on the result, and critically for our framework, we can take a more balanced approach. Many people's goals fail primarily because they set targets that are unrealistic or because they set actions towards them that are unsustainable. They hate what they are doing, burn out or give up. Knowing what we now know, it's time to take a more measured approach and enjoy the journey while we can.

ENJOYING THE JOURNEY

It's important when considering the idea of balance, particularly the balance between our desires and fate, that we recognise that *no one moment or event defines the whole of our life*.

We have times when the world seems to be pulling outcomes in a direction that we would prefer it wouldn't, and we have times when things appear to be going our way. It's essential to see that we can both have times when things don't go our way and still be happy overall. We can both have fallible moments and still be doing well. We can both have failures and still be on target for our goals.

Many memes in culture throughout the modern era have warned us of the fleeting nature of life.

Guy Lombardo once told us, 'Enjoy yourself-it's already later than you think!'

Yet many of us spend so much time waiting for *yet*. We tell ourselves as we enter a period of severe, unbalanced discipline or hard work that when we have/are a specific, different thing (size 8 dress size, immaculate house, make partner of a law firm, etc.) that then we will be happy—then is the time to enjoy our life.

The UK's Office for National Statistics states, 'Life expectancy at birth in the UK from 2018 to 2020 was 79.0 years for males and 82.9 years for females'[58]. That's around 81 years on average.

Without wanting to alarm you, we should be taking this statistic very seriously. It's crucial to consider the brevity of our time on Earth. The Stoics often encouraged thought experiments to test their philosophy against potential loss. The idea is to imagine losing something you value and being comfortable without it. Here I would encourage a similar thought experiment around losing the most valuable asset we have—*our time.*

If we can expect to (on average) live 81 years, then we will have only 81 Christmas Days. 81 birthdays. 81 first days of spring. Just over two months' worth of each of these special occasions. If you see friends once a month and are 41 years old, you might only see them 480 more times in your life. If each visit is 2 hours long, you'll spend only 40 days of the rest of your life with them.

However macabre this sounds; it is a valuable lesson we must learn. We have 4212 weeks of our life, then it's done. Do you want to spend any of that time living *unhappily*? When you begin a 3-month diet so extreme that you are miserable and hungry every day, you are wasting 12 weeks of that precious life. If that diet is to be in shape for a two week holiday, then the payoff isn't cost effective, especially if the reason behind the weight loss target is not authentic. Diet or not - you will still be *you* when you are on holiday.

So, let's understand from now on that the idea of balance is crucial. We must pick goals and actions for ourselves that are sustainable for a happy and content lifestyle. We must enjoy the journey we are on right now and stop waiting for conditions to be perfect.

Most people hear this advice and panic slightly. They picture a slow, minimal approach that doesn't get them to their goals quick enough or makes them feel somehow lazy. Social media is full of productivity content, and we are force-fed ideas that people are all 'on their grind 24/7' (whatever that means!). This is an unfair representation of real life. An edited and airbrushed story that all success is born from blood, sweat and tears (ignoring good fortune). 100% commitment to any one task is often not sustainable—therefore, it will be difficult to maintain *consistently*– thus much more likely to fail. Six months of slower-paced progress is far more effective and enjoyable than six weeks of extreme actions that eventually crash and burn into failure.

We explored in an earlier section why our goals fail—in many cases, it is because the target is too extreme and cannot be achieved (either at all or in an unrealistic time period), or the actions toward it are too severe and can't be sustained. Both adverse sets of criteria are linked to the idea of balance we explore in this section. It is relatively clear that balance is essential to progress, and most of us would advise our friends to be realistic; don't overdo it or let something take over your life. Yet when the time comes to take our own advice, we don't. Often overcommitting to extreme plans.

It is impossible to be content without having balanced expectations and approaches. We swing between highs and lows, successes, and disappointments, or look back on our lives with regret, which is a tragedy. It's essential to be realistic and accepting with ourselves, aware of who we are. Setting a goal that is destined to fail requires you to forgo who you are. All your likes and dislikes should be considered before any journey and balanced accordingly[59]. Instead of being extreme and ignoring your human fallibility, embrace it and have positive changes alongside it.

Life is too short to waste large parts of it doing things you don't enjoy, towards goals you don't really want, in quantities you can't maintain. Building a life story that you can look back on with pride is far more conducive to happiness. So, when we 'look back' at our lives what do we value the most?

Daniel Kahneman and his team performed an experiment where they subjected their volunteers to uncomfortable periods in iced water to record their experiences. The participants submerged their hands in 'painfully cold' water—14 degrees Celsius—and used their free hands to register their pain. The subjects had two cold hand trials:

- The first was for 60 seconds in the painful water, followed by a warm towel.
- The second was for 90 seconds; however, for the last 30 seconds, the water was marginally warmer (still a painfully cold 15 degrees).

The second experiment is more of a painful experience; it is the same as the first trial but has 30 extra seconds of painful submersion. The participants were then told they could choose which trial to repeat in the third and final part of the experiment. Logic would tell us that they would prefer the shorter, less painful trial. However:

'Fully 80% of the participants who reported that their pain diminished in the final phase of the longer episode opted to repeat it, thereby declaring themselves willing to suffer 30 seconds of needless pain in the anticipated third trial.'[60]

This work furthered Kahneman's theory around the two selves we discovered earlier. The theory stands that we have two processors of the experiences we face in our lives: the experiencing self and the remembering self. The former concerns how we feel about events we have experienced in the past. As the experiment above demonstrates, humans put significance into how the story ends (remember how people would be less likely to take a holiday they wouldn't remember after?), and, for that reason, this is a powerful processor that strongly relates to our happiness. The latter processor is how we view the life we are

---

59   It's all well and good aspiring to a solitary life living in a forest self-sufficiently away from society. However, you'll soon be miserable if you like going to the cinema or meeting friends in restaurants!
60   Kahneman, D. (2011) *Thinking, Fast and Slow.*

experiencing right now; it is often swayed towards pleasure as we feel the emotions in the current moment.

In this section, I encourage you to consider this theory's relevance to balance. So far, you could read the information we have seen on balance and conclude that the best thing to do is to live for the moment. After all, *life's too short*. I wouldn't blame you for thinking, 'If almost nothing is in my control, I'm already halfway through my life, and I should enjoy the journey—then LET'S PARTY!!'

Unfortunately, this is *not* enjoying the journey either. A large part of the contentment we are seeking comes from how we remember our life.

Therefore, the ABCD framework must also focus on consistency and discipline. The premise seen in Kahneman's work holds firm for all of us, we must balance out the two processors of our life to live an enjoyable one. Our experiencing self concerns itself with what is taking place as we experience moments in our life. It is related to joy, pleasure, and urges. These are enjoyable on occasion. However, a life dedicated to only optimising how we feel in any given moment is not a content one. It would likely be unhealthy, selfish, expensive, addictive, and even dull. While it is unlikely to be sustainable for these reasons, it also fails to provide us with another of the human needs—*purpose*.

You will have felt the power of purpose and how it is perceived within your happiness. For example:

- You miss a party with friends because another friend is having a tough time. Your immediate experience is one of FOMO and annoyance because we 'have to' help the friend while everyone else is enjoying their night. But looking back on that night in the future, you will see it as a bonding moment with the friend or have a certain glow about you for being helpful to someone else.
- You feel pleased with yourself in the moment for taking some sort of shortcut (the context could vary from study to home improvement and many other areas between). You experience some self-satisfaction and freedom you afforded yourself. Yet later down the line, when you are called upon to recollect that experience, it can often feel tainted or shameful—or worse still, have negative consequences.

The remembering self often views experiences with more reason and aligns with our core values and goals, it is our most powerful processor in this regard. Yet, as with everything, it too must be balanced in our life. I have spent many months miserably slogging toward a goal and neglected my present; it is not a positive approach either.

So, as we begin to create core values and goals, we must remember to keep a balance between the two processors; we want to enjoy the journey but also look back overall and know we acted with purpose and value. We balance (AB) vs (CD) and enjoy the resulting journey.

In selecting balanced approaches that are sustainable in your life, you are effectively allowing yourself to be more consistently in line with the person you want to be. Positive behaviours become more habitual because of this, and real change is made enjoyably. You take the small next steps towards something you actually care about in a way that doesn't overwhelm you or your enjoyment of life. You will find that compared to the overzealous approach you will have tried or seen before, this method *will* lead to lifestyle changes you appreciate. *ABCD* helps you have this in the areas that are important in life with tools helping you visualise how your life interacts overall.

Before I realised this need for a balanced approach, I had many occasions where I was following an overzealous plan with no consideration for my enjoyment of the present and my other values. Having realised that a morning routine could be beneficial to the rest of the day, I decided to incorporate one into my day. Part of that routine was to journal every morning. I set myself the target to journal for 30 minutes *every* day. Within the first week I had already missed several entries – as you all know life gets in the way sometimes. I became irritable because I was 'failing' at this seemingly simple goal. However, it was clear that by setting quite a strict target and not considering the other elements of my life I was doing more harm than good. I'd often obsess on missed journalling and try to fit it later in my day, cutting lunch short, missing time with the kids, and so on. Suddenly, what was intended to be a positive mental experience had turned into a chore that I *hated* and that clashed negatively with my life.

The approach I now take is far more flexible. I write for five to ten minutes most days. Because I know what I am capable of, and what time I have available, this approach is far more balanced and allows for the times when journalling isn't possible – without the disturbances caused by breaking a promise to myself. I'm a person who *sometimes enjoys journalling* – and that is better suited to me.

How will we know if we are making balanced choices? How will we know we are succeeding? How will we know if we are taking the easy route or one that is too hard? One of the first ways will be in how we *feel.* By reducing the number of concerns on our plate to only those that truly matter and reasonably allocating our resources to those tasks in our lives – we begin to feel very different. Rather than feeling overwhelmed, like a failure, not knowing where to start; we start to feel one of the true phenomena of balance. We experience *flow.*

FLOW

Flow is a feeling of contentment that we experience at certain times. Some people refer to it as being 'in the moment.' It is the balancing point where our challenges are equal to our skills. The phrase 'in the zone' is commonly used in sporting circles because professional sports allow participants to use their skills against a certain challenge regularly. Luckily, as I suspect very few of those reading this book are professional athletes, there are many other areas of life where we can find this 'flow state.' We have all been so engrossed in a task that the outside world seems to fade from view; we are totally focused. Often only realising after the moment that many hours have passed or that we were unaware of something happening nearby. This typically happens when we are performing a task that we both enjoy and challenges us.

Mihaly Csikszentmihalyi, the professor and former chairman of the Department of Psychology at the University of Chicago, has dedicated his life to researching flow and related areas. Since the early 1990s, he has been publishing papers on the subject, which led to his now classic work, *Flow: The classic work on how to achieve happiness*, in which he outlines the anatomy of consciousness, happiness, and the enjoyment of our lives in relation to his theory.

'ORDER IN CONSCIOUSNESS: FLOW

The opposite state from the condition of psychic entropy is optimal experience. When the information that keeps coming into awareness is congruent with goals, psychic energy flows effortlessly. Here is no need to worry, no reason to question one's adequacy. But whenever one does stop to think about oneself the evidence is encouraging: 'You are doing all right.' The positive feedback strengthens the self, and more attention is freed to deal with the outer and inner environment.'[61]

Csikszentmihalyi demonstrates many ideas that have become staples in modern thinking around happiness. From the perception of time when we are in flow (time flies when you are having fun), having clear goals and feedback, and the 'autotelic experience,' where one enjoys an activity purely for the sake of doing it – which occurs when the outcome of the activity is less important than enjoying the journey. This is fundamental to this book's work and links back to our ideas on control. The ABCD framework allows you to have more regular autotelic experiences. You might not always have control over the final outcomes in your life, but you do have control of your enjoyment of it.

Within *Flow*, there is a chapter on 'The Conditions of Flow.' Various flow activities are referenced in this chapter, and I found the below graph very interesting because it is similar to the 'X=Y' graphs we previously saw in this book.[62]

The 'Flow Channel' diagram shows that if our skills increase without challenge, we can become bored in any pursuit (moving from a ✓ to ✗ outside of the channel). Equally, if the challenges come to us too soon when we are not ready, we can become anxious (moving from a ✓ to ✗ outside of the channel).

---

61 Csikszentmihalyi, M. (2002) *Flow: The classic work on how to achieve happiness*.
62 It is satisfying to see unrelated resources confirm and re-enforce each other. This is one of the main motivations for me to create *ABCD*.

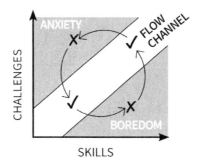

Fig 6.9[63]- Flow Channel

Viewing our core values and goals in this light, we see that we must create balance between realistic ambition toward what we are genuinely capable of *and* still push ourselves enough to benefit from regular flow moments in our lives. *ABCD* makes this possible.

Suppose we accept that those who spend more time in flow enjoy the present moment more frequently (as Csikszentmihalyi demonstrates). In that case, we can see that happiness comes from balancing challenges and skills. This further reinforces that it is crucial to balance the things we enjoy and pick actions we are proud of that challenge us. For this reason, having some intention toward our values, rather than taking the easiest option, is better for us psychologically. We can understand that if we have authentic values and goals we aspire to and we approach them in a balanced way then we create an environment that allows us to be successful and happy. This side of the framework (AB) is balanced by the second half of our ABCD model centred around consistency and discipline (CD), which provide the balance between our flexible, content side and the side of us that aspires for more.

It's this balance that is so often ignored in our daily lives. People are portrayed as either living every moment on their own terms as one big party, or as hungry workaholic go-getters. We will strive for something far more beautiful finding the middle ground that suits us and provides us with more flow in our lives.

EFFICIENCY

It is becoming clear that balance is integral to our mental well-being and happiness. So how do we create balance? Firstly, the understanding and awareness of the information in this chapter are intended to go some way toward this. By knowing and accepting the principles of balance, we can start to see where we are setting extreme goals or overloading ourselves with work towards them. When added to the idea of control we learned from the Stoics earlier in this chapter, we will find that the number of perceived issues we must address

63 Csikszentmihalyi, M. (2002) *Flow: The classic work on how to achieve happiness.* (adapted diagram).

will reduce. However, we're unlikely to reduce that number to ZERO. This leaves us tackling the misbalance often found in how we work towards the authentic goals that remain.

Our earlier discussion suggested we should *enjoy the journey*. I warned that this does not mean the easy route. Some of us are extremely busy, and even with a plenty of introspection, we can't let go of everything in our lives that doesn't directly serve our core values. For a start, most of us have jobs, and though we could decide that is an area we should address or change, it's unlikely to be instant. We also have dependants, friends, family, and our wider community. There are plenty of things we can't control that impact our lives, and while we should be careful to keep our happiness under our control and unaffected by these externals, they can still take a lot of time and effort from us.

I'll end this section with some of the ideas I have seen on efficiency. How can we free space in our routine to focus on our values and goals? Efficiency is important because it allows us to act toward our intended targets without taking too much from our mental and physical capacity. Of course, many thousands of articles, books, and social media accounts are dedicated to productivity, but this is a slightly different concept. In many cases, productivity is how to increase our output in our week/month/life. Generally, this will include some beneficial practices like journaling and planning. However, it often moves toward promoting a lifestyle where you fit so much into your daily routine with the intention of becoming a *super-producer*. You work multiple hours on a variety of projects and achieve considerable results -and this is very appealing, if not a little exhausting to imagine.

Suppose productivity is authentically a core value for you and there is a way to achieve this happily that you can design. In that case, the ABCD framework can absolutely work for large and/or multiple areas of life.

But, for most people's purposes (including myself), we are more concerned with efficiency. That is, getting what you need to get done to move towards an authentic goal, yet taking as little of your mental and physical capacity as possible. The psychological and physical capacity can be allocated to other important areas in your life to have a happy existence. Areas such as: other goals, family commitments, or precious leisure time—all areas of value within your life. We've already seen that our time is precious (40 Christmases and counting for me!), so we improve its use and ultimately have more free time to enjoy.

Once we have a more balanced approach mentally, we need to find *physical* balance in our approach. What resources can we realistically assign to these values and goals?

Stephen Covey has some suggestions that I found most useful when allocating my time. The ABCD framework incorporates some of these important questions when seeking balance.[64]

---

64 Covey, S. R. (1989) *The 7 Habits of Highly Effective People.*(adapted ideas and wording from various sections).

BEGIN WITH THE END IN MIND

Begin today with the image, picture, or paradigm of the end of your journey as your frame of reference or the criteria by which your actions are examined.

ABCD will give you have a set of authentic core values; you can be more efficient because you know what the decisions and actions you will make are going to be.

THE TIME MANAGEMENT MATRIX

How you spend our time can be split into *four quadrants*:

	URGENT	**NOT URGENT**
IMPORTANT	Q1 • Emergencies • Deadlines • Pressing issues	Q2 • Preparation • Self-care • Relationships
NOT IMPORTANT	Q3 • Unstructured tasks • Inauthentic 'needs' • some mail, texts, meetings	Q4 • Relaxing • Trivial work • Timewasting

Fig 6.10[65]**- Time Management Matrix**

People often spend too much of their time on *urgent but unimportant* activities, resulting in stress and burnout. Staying in this quadrant grows it to the detriment of the others, leaving less time to spend on important yet non-urgent tasks such as self-development (See fig 6.11).

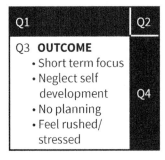

Fig 6.11[66]**- Quadrants Grow/Shrink**

---

65   Covey, S. R. (1989) *The 7 Habits of Highly Effective People.* (adapted diagram).
66   Covey, S. R. (1989) *The 7 Habits of Highly Effective People.* (adapted diagram).

You can analyse the way you use your time each week and determine if you are spending time on what is more important to you. It will be necessary to balance some of the time you spend putting out fires to feel more at ease and free up time for your genuine goals.

P/PC

Most see effectiveness from the angle of how much is produced (P); the more you produce, the more effective you are. It is actually down to two factors, the second being your production capability (PC). You cannot enjoy productivity when neglecting the factors that enable this capability.

This is the aim when we seek efficiency. I have already shown that happiness is more likely when you enjoy the journey, so in setting too many targets, unrealistic goals, and unreasonable expectations (even if they are based on authentic goals), you lack the balance that allows you to carry on producing. This is not sustainable or enjoyable, and in *ABCD*, I will ensure that you assign enough time to yourself and enjoy the present.

EMOTIONAL BANK BALANCE

Much of the ability to produce is dependent on happy relationships with others. Your life does not take place in a vacuum and so balancing how you interact with those around you is important. The excellent idea around the emotional bank balance may not directly deal with efficiency but I believe in improving relationships you naturally improve your ability to give more to achieving your values and goals.

The idea is aimed chiefly at relationships with others and interpersonal dependence. When you take something from someone (their time or efforts), you *withdraw* from your relationship account. When you give something back, you make a *deposit*. When you are 'overdrawn,' the relationship becomes imbalanced, and issues can occur. So, you must know how your accounts sit with others, as many of your values/goals will involve those close to you. There's no point having a value to be a good mother if your bank balance with your children is running on empty.

My children love the ideas of the bank balance. It was a great way to discuss how our actions have consequences and how balancing what we give and take can improve relationships. My children adapted the idea to show a fish tank representing our happiness levels as a group and how water is taken and added depending on how we interact with each other (see fig 6.12 below) – this lead to many discussions about the overall mood of the house being a bit *dry* when we were not considering each other enough.

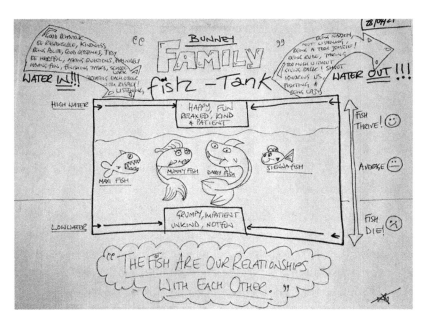

Fig 6.12 – My Family 'Fish Tank'

Balanced relationships lead to happier environments and better ability to reasonably act toward your core values and goals.

As well as withdrawals taken from other people, it will serve us all to remember the idea of making withdrawals from our *internal* bank balance - when we don't treat ourselves well or neglect things that are important to our happiness. For example, not seeing friends because of working too much. We must endeavour to make regular deposits knowing that even though it might slow our progress down, we'll be far happier and more likely to continue than if we don't take of our basic needs.

The popular notion that you must neglect yourself and those around you in order to be successful is a fallacy. Many very successful people have non-negotiables in their personal lives creating boundaries that ensure the balance of a good life is upheld. For example, they may never miss dinner with their family and block it from their diary every day, or only answer emails for a certain period of the day, maybe they haven't missed the community fayre in 10 years. You can both be successfully and enjoy your life.

Sustainable actions that allow us to be comfortable and care for ourselves and those around us will allow us to be more consistent and work healthily towards our chosen targets. If we enjoy the journey, then we can enjoy our lives, and this is all any of us genuinely wants.

We touched previously on the idea of burnout and the regret frequently felt by those who miss large parts of their lives. One final thought in this section is called the 'Negative Pilot,' which is a process that is seen in many industries and personal development arenas, where people are encouraged to remove certain aspects of their lives for a period to see what the adverse effect is, if any.

The idea is excellent in a modern era where many practices are almost unconsciously adopted into our daily lives without noticing.

I might alienate some younger readers, but I remember getting my first mobile phone. I was 17, and it was an exhilarating moment; I spent literal hours on my phone playing *Snake* and messaging friends. I would find codes to change ringtones, learn how to draw 'pictures' in text messages using punctuation, and sometimes I would make calls. Even with such limited functionality, I couldn't imagine I could ever spend MORE time on this device, no matter how much I loved it.

I couldn't have been more wrong – the average person's mobile phone use in the UK is around 4 hours a day[67]. Many of these hours spent on processes that we have adopted as essential parts of our day. But are they really *essential*?

The 'Negative Pilot' approach suggests that if you are concerned with the amount of available time you have or about a particular action you take regularly, you should take some time to remove it from your life. Perhaps a 30-day break from social media, a two-week period where you stop replying to your phone after 7 pm, 90 days alcohol-free etc. You can then see in a controlled environment if your life is negatively affected; if not, you might choose to reduce how often you do it or remove it completely freeing up valuable time. The same applies to perceived *positive* actions too; we will find that we do many things believing them to be beneficial to us, but when we take them away, there is no adverse effect, and we have freed up time in our day and removed some of the pressure we face.

Such an exercise can help aid our efficiency because we can make sure the many activities that have crept into our lives over the years, that we do automatically and without question, are not taking up space that would be used elsewhere. The ABCD techniques will help you bring the ideas of efficiency together and spend time on what is important and beneficial to you.

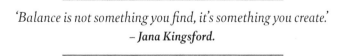

'Balance is not something you find, it's something you create.'
– Jana Kingsford.

SUMMARY

I have shown how having chosen to assess ourselves more authentically, a balanced approach to our thoughts and actions is essential in our lives:

- **X=Y**—No matter how much you want things to go your way, the world is not set up for your success. Fate can always change your life in small or large ways; no amount of wanting can change that. Plus, you are human, and by your very nature, you are fallible. Incorporating the acceptance of this into your lives automatically creates balance and takes you away from extremes.
- **RATIONAL THINKING**—Humans naturally accumulate habits of biased thinking throughout their lives. These can feed into unhealthy negative emotions, which are highly limiting. Applying reason, having healthy negative thoughts, and balancing your expectations is a freeing and beneficial experience.
- **SUSTAINABILITY**—Much of the advice and guidance you receive is not sustainable. The presentation of many lives, techniques, and stories omits the important elements of balance that make journeys to your goals more enjoyable. Slower progress for more prolonged periods becomes ingrained in your life far more pleasantly than short extreme *fads*.
- **ENJOY THE JOURNEY**—Life is shorter than you think and must be put into perspective. Do you want to spend so much of it anxious over what you 'should' be doing? Your actions must be easily integrated into your real life, long term; they become habits of the person you want to be and sit comfortably in your enjoyable life. You must accept who you are and what you are like.
- **FLOW**—Having taken a more balanced approach to your thoughts and actions, you see that taking the easiest route is also a form of extreme behaviour. Humans need to be challenged to have a purpose, which makes us happy. Finding the balance between challenges faced and skills held creates a flow state, heavily linked to human happiness, in a place away from unnecessary extremes that cause you to *Crash and Burn*.
- **EFFICIENCY**—Balance is not passive. You can create an environment that allows you to balance your real life, the things important to you, and your leisure time. As many aspects of normal life cannot be dropped from your routine, it is important to occasionally take stock and ensure you are not overwhelmed or restricted by things that are not as important as they first seemed.

We have covered some more simple yet powerful ideas that have been considered and researched for many years. They help us start to answer the questions we asked ourselves earlier in this book and show us how potent balance is in our lives. We saw that with authenticity, we can spend more time on our actual lives because the areas of concern for us are genuine yet fewer. This is greatly amplified by taking a sustainable and enjoyable approach, remembering not to lose track of what is important. However, it is critical that the authentic areas that we still need to target are given our efforts to bring us a sense of purpose and flow. The purpose, in fact, of the human body is to keep us in the balance of homeostasis; evolution has shown us that imbalance and extremes are not desirable for a healthy life.

The advice is simple: to take small steps towards those targets that allow you to still have flexibility and fun with your precious life. This works perfectly because, unlike those living on the extremes, we are now doing things that are important to us in a way that we enjoy, leading to the next crucial element that the ABCD framework provides—CONSISTENCY.

Pause for Thought – Please take time to make some notes:

CONSISTENCY

I want to start this section with a quote from former U.S. President Calvin Coolidge:

'Nothing in the world can take the place of Persistence. Talent will not; nothing is more common than unsuccessful men with talent. Genius will not; unrewarded genius is almost a proverb. Education will not; the world is full of educated derelicts. Persistence and determination alone are omnipotent. The slogan "Press On" has solved and always will solve the problems of the human race.'

A plethora of content echoes these words, but if it were easy to be consistent, then we all would. The ABCD framework has already given us an advantage in its early stages. We have afforded ourselves some flexibility and self-love with the (AB) elements of the ABCD framework. We have chosen actions that are already authentic and balanced towards a life we enjoy—that makes consistency far more likely. Extremes don't work and putting pressure on things we can't control makes us unhappy. However, as we touched upon in our discourse on balance, inaction is equally as extreme as overaction. We will still have areas of our lives that are important to us and require attention. As they are authentic to us, there is no excuse for inconsistency. Though consistency may still be difficult, regularly taking the small next steps will create habits that align our values with our actions.

CONSISTENCY OVER TALENT

Talent is lauded in our society. Countless movies, TV shows, and literature chronicle the lives of those who have reached the top. The distinction between those who *make it* and those who don't is often (incorrectly) accredited solely to this special talent. It is not possible to be successful if you are not consistent.

David Beckham's famous free-kick technique resulted from hours of extra practice and is often unfairly attributed solely to raw talent. Ed Sheeran, one of the highest-selling pop stars of all time, once sang, 'I've done around about a thousand shows, but I haven't got a house, plus I live on the couch.' Even globally recognised performers like stand-up comedians test new material several times in one night across the smaller live venues and open mics of all metropolitan cities. The point here is that even with the genetic advantage of a natural athlete, vocal cords of an angel, or comedic timing of a great storyteller—accomplishment can only come with consistency and determination.

Writer Tom Clancy said, 'An overnight success is ten years in the making.'

In some ways consistency is worth *more* than talent. Of course, when natural talent and consistency meet, the chances for great success are increased. However, that is for a tiny group of individuals. In the context of our personal journeys, what we strive for is unlikely to be becoming a billionaire sports star. We might want to be a better mother, organise our time more efficiently, or learn a foreign language. In these more relatable examples, the values/goals that we have chosen through parts A and B are more probable if we form new habits we perform regularly.

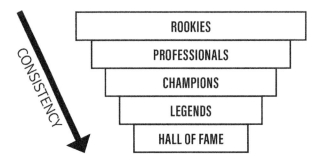

Fig 6.13 – Members of Increasingly Esteemed Groups

Fig 6.13 (above) is a visual representation of how the number of members in a particular group reduces as the level of competency/skill/success in the related field increases. More people are playing grassroots football than those who have won the World Cup. Though when we think of winners, we often think of the star-studded, God-like, and talented. We neglect what we have learned so far about consistency. In this case I reference sports people but the same is true for any field. We can translate this pyramid to the one below (fig 6.14).

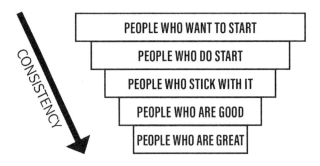

Fig 6.14 – Consistency Pyramid

It's clear that more you stick to something, the more likely you are to improve at it, and given that logic dictates that not everyone will, you will be part of a more and more exclusive group.

In 2008, author Malcolm Gladwell published his book *Outliers: The Story of Success.* The main takeaway from his research and studies was the premise of the '10,000-hour-rule.' By studying the preparation of many successful people (professional ice hockey players, Bill Gates, violinists, The Beatles, etc.) Gladwell found that 'achievement is talent plus preparation.' But the ten-thousand-hour research reminds us that 'the closer psychologists look at the careers of the gifted, the smaller the role innate talent seems to play and the bigger the role preparation seems to play.'[68] Effectively, to harness your extraordinary gift OR to reach the upper echelons of a trainable skill/habit, it takes much practice to become good at anything.

Using myself as an example, I always believed I was capable of writing a book. In *Chapter 10*, I will show you how the ABCD framework can be used to achieve such goals for yourself. However, one thing is crucial to understand is that I would never have written a book without consistency in my writing.

We must not read word *habit* and confuse it with the word *hobby*. For some of you reading this book, the goal may well be related to a pastime - to learn a computer language, integrate a new gait into your long-distance running, or master the cha-cha-cha. However, in any area of your life it is vital that consistency is present yield substantial results.

Greg Plit's goal was to become a fitness model, and however far that aim is from your core values, I think his words are of value:

'You are what you do repeatedly every day. If excellence is something you've striven for, then it's not an accident. It's a habit.'[69]

In consistency acting in accordance with your core values and goals, you make the behaviours of the best version of yourself – habitual. They become your natural response to life's challenges each and every day. It's this alignment that makes you both successful and happy.

When we add consistency into the ABCD framework, we see the need to break down our goals into smaller pieces (like the elephant in the *Preface*) so that we look at more manageable next steps toward our goals. In the next section, we will explore the *Small Next Steps* idea in more detail.

But first, I will address another vital idea around consistency.

When we find consistency in what we are doing, aside from the more flow we can experience, we also develop *case studies*, which are examples of positive behaviour or success in our journeys. They are more realistic than previously held opinions of ourselves because they are current and begin to take the place of our old internal story. We take back authorship of our story in the present.

The young girl told by classmates that she is a loser in her sometimes-cruel adolescent years may start to believe this to be true and adjust her responses to situations to be quieter and to stand back from the group. It becomes a self-fulfilling prophecy. Unfortunately, this is not uncommon in schools worldwide; thankfully, many more positive events can often follow. When the girl joins a university or workplace, a new club or social group, she will

---

68 Gladwell, M. (2008) *Outliers: The Story of Success.*
69 Similar to Aristotle: 'We are what we repeatedly do. Excellence therefore is not an act but a habit.'

realise that she is not who she was told she was. People love her, she has a particular skill, or she displays kindness and support for others. As her personality is given the environment to be consistently genuine, a series of examples and experiences (case studies) build up that dissolve the unfair rhetoric of her youth and allow her to have confidence in herself and develop the self-esteem she deserves.

The case studies we build on the journey when we are consistent are reminders of who we *really* are. They provide quiet confidence that we are capable, that even when the going gets tough, our best has been and will be good enough. This is hugely empowering, from discovering ourselves after a dreadful school experience to knowing you can socialise with your friends happily with a soft drink, having given up alcohol. The early part of the journey can be scary, but as you move down the steps of the consistency pyramid, you discover that *you can do it.*

We're seeing that by being consistent, we are likely to become the sort of person we'd like to be either by our successes or the habits we can establish that improve us. We're regularly acting in a way that reflects who we want to be, and in those actions, we are far more likely to reach the targets we are aiming for. Although it is not in our control, far fewer people will be up to your level. The slightest amount of consistency can lay the groundwork to catapult you towards achieving things in the future that you once may have found difficult. That groundwork starts with small steps you can take now, in the present.

'Today I will do what others won't, so tomorrow I can do what others can't.'
– Jerry Rice[70].

SMALL NEXT STEPS

We have seen in our discussions on happiness and control that much of what we seek to achieve is not entirely down to our own actions. Many of the challenges we decide to take on when we assess our authentic wants and needs will doubtlessly be only partially within our control. We saw earlier that these preferred indifferents are outcomes that we would like to happen, but we are aware that, as they are out of our control, we must also accept the outcome either way. This way, we are not rooting our happiness in externals, and we can keep our inner sanctuary protected. When learning about balance, it became clear that to save that inner sanctum when we embark on our journey, a certain level of realism must be applied to our expectations of our results and our capacity to work towards them. We take a balanced approach or risk expecting too much or promising to give far more of our efforts than is possible or enjoyable.

Let's say that you have an extensive renovation project that you intend to undertake. There are several rooms of the house requiring work and several different types of work

---

70   Again, from the Indian Proverb quoted by Mat Fraser earlier.

required across the house. When you begin this project, you will likely have an idea of what you expect the house to be like when you finish. You might even have a timeline in mind for completion. These are both reasonable targets to have and allow a view of where you are heading.

It's also fair to say that with so many moving parts, you cannot be in control of all of them. From the obvious elements such as weather, cost, availability of resources and so on, anything could happen to delay or change your plans. This stretches to less-tangible factors such as your work situation, illness, or unexpected building regulation changes.

I even had a close friend have some building work delayed because builders found a skeleton in a wash basket in his loft. Police had to investigate only for forensics to find it was a fake skeleton used for medical studies by a previous owner!

My point is that anything can happen—and almost always does. In our renovation example, it's standard for the finished article not to be exactly as planned, for budgets to be busted, and for families hoping to be finished by Christmas to be still living in a building site by Easter.

However, when beginning the project, do we think all at once about every possible unknown, overwhelming ourselves? Most likely, we do not. A friend of mine spoke to her therapist about a similar project where they 'Didn't know where to start' to be given some simple advice, 'Start small and make small steps toward easy wins; focusing on everything at once will paralyse you.' We must break the journey up into east to manage parts.

'oneinarow
Any success takes one in a row.
Do one thing well, then another.
Once, then once more.
Over and over until the end.
Then it's oneinarow again.' [71]
– Matthew McConaughey.

You'll naturally feel like you don't know where to start when working toward something large. You will all have identified a goal and felt it was so far away and unrelated to the present that you found it hard to begin.

Using the lessons in this chapter, any personal notes you have made, and the ABCD framework, you will pick authentic and balanced goals, bringing you to a better starting position. You will care about what you are doing; it's your own choice, you will have an end in mind that is reasonable, and you will choose actions that suit your life. These actions

71 McConaughey, M. (2020) *Greenlights.*

will lead you to be consistent by their very nature. But much like the elephant example in the *Preface*, the renovation example above or any number of real-world examples, your goals may still be very large and important – life-changing. The scale can still be daunting no matter how important or realistic they are to you. It's important to break them down into smaller, easier to swallow, components.

This is where the idea of *Small Next Steps* comes into our framework. When building consistency, we must have reasonable actions that we can be consistent with, that we control, and that happen in the short term—regularly.

If we have a large value, goal, or solution that we are working towards, it is difficult or even impossible to consistently achieve anything without this step. It is too vague.

For instance, continuing the example of writing a book.

The goal I had assigned value to was to – *Write a Book*. I had already assessed why this was an important and tangible goal. I have even evaluated reasonably that I was capable do so and had enough knowledge of the subject matter to create the content.

However, *Writing a Book* is NOT what I needed to be consistent at. That is too vague, and too many bored party guests have heard that someone is in the process of becoming an author only to discover that their pen hasn't touched paper.

I needed to create another layer of smaller behaviours/actions that sum up the habits of an author. Most notably—writing. So, the action was to write for two hours a week, and there were other similar actions to read, research, or annotate, but they can be similarly broken down into small next steps that roll up into the overall core value/goal[72].

Applying this practice to larger projects gives us the freedom to view the bigger picture and balances the manageable behaviours with other parts of our lives. We can see these small victories being won each week, and the distance to the end goal diminishes. We gain confidence in ourselves and reassurance that the job is not as big as first thought - we have begun our journey.[73]

In a 2017 research paper led by a Marketing Professor from Stanford Business School[74], several hypotheses were tested in four central studies. The aim was to ascertain if 'Sub-goals' sufficiently increased motivation to succeed compared to larger goals.

- Study 1—Participants were examined for their motivation to achieve a calorie-burning goal. One group was asked to burn 200 calories while another group was split into four 50-calorie sub-goals with feedback as each goal was reached.

---

72 This example is used later to demonstrate the ABCD framework in action

73 Many seemingly impossible lifesaving journeys away from addiction are taken one day at a time.

74 Huang, S. and Jin, L. and Zhang, Y. (2017) 'Step by Step: Sub-Goals as a Source of Motivation' –– *Organizational Behaviour and Human Decision Processes*, July 2017, Vol. 141, Pages 1-15

- Study 2—Participants were asked to write restaurant reviews to earn points for a new social media platform. One group was told to earn five sets of 20 points and another, one set of 100 points. Motivation and belief in their success were recorded at 30% and 70%.
- Study 3—Participants were given transcription work paid by the word with a maximum of 100 points earned. The groups were split similarly to Study 2.
- Study 4—Participants, over several days, were asked to upload books to a website. This time, three groups were set; one that was given an overall goal, one was given a set of sub-goals, and one was given four days of sub-goals followed by four days of knowing the overall goal.

The research findings are interesting and demonstrate the psychology of performing tasks, which fully supports the ABCD idea that we must define larger goals and then take 'Small Next Steps' towards them.

- Study 1—The participants that had some form of feedback provided from the sub-goals they were performing reached their goal quicker and were more motivated to achieve it (they took faster steps once they saw the 1st Sub-Task completed).
- Study 2/3—However, on larger tasks where motivation was tested at 30%/70% completion, the results showed that participants at the early stages (30%) of a task were more motivated by sub-goals than by overall goals. However, when nearing the end of the task (70%), the group with the overall goal started to become equally as motivated (if not more) than the sub-goal group.
- Study 4—Furthered this when the 'hybrid group' uploaded close to 50% more books over the period.

Huang summarises:

'We found that when progress is low, people's source of motivation lies in the perceived attainability of the goal; when the progress level increases and the end point is within reasonable proximity, the source of motivation shifts to the value people attach to their actions (e.g., Studies 2 and 3). As a result, the impact of a sub-goal structure depends on the dominant source of motivation at a specific point of the pursuit. As shown in Study 4, a hybrid structure that highlighted sub-goals early on and then removed the sub-goal when employees reached the advanced stage of the task could help to leverage the driving forces in both stages and maximize their total effort and performance.'[75]

In other words, when we start on our journey, we need to take the small next steps to create accomplishments that encourage us to continue and work harder. In the ABCD framework, we will be choosing sub-goals/principles that allow us to break down larger goals/values and have the motivation to maintain consistency. But as this study shows, we must also

---

75 Huang, S. and Jin, L. and Zhang, Y. (2017) 'Step by Step: Sub-Goals as a Source of Motivation' –– *Organizational Behaviour and Human Decision Processes*, July 2017, Vol. 141, Pages 1-15

have a picture of the authentic core goals and values in our minds because it appears our source of motivation moves from completing smaller tasks to our perception of how close we are to finishing the goal as we progress.

The ABCD framework ensures that we maintain both without being overwhelmed into inaction or stuck on things that don't truly matter to us.

This means we accept life as a journey that we can enjoy if we only concern ourselves with our part in it, choosing actions that are our responsibility. Many successful people attest that when they began to concentrate only on their own part of a process, however small, and let go of the will to control the things they couldn't, they became the most successful they had ever been. It is relatively common that when you take this approach, the end goal is accomplished. Should the end goal never come to fruition, we will still feel a sense of achievement that comes from doing what we set out to do, from keeping our end of the bargain, from keeping promises to ourselves.

When we fail to keep promises to ourselves, much like when others let us down, we damage our trust in ourselves. We have all been in situations when our good intentions slip, and we act inauthentically. It is often followed by an uncomfortable feeling of shame and guilt, which are both unhealthy negative emotions. Not doing as intended set us off on a fairly lousy day emotionally. Of course, we can adjust how we think about events and regularly reframe them. We'll tell ourselves, 'Actually, I didn't fancy that swim, anyway.' Significant mental harm can be caused by the cognitive dissonance created by setting out to do something we later fail to do. This is where many of the readers of this book will have found themselves at one stage or another. The lethargy, lack of motivation, and uneasiness can be traced back to our inconsistency with the values that we hold dear.

Luckily for us, the ABCD process we are building acknowledges that just as consistently breaking promises to yourself can cause distress—*consistently keeping promises* is extremely powerful. When these promises are authentic and balanced, and we do them regularly, we build confidence in ourselves. Case studies that we are capable of what we set out to do and a much more contented mindset all around.

Our small next steps will lead us to form habits. Even before the 10,000 hours needed to perfect them, the mental response is almost immediate. We have all felt in a rut one day to have a small victory and feel relieved the next. Our external actions match our internal values. We're being principled and can choose behaviours that match these principles. The seemingly thousands of overwhelming decisions we face can be made with greater ease because our choices are now automatically authentic. Success and calm are achieved when you know how best to behave before you are required to.

Bill Walsh, the legendary San Francisco 49ers head coach, would devise a 15- to 25-play script for his offence to follow. 'Scripting is planning; it's contingency planning,' Walsh told *The New York Times*... 'The fewer decisions to be made during the game, the better.

You don't want to live by your instincts. It's isolating each situation that comes up and establishing what comes up.'

In setting his team up to follow a script for a short period of the games, they would settle into the environment around them, knowing what would happen early on. Of course, as things change and external factors appear, the game must be played in response, but by creating a sense of calm, they won three Super Bowls in seven years and became one of the most successful teams in NFL history. Taking those first steps confidently can have tremendous power over our mental performance.

It all starts the second you wake up.

DAILY ROUTINES

Have you ever overslept one morning when you had intended to wake up early? Perhaps you were supposed to go for a run before work, prepare the house for a visitor, or even just spend some time alone before the house bursts into life. We all make plans of this type. Sometimes it's a permanent change of lifestyle, and others we simply just have things we'd like to do. A sense of pride is associated with being up while others are still asleep. Though it is not for everyone, many successful people swear by early mornings. In a recent presentation for college students, Dwayne 'The Rock' Johnson made a rousing speech about how he wakes up early each day, anchoring his belief that 'No one will ever outwork me.'

The benefits of waking early could be down to the smug effect of doing something others find difficult, but some science suggests the body benefits from earlier nights and mornings. This is because our 'Circadian Clock,' which regulates our physiology, can be disrupted and cognitive function impaired when sleep is not taken at night (seen in studies of shift workers[76]).

When writing this book, I had to be careful not to overdo it and stray into obsession. The body is constantly taking biological action to bring our body into homeostasis and to protect us from changes to our environments—and ourselves—often in subtle yet astounding ways.

We must do the same with our mental approach.

We're working through a framework that balances our theory's happiness (AB) and hard work (CD) sides. So, it's crucial in this section that I do not suggest early nights and mornings for those to whom they are not suited. Many people work long hours and shifts, others feel unable to sleep and/or get up early, and some may feel that they require eight or nine hours a night while others operate well on six or seven.

---

76 Jagannath, A. et al. (2017) 'The genetics of circadian rhythms, sleep and health' –– *Human Molecular Genetics*, Volume 26, Issue R2, 01.

However, when we snooze the alarm for the fifth time and reluctantly flop out of bed an hour later than we intended, more than just the annoyance of the resulting mad rush remains. There is often a sadness or remorse left over from not doing as we had promised ourselves. We know the extra time would have helped with the efficiency we discussed in an earlier section, or the spare time to prepare could have made a later task far more manageable. Even if the time was intended for some personal time, it might feel a bit disappointing if we miss out on that time to sleep in.

When asked why they can't follow through on a specific goal, many people will answer that they don't have time. Yet, many of the same people sit on their phones late at night and only wake up with barely enough time to rush to work, tired and lethargic.

If this sounds familiar to you, and you have worked through the ideas seen so far in the ABCD framework. It might be interesting to experiment with keeping that first promise to yourself each day; gifting you the time to work on your authentic goals without having to shoehorn an overwhelming extra hour into your day later.

The power here lies more within passing the day's first test than in the extra time earned. This doesn't have to extend to an insane daily routine like Mark Wahlberg's (look it up if you aren't aware of it), which may help Mark keep balance in his life. It allows him not to miss family meals or school drops, but for most of us, a far smaller change to our routine can be equally powerful.

We're trying to create consistent intention toward objectives we are passionate about. We have some easy consistency by having some small elements of our day that we can rely on. We're keeping promises to ourselves and taking small steps, which allows us to develop consistency as a habit that we can call upon when needed.

It might be as simple as getting up and making your bed[77] as a principle. It stops you from snoozing your alarm in the morning, and when you have another opportunity in your day to take positive action, it is easier to stay committed when you have a precedent set.

It may sound far-fetched, but I implore you to give any of the below a try. Setting up in the right way has added a great sense of positivity to my day :

- Avoid the snooze button.
- Perform daily gratitude.
- Make your bed.
- Eat breakfast.
- Take a cold shower.
- Meditate/Reflect.
- Complete a puzzle/crossword.
- Stretch.

---

77 McRaven, W. H. (2017) *Make Your Bed: Little Things That Can Change Your Life…And Maybe the World.*

- Light exercise.
- Phone family/friends to check-in.
- Reading five pages of a book.
- Journal.
- Plan your day.
- Complete your morning routine before you look at your phone.

These may not be appropriate for you but you will no doubt be able to think of your own.

We're not trying to create a military process. Still, as many soldiers report, when some of the decision-making is taken away from their daily routine, it allows them the mental capacity to focus on the job at hand. It's why Mark Zuckerberg and other CEOs wear the same clothes each day.[78] It's the first decision made for them.

In a recent book, Dr Rangan Chatterjee discusses the idea of Micro Stress Doses (MSDs) and their effect on your overall resilience.

'(MSDs) are the tiny moments of anxiety, frustration or fear we get from watching the news or seeing something triggering on social media, or from leaving the house late and having to deal with heavy traffic...In isolation, we can usually cope with MSDs just fine. The problem comes when they start to build up. The more MSDs we absorb in a day, the closer we'll be pushed to our own personal stress threshold...Every time you time you make an unnecessary choice; you're creating tension and stress in your mind and body.'[79]

When an event occurs in our day, we have a mindful gap between the event and our response, in which we make our judgements. We discussed earlier that being stressed, tired, and hungover can make it difficult to respond reasonably, making us more reactive. Chatterjee suggests that we have a threshold of stress we can take in our day—our resilience limit. By engaging with small stressor events, we have MSDs that build up to this threshold, making us more stressed later. We have discussed that regular stressors or moods will reduce our ability to *mind the gap* and make reasoned judgements of events, so we become unable to respond how we desire. If we are not behaving in accordance with our values, we lose our ability to be balanced and authentic.

Having some structure to our day/week not only honours our set of values but reduces the probability of MSDs created by the unknowns we face each day. For example, if we have a plan, then some decisions are made before we reach them—we are proactive. If we

---

78 'I really want to clear my life to make it so that I have to make as few decisions as possible about anything except how to best serve this community. There's actually a bunch of psychology theory that even making small decisions, around what you wear or what you eat for breakfast or things like that, they kind of make you tired and consume your energy. My view is I'm in this really lucky position where I get to wake up every day and help serve more than 1 billion people, and I feel like I'm not doing my job if I spend any of my energy on things that are silly or frivolous about my life, so that way I can dedicate all of my energy towards just building the best products and services and helping us reach our goal and achieve this mission of helping to connect everyone in the world and giving them the ability to stay connected with the people that they love and care about. So, that's what I care about. Even though it sounds silly that that's my reason for wearing a grey t-shirt every day, it is true.' – Mark Zuckerberg (Facebook Q&A November 2014)
79 Chatterjee, Dr R. (2022) *Happy Mind, Happy Life.*

don't, we constantly react in real-time, which can cause us stress. Perhaps wearing the same clothes every day is a step too far, but some routine can significantly benefit us mentally.

Just remember, as with any of these topics, we are fallible human beings, and we should afford ourselves some flexibility. An element of trial and error will help us find the right balance. Personally, I have been in periods where I have tried ALL the habits I mentioned above, and I found it too much pressure to maintain. This swung me away from balance and mad my life less enjoyable.

Choose a few practices that you know will benefit you and try to work them into your day to have a spine of consistency. You become 'the type of person who....' and this lets you know something about yourself and build some quiet confidence in your ability to act intentionally and keep promises to yourself.

'Courage wasn't a matter of taking the whole mountain in a single massive leap. Courage was taking it one step at a time, doing what was necessary now, preparing for the next step, and refusing to worry about whether some step in the future would be the one that would break him.'[80]
– Lando Calrissian.

SUMMARY

Having applied reason and flexibility to choose our plans of action with balance in part two, I have used the third part of the ABCD framework to show that consistency is more potent than many environmental and ability-related factors. Being consistent is crucial and doesn't have to be as tricky as we are led to believe:

- **THE POWER OF CONSISTENCY**—Consistency has the power to trump talent, take small steps, and turn them into giant leaps. Anyone can talk about wanting to achieve something, but few start and fewer still become great. You can find this consistency far easier when you have something you care about and a balanced approach.
- **CASE STUDIES**—By having consistency, you give yourself a new set of examples to build a new story. These examples are of you being the person you want to be. As time goes on, you can have a quiet confidence that when challenged, you will behave in ways where your external actions align with your internal values. This confidence will bring you happiness.
- **SMALL NEXT STEPS**—Having you goals and values in mind is extremely important. But so is NOT having the same global view on a daily basis. Taking the next small step required, you build accomplishments that develop into larger successes.

---

80 Zahn, T. (2013) *Star Wars: Scoundrels.*

- **DAILY CONSISTENCY**—It will be helpful, if you so choose, to implement a few pieces of consistency into your daily routine. These vary in type and magnitude; the action is unimportant in many ways. What matters is keeping promises to yourself, showing up, and reducing the build-up of stress from being faced with the unknown less regularly. There will also be room to remove things you don't need to do if they aren't equally important to you, giving you less pressure and more time for the present.

Here we have learned that consistency is a strong driver of success and that small levels of consistency can improve our overall happiness. We have some ammunition for the tough questions asked in *Chapter 3*. Many ideas around consistency seem small and easy, but as we know, developing any habit takes time. Now that we have addressed the (AB) side of our framework, we can start to see why it requires a work ethic and resilience side to add further balance. We must have (CD) to have (AB). The final part to the ABCD framework is D – DISCIPLINE.

Pause for Thought – Please take time to make some notes:

DISCIPLINE

Consistency and *discipline* (much like *authenticity* with *balance*) are closely intertwined. They comprise the side of our ABCD framework, primarily concerned with happiness brought to us by *virtue*. Without our model's (CD) side, we could simply take the easy route in all we do, deciding that nothing is as important as our ability to relax - interpreting inaction as 'balance.'

This approach isn't balanced at all; rather than fearful that we can't cope, we are at the other end of the spectrum that leads to boredom—it's another extreme. Fortunately, our framework *promotes* balance and takes both sides of the equation into consideration. We have elements that ask us to be more considered, genuine, easy-going, flexible, authentic, and balanced. Now we look at discipline, or, more accurately self-discipline, which, paired with consistency, shows us that once we have identified what is important to us and have a reasonable way to achieve it - hard work and character are necessary to be happy.

DISCIPLINE-NOT TORTURE

Familiar negative images tend to spring to mind when picturing discipline. We might picture the focus required to survive SAS training, the sacrifice needed to qualify for the Olympics or the single-minded ruthlessness of a Fortune 500 CEO. Ultimately, the message we have been fed is the same — discipline is reserved for other people, for exceptional cases.

When prioritising our goals, we may authentically target winning the 100m final at the 2024 Olympics. We could assess that, on balance, this is a reasonable expectation and the future eventuality of us accomplishing this is not only life changing, but possible. If that is the case for you, I am very grateful for someone with such considerable goals to be using this book!

For most readers though, including myself, the A,B, and C stages of the framework are there to lower our expectations and find the small changes that can improve our life. These will be equally life-changing; however, as we saw in *Chapter 4*, they are likely to be far more modest and common changes that can be made easily to great effect.

It will become clear that the regiment required to reach an extreme goal will need a radical approach. This is likely to be unsustainable. So, we will refocus our efforts on essential concerns that are realistic to us. This might be letting go of the desire to be a millionaire by the time we are 21 and instead seeing that we can aim to be financially stable and content. The steps toward this goal are much closer to our control and simple enough to gain consistency. We may wonder why we placed so much importance on becoming a millionaire in the first place, as the pressure involved was causing us stress. And if fate allows it, our new calm attitude to taking these steps may well lead to us being both happy and wealthy – under far less stressful conditions than before.

Crucially, whatever the objective; without discipline, even simple and heartfelt targets won't be reached. The ABCD framework does not seek to reduce expectations and progress to *zero*.

You will unearth areas you would genuinely like to improve. For that reason, you will need some discipline to keep your lives pointing in the right direction. Maybe not as extreme as the pledge of the silence of a Carthusian Monk or the broccoli and chicken Tupperware life of a bodybuilder (unless you want it to be). I'm just encouraging some form of hard work, resilience, persistence, and determination - *putting your money where your mouth is*. The effort it takes to act with intention so that your behaviour matches your values is tough to find at times. Luckily for you, by using *ABCD* to choose aims that are authentic to you and a balanced approach, both the consistency and discipline required to follow through needn't be torture.

DISCIPLINE IS A VIRTUE

'Self-discipline is that which, next to virtue, truly and essentially raises one man above another.'
– *Joseph Addison.*

Discipline makes us happier by creating a confidence within us. This comes not from limiting our efforts solely to the actions that we take, but also to how we chose to think. Almost every ABCD element we have explored in this chapter will require some form of self-discipline to being to mind when we need it:

- Accepting what we can and cannot control can be difficult.
- Balancing our actions and expectations. We can easily stray into too little or too much focus on our values and goals.
- Consistently performing even the smallest of actions will demand discipline.
- No matter how much we want to act and be a certain way we will be challenged by our old behaviours and story – discipline is essential to take back authorship.

Obtaining happiness is not passive but *active*. As Matthew McConaughey says in *Greenlights*:

'just keep livin... lower case because life is nobody's proper noun, and there's no "g" on the end of livin because life's a verb.'[81]

However much you connect with any of the contents in this book, adopting them into your lives will require you to *try*. It won't happen by chance.

---

81 McConaughey, M. (2020) *Greenlights*.

Intention is a powerful determinant of happiness. Those who regularly act intentionally and with purpose are far more likely to be content with their efforts than those who regularly fall at the first hurdle, fail to turn up for themselves, or lack purpose to begin with.

Former President of the American Psychological Association and pioneer in *Positive Psychology*, Dr Martin Seligman believed that a shift was needed in how we view mental illness. Previously treated around the pathology of a sickness, Seligman wanted to use his platform to move this toward guidance for positive living and wellbeing. In 2012, he designed the PERMA model,[82] which outlined the characteristics of a flourishing individual:

- Positive Emotion.
- Engagement.
- Relationships.
- Meaning.
- Accomplishments.

We have discussed some of these factors already as we build the ABCD framework. This association continues as we think about the role discipline plays in maintaining intention of our actions: *meaning* and *accomplishments* are crucial to mental wellbeing.

To have meaning, we need to act with purpose; we purposefully make decisions about how to work that will make us happy. We can see accomplishment if we maintain some form of discipline. Many believe, like Seligman, that these factors contribute to our happiness.

By being authentic in what you choose to pursue, you will take a step closer to the purpose of your life in the near term – and making an effort towards this purpose is enriching – not strenuous.

Windy Dryden addresses the subject of frustration tolerance in his work. The idea is that to be content and happy; we must develop a certain level of 'high frustration tolerance.' This is the ability to firstly accept that the world is not operating to make sure you are comfortable. Things will happen that you don't like/enjoy, and you will certainly not always get your way. Secondly, as we saw with our flow discussion, understanding that hard work is required to live a happy life is essential.

Those with 'low frustration tolerance' tend to 'lead an undisciplined lifestyle' and 'frequently fail to persevere at tasks that it would be in your best interests to stick with,' Dryden explains, because they have low frustration beliefs, such as 'I must not be frustrated, I must be comfortable, and I must not experience any negative feelings.'[83]

---

82 Seligman, Dr M. (2012) *PERMA*.
83 Dryden, W. (1994) *10 Steps to Positive Living*.

Having these beliefs will mean that when the world doesn't move in the ways that you would want, you will be frustrated, uncomfortable, and low. You will not handle it as well as someone with a more realistic outlook. By having an 'I can stand this' philosophy, you improve your chances of coping with life and being happier. In other words, if you can demonstrate some discipline and resilience in the face of challenges, you will have a greater sense of wellbeing.

We would all advise a friend, who was hoping for miracles in any field, to lower their expectations. It is a far more reasonable approach and far less open to disappointment. Dryden's seminal work, *10 Steps to Positive Living* was one of the first books I was recommended when I tried therapy in 2016, and once you get past the title, you find that the author often takes a tact that is not as upbeat as the cover suggests. It is helpful here to consider these steps because rather than instructing us to *be positive*, they require us to accept what life throws at us and take ownership of our part in it. This requires mental discipline.

They are:

- Assume personal responsibility.
- Adopt a non-demanding flexible philosophy.
- Accept reality.
- Develop high frustration tolerance.
- Develop a healthy attitude towards yourself.
- Allow yourself to experience healthy negative emotions.
- Think critically, think creatively.
- Develop vitally absorbing interests.
- Improve relationships.
- Personal change: develop a realistic outlook.[84]

These steps call back to many ideas we have covered in the ABCD framework. Notably, most of these steps require some instruction to 'develop' or 'adopt.' As McConaughey reminded us earlier, it appears that happiness in life comes from *action*. It's within the intention and discipline of our actions that we find purpose and greater contentment—a process the ABCD framework will facilitate.

Discipline is not only prescribed to us in our actions. It is also virtuous to our existence because it feels good. Both physically and mentally.

We have touched on homeostasis on several occasions in this book. The human body is a wonderfully complex series of systems and controls. Many of these are evolved to maintain a level of balance, which keeps us functioning at a healthy and efficient level.

---

84 Dryden, W. (1994) *10 Steps to Positive Living.*

We saw earlier that homeostasis is at work when we have joyous or rewarding moments. The body secretes dopamine, and, following the passing of pleasure, the body tries to regulate us down to a normal state again.

In a recent interview discussing her book *Dopamine Nation*, Dr. Anna Lembke explains why this 'cruel joke' was helpful in our evolution.

'It seems like nature's cruel joke to require that for every pleasurable experience, we will experience pain. But if you, again, think about the way that humans have survived on this planet over most of human existence, it's absolutely genius, because no sooner have we found some kind of rewarding substance or behaviour than our brain plummets us into this dopamine deficit state, which has got us going, looking for that next thing. The problem is, we're no longer living in that world of scarcity and ever-present danger. We're now living in a world of overwhelming abundance, where all of our basic survival needs are met.' She summarises, 'The central sort of takeaway from the way that our brains restore homeostasis, which is not just to bring dopamine back to level baseline – because we're always secreting a tonic baseline level of dopamine – but actually to bring it below baseline. So, that's really the key neurobiological concept that I want people to grasp. It's not just like you use up the dopamine you have and then you've run out and you're even again. The way that the brain restores homeostasis is to go below baseline and put us in this dopamine deficit state, which is essentially akin to depression.'[85]

Of course, this is also true (on a smaller scale) with low frustration tolerance behaviours: eating junk food regularly, sleeping in instead of going to the gym, cheating on a test, and making poor decisions to satisfy the need for an easier life. We feel somewhat depleted and sad after we indulge these unhelpful urges, especially if they were done whilst breaking promises to ourselves or others. This may feel like shame or guilt, but it is also physiological as the body brings the dopamine back to normal levels with a hefty dose of sadness.

This may sound a little bit glum; joy brings us pain, so what's good about that?

Thanks to homeostasis, the opposite is also true.

As a reverse dopamine response to facing painful or challenging experiences, the body releases endorphins to help us deal with pain. Endorphins help the body reduce pain if we hurt ourselves, are scared or go through a trauma (including childbirth). It's why we can survive such events; our system is providing us with our own painkiller, aesthetic, and antidepressant all in one as it fights for balance. For this reason, choosing to have discipline and regularly facing challenges naturally increases our dopamine baseline making our 'normal' state a happier one.

You might have taken on a fitness challenge, public speaking task, acting role or any challenge that takes you out of your comfort zone. Almost immediately upon completion, there

---

85 'Dr. Anna Lembke: Pain, Pleasure, and the addictive chase for Dopamine.' – *www.findingmastery.net*

is an elation you feel. Akin to relief, you feel positive and motivated; you feel proud; not solely because of the mental interpretation of the event, but also physiologically, the brain has released feel-good hormones into the system in the same *fight or flight* response as for more painful or challenging events. It's clear that to feel a steadier state of contentment - challenge and discipline are far more effective than inactivity and boredom. Essentially, you can live with a reverse hangover by keeping yourself challenged. This is why discipline is such a crucial element of the ABCD framework.

Another facet of the virtuousness of discipline stems from the fact that humans frequently underestimate themselves. *Imposter syndrome* is the feeling of being underqualified for a challenge; most commonly, when we are promoted or enter an environment, we feel we don't have the credentials for. We all feel this way at some point in our lives, only to realise we are perfectly capable of existing in the new environment (we may even realise others at our new level feel the same way). Michael Easter, the author of *The Comfort Crisis*, encourages us to push through what we thought we could do with regular life challenges. Over time this removes the fear and builds a sense of confidence in us which is very enriching – similarly to the 'Case Studies' we have mentioned previously. In effect, we will be in flow more frequently because we balance our challenges versus the acknowledged, increasing skillset we possess.

What this means for the ABCD framework is that if we have authentic goals that we care about, a balanced approach that has realistic expectations, and because of this, we can gain some consistency – then we can have the benefits of discipline, without the tyrannous overbearing distress that is often associated. We can easily be disciplined because we choose to be disciplined in things we value, which make us the person we want to be. And if these goals or actions are challenging, we'll feel the benefits even more. We stop falling down the hole in the road of chasing targets that aren't in line with our values, and we have more intention – we are more like *us*. We align our internal values with our external actions and find it far easier to be content, happy, and confident.

FAILURE

Before discovering the ABCD techniques that will enable us to find the crucial elements we require for happiness, it's important to briefly mention failure as it relates to discipline.

Failure is somewhat of a big word. Like discipline, it conjures up certain images, and when those images are drawn from our past experiences, they can elicit a shameful or guilty response. We often blame ourselves for the failed marriage, the failed business, the failed health kick, and the failed job interview. It is important to remember that we were rarely in control of all the parts of these events; they were externals or, at best, *preferred indifferents* to us. We may have done our best (or not) but feeling disturbed about these past events now in the present is pointless.

We all make mistakes; they are an inevitable part of life (it's why there are rubbers on pencils!) – they reflect the always-present fallibility and beauty of humanity.

No honest reader will be thinking, 'Not me. I've never made a mistake in my life.'

It is the way we decide to respond to these failures that makes the difference. It builds character. We have already seen that many of the great minds we are drawing from, as well as more recent scientific research, demonstrates that discipline is a virtue; well, there is nothing more disciplined than falling and getting back up again.

One example that stood out to me was US baseball player Tommy John who played 26 years at the top of his sport. He faced many failures and obstacles in his career but never gave up. From pioneering surgery, the near-death of his son, and his ability being tested. While he could still do his part – he always would. His almost mythical level of discipline - to do everything in his control - is summed up nicely by the following quote by Ryan Holiday,

'The things that Tommy John could change – when he had a chance – got a full 100 percent of the effort he could muster. He used to tell coaches he would die on the field before he quit. He understood that as a professional athlete his job was to parse the difference between the unlikely and the impossible.'[86]

He would show the discipline to go again if there was still any chance of success. *Would you?*

'It's better to have tried and failed than to live life wondering what would have happened if I had tried.'
– Lord Alfred Tennyson.

SUMMARY

Having shown that consistency in our actions is invaluable to achieving our goals in part three, in the fourth and final part of the ABCD framework I have demonstrated that discipline is more than just self-flagellation and misery. Being disciplined can bring us happiness, and it's not as traumatic as it might first seem:

- **DISCIPLINE NEED NOT BE FEARED** – The archetypal example of discipline is often full of negative imagery. This doesn't have to be the case. What you actually fear is *too much discipline* causing life to be miserable. When you learn that balance is integral to a happy life, you take an approach that allows you to be disciplined but to a level that suits your life and goals. Effort is required – not suffering.
- **DISCIPLINE BRINGS US HAPPINESS** – When you possess a higher level of frustration tolerance – you can spend much of your time in flow. Put simply; it's

---

important to have a work ethic in the areas that matter and to avoid the temptation to be lazy; when you do, you feel *in the zone* and can look back on your efforts with pride.

- **CHALLENGES OVER JOYS** – Your body also *physiologically* responds to challenges to give you a dopamine response - a buzz when you survive or achieve something. By pursuing challenges in areas you deem important, you get this response more frequently and increase your general level of happiness.
- **YOU WILL FAIL** – The universe is not set up for your success. Because you already know that the course of your lives will follow the X=Y seen in earlier chapters, you will likely face some difficulty and failure along the way. Rather than fear this eventuality or use it as an excuse, you can use any instances of an actual or perceived failure to your benefit and learn from them.

Here we have learned that discipline can make us happy and doesn't have to be extreme. Following the above areas, we have ample knowledge to consider the questions asked in *Chapter 3*. We have addressed the (CD) sections of our framework so we can appreciate the need for all four elements of ABCD; without every aspect, there is a chance of losing another.

Consistency is difficult if you don't believe in the goal, discipline is hard if you don't take a balanced approach, balance is impossible to maintain, with zero discipline, and nothing is enjoyable if you are behaving in ways that are not authentic to yourself.

We commonly find ourselves anxious and worried because we have one of these elements missing. In that case our approach is too rigorous and needs some *AB* attention, or it is too flexible and lacks *CD*. Whichever is true, addressing the issues doesn't happen on its own; you must be intentional, or the old story, past experiences, and influences of others can take over. We're left feeling out of control and disturbed.

You are now ready to look at the simple techniques you can follow to achieve the four elements of the framework and develop some core values and goals and the small next steps towards them.

But first, let me speak to the voice in all of you that says you don't need help - the voice of *doubt*.

Pause for Thought – Please take time to make some notes:

7

WHY *ABCD* MAY NOT HELP YOU – BUT PROBABLY WILL

'*The definition of insanity is doing the same thing over and over again and expecting different results.*'
– *Albert Einstein.*

SO, YOU DON'T NEED HELP?

YOU MIGHT BE THINKING that the lessons presented in this book are fairly obvious, and you'd be right. The topics in the previous chapter are not difficult to understand. They are primarily ancient teachings from the Greeks and Romans, which were later embraced by modern religions[87], and later still in therapies and counselling. A large section of psychotherapy through the past three hundred years has helped humans overcome the anxieties they have faced in the ever-changing world they inhabit. More recently, self-help books, productivity gurus, and positive vibes meme accounts on social media regularly quote the findings we have dissected in earlier chapters.

If I could wish anything for the readers of *ABCD*, it would be that these helpful thoughts and behaviours already come easily to you. You know yourself well based on your considered life, not the life of others or your past. You take a balanced approach to life and never find yourself with urges or behaviours that lead to disturbing thoughts. Along with these cornerstones of self-love being constant in your lives, you also challenge yourself regularly and experience the life-affirming feeling of flow, frequently throughout your day. In short – you don't need my advice.

---

[87] One good example is the *Serenity Prayer* from Christianity, which adopts the 3 Stoic Principles we saw at the beginning book, and is also read allowed within 12-step fellowships globally.

Of course, I am being facetious, and many people who do not have life perfectly sewn up, live perfectly happy lives. It might simply be that there is enough right that the effort to improve further is not of value. The juice is not worth the squeeze.

As *Spider-Man* creator, Stan Lee once said, 'With great power comes great responsibility.' You might find the comparison between happiness and a superpower to be a bit of a stretch of the imagination. However, I believe that being perfectly content without room for improvement or growth is equally as rare as being able to fly or swing between skyscrapers.

In March 2020, much of the world found itself in an unprecedented and undesirable situation. Due to the coronavirus pandemic's aggressive spread from China to Southern Asia, to Europe, and then onto the rest of the world, governments mandated their populations to stay at home, keep safe, and lockdown. LOCK - DOWN. The phrase still fills me with dread, and I'm sure it's not the first word that comes to mind when thinking about how best to spend the summer holidays.

We have previously referred to human needs such as certainty, purpose, and connection. While many front-line workers (though facing new challenges themselves) will have found increases in these metrics; in general, populations globally saw the disappearance of many necessary conditions that are vital to a happy life. Laughter, connection, employment, certainty, collective family grieving, fitness, adventure, sleep, fresh air, and so much more were lost for an extended period.

Collectively, the mood of many nations changed. Sometimes for the better as early hope, purpose, and responsibility increased, but many people struggled with the negative effect on mental health. Though there is no evidence of increased suicides over the COVID-19 lockdowns, people were still changed forever, and like so many people in our *look how great I'm doing* era, they suffered in silence or put on a brave face.

So please, if you have a good handle on your existence, reach out to those close to you and check in with them. Your own experience or the contents of this book could help someone who needs it, especially in a post-pandemic world. We'll cover this in more depth in a later chapter.

Unfortunately, suicide is not a modern phenomenon. It plays a prominent role in ancient legend and history. Shockingly, early as the 1800s, research began to look at a 'Sickness of Our Time,'[88] and suicide statistics for the most recent 20 years are not particularly cheery reading[89]. From ancient civilisations right up to today, the stresses, anxieties, and mental illnesses associated with being human are ever-present.

Therefore, the lessons in this book have been reiterated and regurgitated hundreds of times—rediscovered and repurposed by great minds of every generation. The struggles common with the human condition are not something that can be solved and then

---

88   Durkheim, E. (1897) *Le suicide: Etude de sociologie.*
89   'Suicide rate in the United Kingdom (UK) from 2000 to 2020' – *www.statista.com*

consigned to history like dated technologies. We're yet to upgrade to *Mental Health v2.0*, allowing us to all be naturally happy and stress-free. Similar struggles remain present, and the longevity of the use and efficacy of these valuable lessons is proof that they are as helpful now as they have been each time they are brought into prominence.

That is the inspiration for *ABCD;* to share the philosophies that have helped me be the happiest I have ever been and pay them forward to others who will undoubtedly need them.

Personally, I found the lockdown difficult, as many of us did. It was a big adjustment to work from home and spend much of your time with the same people. The exciting period of clapping the NHS and baking banana bread soon faded into the numb feeling of emptiness associated with uncertainty and lack of perspective. These lowered mental health metrics interfered with my ability to judge my thoughts and actions rationally. It became paramount to regain awareness of how I perceived the world and stop acting out of line with my values.

Recovery programs sometimes advocate using a daily checklist for the mindful assessment of someone's feelings at a given moment.

H.A.L.T.S.

Hungry, Angry, Lonely, Tired and *Serious/Stressed* moods can cloud the judgement process we saw earlier. We often make more reactive choices when we are experiencing any of these. So many of us are agitated when hungry that it has its own portmanteau-*Hangry!* By 'lockdown two' at the end of 2020, anyone who wasn't feeling several of these emotions regularly was superhuman.

Though mine was a similar experience to many, it felt slightly more frustrating.

You see, I had read endless books on philosophy, therapy, and mindset *before* coronavirus was even in the public eye. I had continuously taken in information and assessed my life to be more considered and true to myself. I assumed that *nothing* could affect me negatively, and I was smugly going about my life with the aloof mannerisms of a modern-day Epictetus. I looked down my nose at those unfortunate enough not to have learned what I had learned - I had the secret.

In short, I was an unlikeable and cocky so and so.

My dad used to say, 'Empty cans make the most noise.' This became incredibly timely after years of preaching my newly found awareness to those around me. Because knowing something doesn't mean that you are *doing* it. Anyone who has ventured on a new diet can confirm that if the knowledge of how to lose weight was the only requirement, then obesity would be a thing of the past.

The truth is that the human mind is complex and can take on many characteristics from our past and the world around us. So, the success of ideas relies on practical application in our real life more than it does on reading books and *liking* memes. We must spend more time doing than we spend planning. We must 'sharpen the saw' (as Covey puts it) so that when it is time to apply these helpful ideas in challenging moments, they are already habitual.

I had missed that memo, which meant I paid the price with a pretty miserable 2021 for which I was thoroughly unprepared. I was truly lost and felt ashamed that I had proclaimed to be so empowered whilst unable to keep that power to hand when challenged.

So how do we turn knowledge into power? When my wife advised me in my moment of need, I realised that I needed a framework to build the ideas and insights I had accumulated into a usable model. Simple steps and guidance to turn the words on the page into processes galvanising my learning.

Even if you feel that you have everything under control, take time to consider if you have the right tools to apply your happy philosophy when times are tough? If not, *ABCD* can help you develop this vital last step.

SMALL CHANGES MAKE BIG DIFFERENCES

As we have seen in the previous chapter when referring to small steps toward a goal, the benefits from making seemingly insignificant changes can be substantial. This is especially relevant when it comes to starting your ABCD process. The aim is not to overwhelm you with tasks and create a dogmatic approach by which you are held accountable. The purpose is to understand yourself and what you stand for better. Then plot a journey towards upholding your values - quite frankly - with as little disruption or effort as possible. Much of what I describe in this book can be taken seriously or with a pinch of salt. If you decide that one area in particular needs some work, you can take some of the advice in the following chapters, scaling up or down depending on your requirements. Following the entire process is not mandatory – application and action are the only important commonality between any approach.

This rationale carries through to the people I am addressing in this chapter. Those readers who feel that they don't need to work on anything and are doing just fine. It could be something so small that you learn from the ABCD framework that makes an unexpectedly significant difference in an area of your lives.

'It has been said that something as small as the flutter of a butterfly's wing can ultimately cause a typhoon halfway around the world.'
– Chaos Theory.

Though it sounds grandiose, much like a butterfly flapping its wings can cause a typhoon across the globe, a slight change of routine or attitude might cause a metaphorical typhoon of favourable results in other areas of your life. So don't miss the opportunity to explore these possibilities.

Our mind often stops us from operating on a higher level than we feel capable of. We undersell ourselves and feel out of place, as though everyone around us has their whole life together. When we take steps to improve ourselves, whether in our career, education, or health, we often have an uncomfortable feeling where we 'doubt our own skills, talents, or accomplishments and have a persistent internalised fear of being exposed as a fraud.'[90] This imposter syndrome exists within most of us at some point, and our early taste typically comes on the first day of secondary school or first days in a new job.[91]

Evolutionarily, it would have been beneficial to take fewer risks. Still, I believe that we often find ourselves in low frustration tolerance mindsets, where we are unmotivated and bored in equal measure. We've settled with our lot, not making even the smallest of improvements. Some of the reasons will be the fear of failure and a large portion of feeling like we don't believe we are capable.

If it is the case that you have settled or think that you aren't the type of person who could make a change in your life. Perhaps you feel that you could benefit from this book's guidance but that you don't deserve any better. Please don't let that be a reason not to try. We're all valuable people and deserve the opportunity to find some happiness and success if we choose to. If nothing else, I implore you to absorb some of the content on authenticity and happiness found earlier in the book. Taking on the ABCD framework is a challenge that brings some healthy discomfort and increases your opportunity to experience regular happiness.

The reality of the situation is often that only by pushing yourself that little bit further than you are comfortable with do you discover your true capabilities. This will raise self-esteem for the better. It is entirely in your hands to do so. You need to find some awareness using the subjects covered in *ABCD* and permit yourself to make even the most minor changes for the better.

SELF-IMPROVEMENT IS NOT PASSIVE

When I began to do the work that later formed the bulk of the ABCD framework, I noticed significant changes with minimal effort. I stopped assuming I was spiritually enlightened simply because I had read a few books. I stopped giving so much advice to others and providing opinions to everyone on every subject. I cut myself a lovely, big slice of humble pie and realised I was not *actively* working on myself. As a result, the first unexpected challenge

---

90   'Imposter Syndrome' – *www.wikipedia.org*
91   And ironically, even when you have tonnes of experience it can still be a factor!

and my values had gone out the window, and I was acting like I always had, rather than how I 'knew' would make me happier. I realised that I'd been lucky so far, but I needed to be more pragmatic when the world became more challenging. I recall a quote I like from the American author Coleman Cox:

'I am a great believer in luck. The harder I work the more of it I seem to have!'[92]
– Coleman Cox.

One area I had battled with recently was SLEEP. Anyone who struggles to sleep at night will know it has a huge impact on one's life (we saw in *Chapter 4* why it is so important) and can make you irritable and unmotivated, preventing productivity and clouding judgement, often leading to poor relationships.

I'd always assumed feeling this way was just how it would be for me. I wasn't perturbed about anything at night, but I went to bed late and often woke multiple times through the night before waking early, snoozing the alarm several times and flicking through my phone before getting up. I had read some literature on getting a better night's sleep, seen the pop journalism pieces on the *Top 5 Sleep Hacks* and searched for devices that offered miracle cures to poor sleep. The problem was not significant enough to warrant the over-whelming work required to fix it. Most people around me existed in the same way (in fact, in a 2018 UK study, it was found that almost 23% of us only get between 5-6 hours of sleep per night, giving them a heightened risk of respiratory problems, heart disease, diabetes and obesity.[93])

However, when I finally accepted that having poor sleep hygiene was causing me more of a problem than I had thought, I decided to act. Improving my sleep was a core value that touched several other areas of my life. Using early incarnations of the ABCD framework, I soon realised that small changes could be made to my sleep pattern with positive effects.

I narrowed it down to the following actions (Sunday to Thursday[94]):

- Putting my phone away an hour before bed.
- Reading for 15-30 minutes before sleep.
- Wearing an eye mask.
- Turning phone notifications off when in my bedroom.
- Allowing one snooze only.
- Splashing cold water on my face as soon as I got up in the morning.

---

92 Cox, C. (1922) *Listen To This.*
93 'Sleep Survey' – *Chemist 4 U* (carried out by One Poll 2018) - *https://www.chemist-4-u.com/sleep-study/*
94 Let's leave a little room for adventure at the weekend!

They are all reasonably small actions and as I had established the issue was authentically crucial to me, it was relatively easy to enforce them consistently enough to see results. I had planned to apply some balance and consistency to my evening routine without making considerable changes to my day.

Rather than thinking about the multitude of advice or the end goal of *sleeping well*, I just set about using the information I thought was relevant and taking these small steps regularly.

Within a few weeks, I was falling asleep relaxed in bed (not on the sofa in front of the telly or thinking about an email I had just read), I didn't feel I was missing out on whatever my phone offered late at night. I slept like a baby, and crucially I woke up with natural alertness I could have only dreamed of.

The knock-on effect was profound. Extra time in the morning allowed me to move my gym sessions to before work (where I met a community of like-minded people who are now some of my closest friends), freeing up time with my family in the evening. I shared more family meals and was awake enough to take the time for bedtime stories with the kids and bedtime activities with my wife (wink wink).

The point is that losing the extra hour of Netflix I watched each night, replying to late messages in the morning, and spending £9.99 on an eye mask were relatively small actions that now aligned with my internal values—and the results were incredible. This routine is still part of my daily life two years later.

To think that without taking a modest amount of action, I might still be behaving like a substandard father and would not have met many of my closest friends is a clear example to me of how this process works. Even in lesser doses, it can add more contentedness to your life than you would ever expect.

WHY YOU PROBABLY COULD GIVE IT A SHOT

How ABCD can help you:

HUMAN EXPERIENCE

- The themes and ideas that form the foundations for the ABCD framework have been passed down for millennia. The problems they solve in our lives are a part of what it means to be a human. They are ingrained in the human experience and always have been.

PREPARATION

- When things are going smoothly, you tend not to value introspection. But like many people during the pandemic (and anyone who has had their relationship fall apart due to grief, illness, or financial struggle), you will soon regret not doing the work to ensure you are robust when tough times come...which they will.

TAKING ACTION

• Being aware of the ideas I have presented in this book is the easy part; the action and work you do to make them part of your life is where the changes are found. In doing so, you will find that you are capable of. American philosopher William James said, 'Action may not bring happiness, but there is no happiness without action.'

SMALL NEXT STEPS

• When you take a more significant problem and break it down into smaller parts, you can adopt life-changing actions with minimal effort. The next small step towards what you want is often relatively simple and far less overwhelming than thinking only about the end goal.

ABCD

• *ABCD* offers a refreshing alternative to many of the other, less flexible self-help structures that exist. If you want a flexible, light antidote to anxiety around your best actions and why you choose them – it is perfect.

Finally, here are some other thoughts on why it is worth reading on and seeing if there is anything of use. Some we've seen already, and some are new, but many of them will factor in your decision to continue:

HUMAN NEEDS

• Humans need *purpose*. You can find something to give you intention and motivation to fulfil that need. Action is the antidote to anxiety.

YOU CAN'T POUR FROM AN EMPTY CUP

• Taking time and energy to improve yourself will make you better equipped to help those you care about.

FLOW

• You will find it harder to find precious flow moments if you are not challenging yourself. If frustration tolerance is a reason not to make improvements, you are missing out on the *true joy* of being in the zone far.

PERFECTIONISM

- Waiting for the right moment to make changes will never come - happiness must be found today, not tomorrow.

TECH ZOMBIES

- Notice how much time you spend on technology. The average screen time is in the region of 7 HOURS A DAY! If you feel that you do not have the time to make positive change, please ensure that time isn't lost *scrolling*.

OVEREXPOSURE

- The cacophony of voices vying for your attention is vast. You rarely spend a minute of your life unoccupied by information, and attention spans are falling to alarming levels (for teenagers in 2016, it was already at 8 seconds[95]). Don't confuse a busy mind with a mind that is serving you well. Just because loads is going on, make sure that some of it is helping you live a better life.

PRIORITIES

- When you are unaware of your core values and how to act in accordance with them, you open yourself up to disappointment. Knowing what your responses will be in advance prevents you reacting to life. This is incredibly effective at reducing stressful, overwhelming, and exhausting decision-making.

FUTURE PROOFING

- With a bit of intention, you can ensure that you are futureproofed against changes in life that might see it passing you by. As actress Lauren Bacall told interviewers, 'Standing still is the fastest way of moving backwards in a rapidly changing world.'

We can address all of this and so much more by focusing our attention on being authentic, taking a balanced approach in life, having some consistency in doing so, and then applying discipline.

After an excruciating teenage break-up, I once drew some inspiration from an Argentinian proverb, 'A man who develops himself is born twice.' At the time, my rebirth was to be watching TV and eating takeaways whilst feeling smug about having painted a quote on my bedroom wall.

---

95 'You Now Have a Shorter Attention Span Than a Goldfish' – *www.time.com*

Had I known the proverb's actual truth – that only in action can we truly develop - I would have taken it more seriously at the time. The phrase stuck with me; many years later, I finally began to follow its lesson. I would say the best thing I ever did was to take a closer look at my life and the story I was letting lead it, even if it was 20 years later.

Pause for Thought – Please take time to make some notes:

8

THE ABCD FRAMEWORK

'That's why the philosophers warn us not to be satisfied with mere learning, but to add practice and then training. For as time passes, we forget what we learned and end up doing the opposite.'[96]
– Epictetus.

THE FRAMEWORK

I'M GOING TO START THIS CHAPTER with a few assumptions:

- You started reading this book because you were curious about a process that would improve your results in specific goals in your life.
- You had one (or more) goal in mind when you picked this book up. A dream that you were struggling to achieve or several goals that were overwhelming you .
- Equally, you may have felt discontent with your actions in general. Not living to a high enough standard compared to your perceived values.
- If you were to question yourself, you would not be able to give healthy and thorough reasoning as to why you wanted the values and goals you were chasing.

In this chapter, we will explore some straightforward techniques I have formulated. It is important that the below is true:

- You can see that the lessons covered can improve your situation, if applied correctly.
- If you didn't start with a specific area of your life in mind, you have a better idea of where to start.

---

96 Epictetus. (c108AD) *Discourses*, 2.9.13-14.

- You can agree that *authenticity, balance, consistency,* and *discipline* are four fundamental principles that won't only make your actions more effective but have the power to improve your life overall.

If the above statements are true, you acknowledge that understanding the subjects you have seen, and their value is important. However, Epictetus reminds us that simply knowing the information isn't always enough.

Even though I felt I knew it all, I had to reframe what I learned when struggling. I had to turn understanding into application.

It was clear that I needed ways to bring the lessons I had learned to life. They would only come to me when I needed them most if I made them habitual. So, I drew similarities between the four key elements and how each of the ideas interacted. They are all closely interconnected. Improving one or more of them can help improve all the others. That is a powerful idea because in practice, the four pillars are inseparable: if you can reach a place where you have some intention and progress in one – you are more likely to do so in the other three.

I started to combine some of the techniques I'd seen and make some simple processes that I could use in my daily life. The idea was that because of the interconnection within *ABCD*; I can apply any of the tools to any area of my life. In some cases, I need to work through them in detail before embarking on a challenge requiring more attention. In other areas, I only need a light version of one of the tools. The magic of understanding and accepting these philosophies into our lives, as so many successful people have before us, is that it isn't one size fits all. Humans are similar enough to all benefit from historical teachings but brilliantly individual to take their own approach. If we are authentic in what we choose and know what we are capable of, then we can decide for ourselves how we proceed.

With the help of a simple personal example in *Chapter 10*, it will become clear that if you want to use part or all of the techniques within the ABCD framework, you can do so, though many benefits from one will feed into the next. They don't only work if utilised on a specific goal, but also when applied more broadly to your life—acting more authentically, in general, will improve your life, and the other factors allow you to create actions in line with your values. I have covered the areas in depth; you know and accept that the ideas and themes are sound so that you can be honest with yourself regarding your adoption of them. Only you know what is best for you.

Unlike much self-help literature, this is not a quick fix, a one-size-fits-all, strictly prescribed set of *rules*. You will be beyond this notion just having read this far. You are beyond being told precisely what to do and then feeling like a failure because the method doesn't work for you. Life is not that simple, and humans rarely are either; we too often set ourselves up for failure by thinking that they are.

It isn't a popular view—that we can trust ourselves to decide how to act instead of being told—but it is what *ABCD* is built upon. I trusted myself, and you can, too, regardless of what other people might want you to believe. We've covered the lessons together as I did, and now, we can look at some methods I have used and decide if these, something like these or something different, can be helpful to you.

If you accept that you can improve these factors in your lives, accept that they are connected and influence each other, and accept that by acting with some more purpose within these areas, you will be happier – then I have achieved what I set out to achieve.

These are not just a few tactics to help you hit a goal; they guide you in many of the crucial actions you take in your life that add up to the values and principles you hold dear across several areas of your existence. When you have this purpose and knowledge of yourself, you can reduce the anxieties you were once facing and feel confident and happy in your life.

You can generate the balance of the factors that allows you to experience regular flow moments. Then, like me, you can move from an anxious mindset into the happiest you have ever been.

Let's turn our passive knowledge into meaningful action. We have the power to improve our lives.

VALUES, PRINCIPLES, AND ACTIONS

Throughout the following sections, I will regularly use the terms:

Value – noun

'Principles or standards of behaviour; one's judgement of what is important in life.'[97]

Principle – noun

'Fundamental truth or proposition that serves as the foundation for a system of belief or behaviour or for a chain of reasoning.'[98]

Action – noun

'The fact or process of doing something, typically to achieve an aim.'[99]

It is crucial to define these separately.

In everyday language these terms are often substituted for each other, and their meanings appear interchangeable. However, within *ABCD* they are their own stand-alone parts of the

---

97 'Value' - *www.OED.com* (via Google/Oxford Languages)
98 'Principle' - *www.OED.com* (via Google/Oxford Languages)
99 'Action' - *www.OED.com* (via Google/Oxford Languages)

framework. This becomes important as you build the framework towards your intended targets. (Many of which will come from the *5 Key Areas Of Life* chapter we covered earlier[100]). The terms feed into each other and develop as you follow the process.

Whether you are seeking improvement in one particular goal/objective/target.

OR

You hope to uphold a core value such as curiosity, family, integrity, compassion, nature, loyalty, kindness etc.

The starting point is the same:

Core Values = Core Goals

These are the overarching target – the end in mind.

Using the ABCD framework you will break these larger items down into the smaller principles or sub-goals that they comprise of.

Principles = Sub-Goals

These are the smaller areas that relate to the value/goal and are easier to visualise and attain. Bringing these to focus will reduce the overwhelming nature of many of our priorities.

Finally, are the detailed yet simple *Small Next Steps* that you can take toward each principle/sub-goal.

Actions

These are the very small behaviours that, when shown consistently, add up to your principles and sub-goals.

The ABCD framework aims to provide you with tools to understand and prioritise your values, principles, and actions (or goals, sub-goals, and actions) and work towards them. Safe in the knowledge that they are all true to you and within your capabilities.

You will end up with a personal version something like below (fig 8.1):

---

[100] Mindset. Relationships. Movement. Diet. Sleep.

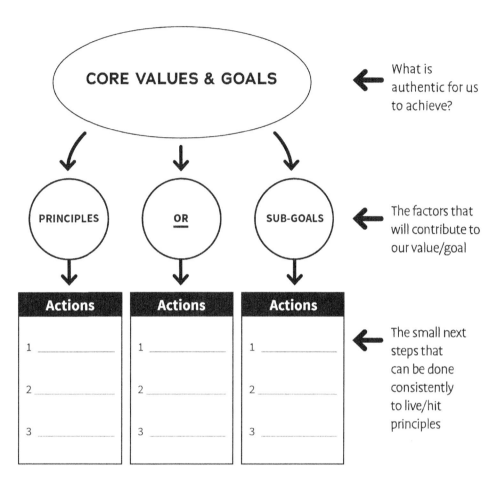

Fig 8.1 —Use ABCD to Create Your Own Map

Pause for Thought – Please take time to make some notes:

AUTHENTICITY TECHNIQUES

Authenticity (Philosophy) – noun

'Authenticity is a concept of personality in the fields of psychology, existential psycho-therapy, existentialist philosophy, and aesthetics. In existentialism, authenticity is the degree to which a person's actions are congruent with his or her (sic – or their) values and desires, despite external pressures to social conformity…In human relations, a person's lack of authenticity is considered bad faith in dealing with other people and one's self, thus, authenticity is in the instruction of the Oracle of Delphi: "Know thyself."'[101]

'Authenticity is the daily practice of letting go of who we think we're supposed to be and embracing who we are. Choosing authenticity means cultivating the courage to be imperfect, to set boundaries, and to allow ourselves to be vulnerable.'
– Brené Brown.[102]

The first element of our ABCD framework is authenticity – what is authenticity?

Being authentic, in a nutshell, is being true to yourself. Acting on the OUTSIDE how you want to be on the INSIDE.

We have discovered that in the broader context of our lives, we are authentic when we realise truths about our happiness and the part we play in it. Our past has created a story that might not align with the genuine desires of the person that we are now and the person we want to be in the future. Our control is limited to two things: our thoughts and actions. We can be more considered in our approach to both and align how we act with how we feel—removing the items outside our concern from places of power in our lives. In this relinquishing of control, we find calm, contentment, and happiness.

More specifically, relating to what we choose to do, our *values* and *goals*, we can genuinely assess what we are striving for and WHY. This way, when limited to our circle of influence, we can ensure we choose the few authentic areas that will make the most difference to us.

In *Chapter 3*, after exploring these ideas, we posed some questions we would need to answer to attain authenticity.

---

101 'Authenticity (philosophy)' – *www.wikipedia.com*
102 Brown, B. (2018) *The Gifts of Imperfection: Let Go of Who You Think You're Supposed to Be and Embrace Who You Are.*

These questions centred around the following themes:

- Letting go of what you can't control.
- Judgements.
- Defining issues and goals that matter to you.
- Differentiating between good and bad advice (internally/externally).

From the various sources analysed in *Chapter 6*, it became clear that the answers to these questions lie within the ideas we have seen:

CONTROL

Knowing that you can only control your thoughts and action and relinquishing control removes disturbances from your lives.

JUDGEMENT

Applying reason to your judgements (of yourself and others) so that you can respond rather than react.

CONSIDERED LIFE

Knowing your old storyline doesn't define you in the present.

VALUES

Using introspection to question WHY you want and act how you do. Realising where your effort must be directed (and where it must not).

We have covered much ground to find such simple, clear focal points. Some of that is from the magic of editing (behind the ~~magician's~~ *author's* curtain, if you will). The fact is that the literature frequently points in the same direction, which makes a compelling argument for upholding ABCD elements in our lives.

Let's explore some of the tools I have created to ensure regular authenticity in my life. The simple techniques, adopted either partially or in full, can vastly improve your life[103]:

---

103 As with all these simple techniques, if you are addressing a particular goal, you can take fewer or less detailed steps as you see fit—though, as you'll see later, there is valuable interaction between your individual goals and other core values. These goals often reveal some value you have and vice versa.

CORE VALUE PRIORITISATION

GENERAL VALUES QUESTION[104]

- What core values does the type of person I want to be hold?

GOAL SPECIFIC QUESTION

- What goals are important, so that I live in line with my core values?

TECHNIQUE

These are simple questions, but people rarely ask them, already caught up in a storyline provided to them that might be untrue. If you want to be more content and confident in who you are, you must be more considered.

So, with this technique, you will take time to analyse who you want to be, what values that person has, and finally, which are the most important — your *core values*.

Complete Worksheet 1 as follows (see Fig 8.2 for reference):

- **Step 1** – Pick up to 10 areas of your life that are most important
- **Step 2** – Can you control outcomes in these areas – YES/NO/PARTIAL?
- **Step 3** – If you have partial control, what part can you control?
- **Step 4** – In 2-3 words, how does improvement in these areas enrich your life?
- **Step 5** – Considering Q1-Q4, honestly select up to 5 areas to focus on
- **Step 6** – With possible core values/goals in mind, re-phrase Q5 as:
  I am the type of person who...
- **Step 7** – Considering Q6 – write your CORE VALUES/GOALS in full:
  My core values/goals are...

---

104 For each technique I will pose a question that broadly sums up the purpose of the tool. These will be split into questions specifically for 'Values' – who do I want to be? And for more specific 'Goals' – what do I want to achieve? The process is the same but posing the question separately is helpful at the outset.

CORE VALUE PRIORITISATION[105]

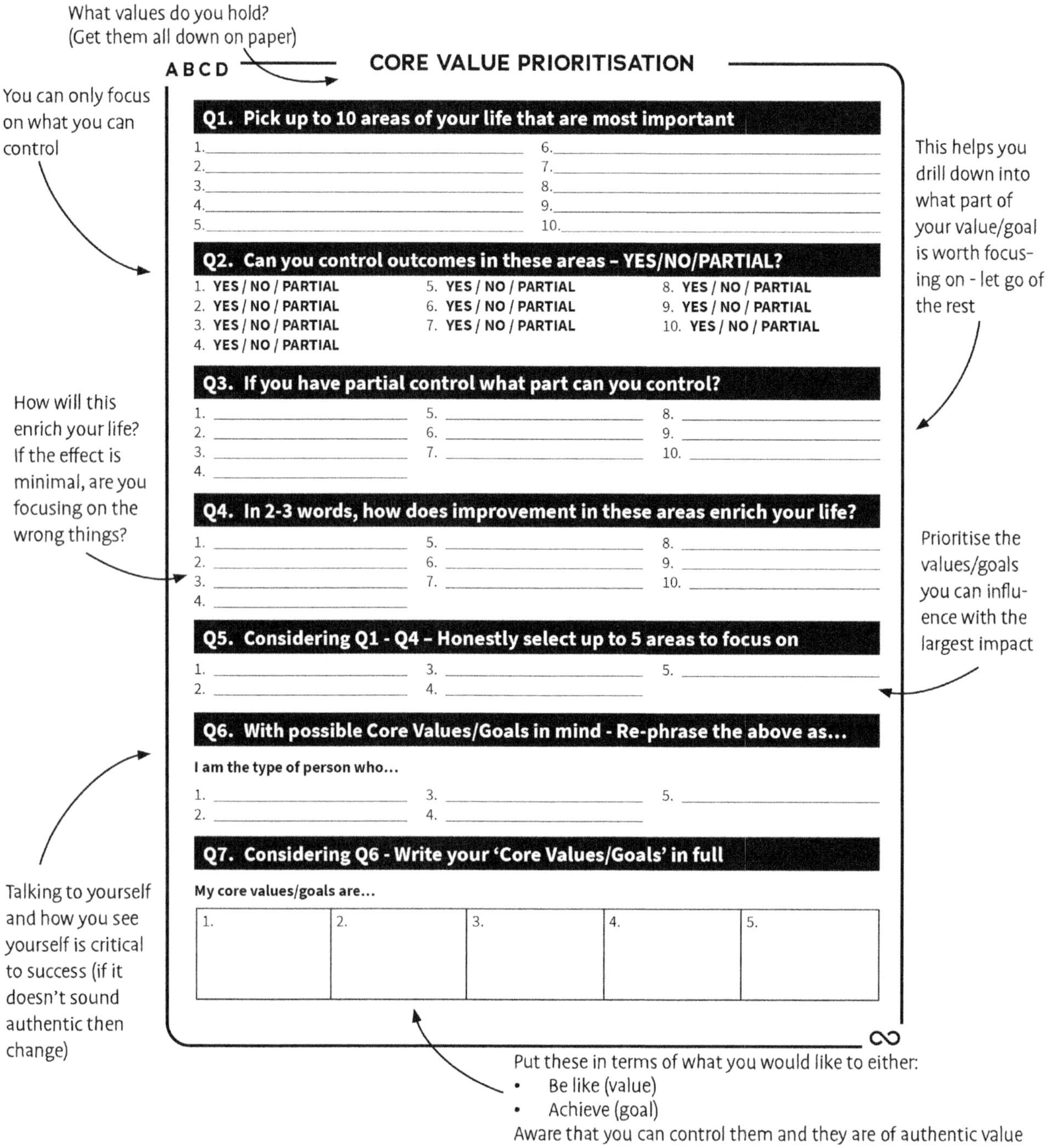
What values do you hold?
(Get them all down on paper)
ABCD
CORE VALUE PRIORITISATION
You can only focus on what you can control
Q1. Pick up to 10 areas of your life that are most important
1. 2. 3. 4. 5. 6. 7. 8. 9. 10.
Q2. Can you control outcomes in these areas - YES/NO/PARTIAL?
1. YES / NO / PARTIAL
2. YES / NO / PARTIAL
3. YES / NO / PARTIAL
4. YES / NO / PARTIAL
5. YES / NO / PARTIAL
6. YES / NO / PARTIAL
7. YES / NO / PARTIAL
8. YES / NO / PARTIAL
9. YES / NO / PARTIAL
10. YES / NO / PARTIAL
This helps you drill down into what part of your value/goal is worth focusing on - let go of the rest
Q3. If you have partial control what part can you control?
1. 2. 3. 4. 5. 6. 7. 8. 9. 10.
How will this enrich your life? If the effect is minimal, are you focusing on the wrong things?
Q4. In 2-3 words, how does improvement in these areas enrich your life?
1. 2. 3. 4. 5. 6. 7. 8. 9. 10.
Prioritise the values/goals you can influence with the largest impact
Q5. Considering Q1 - Q4 – Honestly select up to 5 areas to focus on
1. 2. 3. 4. 5.
Q6. With possible Core Values/Goals in mind - Re-phrase the above as...
I am the type of person who...
1. 2. 3. 4. 5.
Talking to yourself and how you see yourself is critical to success (if it doesn't sound authentic then change)
Q7. Considering Q6 - Write your 'Core Values/Goals' in full
My core values/goals are...
1. 2. 3. 4. 5.
∞
Put these in terms of what you would like to either:
• Be like (value)
• Achieve (goal)
Aware that you can control them and they are of authentic value

Fig 8.2 – Core Value Prioritisation (Explained)

---

105 Blank Worksheets for your own process can be found in Chapter 14 – *ABCD Worksheets*

TIPS & PITFALLS

- The aim here is to bring awareness to what really matters in your life.
- You might start with values you feel are essential, and it is hard to let them go.
- Be honest with yourself.
- If you can't control the outcome of a value/goal – you must let it go.
- If you can partially control the outcome of a value/goal – focus on the part that concerns you.
- It's okay if you have less/different values when you finish; the idea is that you are being considered and, therefore, authentic.
- Keep it simple. These are the overall values/goals, not the steps needed to complete them.
- Feel free to edit this flow of questions to suit you. It is a personal conversation with yourself.

WHAT DOES SUCCESS LOOK LIKE?

- You will have taken time to consider what is worth placing focus on; some clarity we rarely give ourselves.
- You will feel proud to describe yourself as a person who behaves like 'XYZ.' This makes the values/goals feel more personal to you.
- You will have reduced or removed several external concerns and feel more focused.
- By investigating your values, you will reduce overwhelm by knowing what matters and ceasing to worry about the rest.

ABCD INTERACTION

- This is a far more *balanced* approach to understanding what is important to you and will give clarity to what direction you will want to take and how you balance these values/goals with each other.
- Having *authentic* values/goals, you reduce the likelihood of being overwhelmed, and so find time/effort to *balance* your behaviours.
- When deciding actions needed to uphold these values or achieve these goals, you can ask yourself what the type of person-who has these values-does to encourage *consistency*. Prioritising means there is less to focus on.
- When you need the motivation to apply *discipline*, you can trust the fact that these are things that you sincerely want so being true to them is being true to yourself.

WHY? WHY? WHY?

GENERAL VALUES QUESTION

- Why do I hold these values?

GOAL SPECIFIC QUESTION

- Why do I want to achieve this goal?

TECHNIQUE

The basis of this technique is a simple question. But how often have you thought about why you do the things you do?[106] Quite often, when you start a process, it can be very easy to lose track of why you started it in the first place.

So, the technique is really to ask yourself the question, *why?*

Hopefully, this iterative process will find the authentic reasons behind your values and goals. Perhaps you were struggling with overcoming a challenge and realised that your focus was on the wrong thing. There will be many different paths you can follow if you know your true intentions.

Extreme athlete Wim Hof put it perfectly in a recent BBC show[107]:

'Criticism polishes the diamond of truth.'

Complete Worksheet 2 as follows (see Fig 8.3 for reference):

- **Step 1** – Why is this core value/goal important?
- **Step 2** – Why?
- **Step 3** – Why?
- **Step 4** – Why?
- **Step 5** – Why?
- **Step 6** – Re-write/amend your core value/goal *authentically*:
  My core value/goal is...

---

106 Personally, the answer was NEVER!
107 *Freeze the Fear* – BBC1 (April-May 2022)

WHY? WHY? WHY?[108]

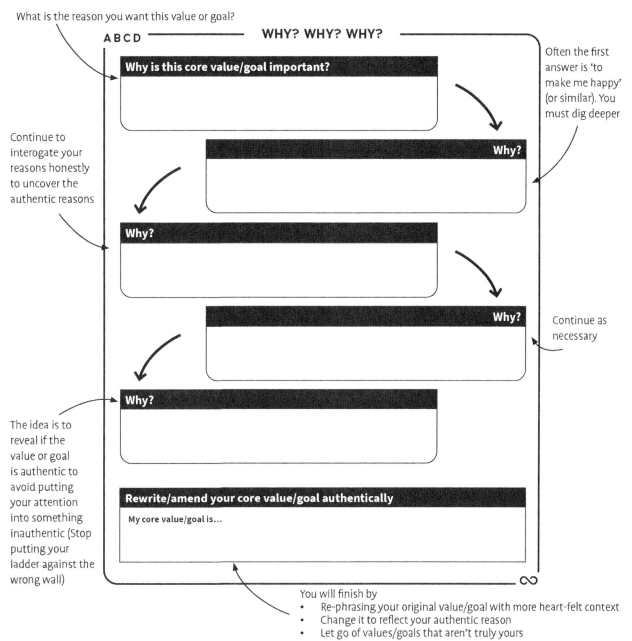

What is the reason you want this value or goal?

ABCD ———— WHY? WHY? WHY? ————

Why is this core value/goal important?

Often the first answer is 'to make me happy' (or similar). You must dig deeper

Why?

Continue to interogate your reasons honestly to uncover the authentic reasons

Why?

Why?

Continue as necessary

Why?

The idea is to reveal if the value or goal is authentic to avoid putting your attention into something inauthentic (Stop putting your ladder against the wrong wall)

Rewrite/amend your core value/goal authentically

My core value/goal is...

∞

You will finish by
- Re-phrasing your original value/goal with more heart-felt context
- Change it to reflect your authentic reason
- Let go of values/goals that aren't truly yours

Fig 8.3 – Why? Why? Why? (Explained)

---

108 Blank Worksheets for your own process can be found in Chapter 14 – *ABCD Worksheets*

TIPS & PITFALLS

- The aim here is to ensure your 'ladder' isn't up against the wrong wall. You question your reasons for wanting something in the hope that you will uncover your authentic desires.
- Don't be scared to discover that there is an ulterior motive for your values/goals.
- Challenge why you want things as it might reveal a storyline that you no longer wish to be part of.
- At first, you might be scared to change long-standing values and give marginal answers. There is less value in keeping hold of old ideas than discovering new ones. If the old story is genuine, it will remain when challenged.

WHAT DOES SUCCESS LOOK LIKE?

- Values/goals will be worded to reflect your true intentions.
- You will find it takes a far less rigorous approach to find satisfaction. You will discover a happier journey toward a more genuine target.
- Reframing your values/goals in a more positive and honest light is essential (as shown in CBT and dialectics).
- You will be motivated towards success more when the values you hold are authentic, and you understand your motivations.

ABCD INTERACTION

- Firstly, some self-awareness and acceptance that you find here improves your abilities in *all* other areas making you happier.
- Having reviewed why you want what you want leads to knowing how much effort and time you want to put into achieving it. Honesty allows a *balanced* and sustainable allocation of your efforts.
- Reducing the noise, you will have fewer, but more mindfully selected priorities. *Consistency* is far more likely in this way.
- When you face choices around *discipline*, having an authentic answer to 'Do really I want this?' will help you stay on track.

Pause for Thought – Please take time to make some notes:

BALANCE TECHNIQUES

Balance – noun

'Physical Equilibrium

Equipoise between contrasting, opposing, or interacting elements

Mental and emotional steadiness'

Balance – verb

'To bring into harmony or proportion'[109]

'Virtue is the golden mean between two vices, the one of excess and the other of deficiency.'
– Aristotle.[110]

The second element of our ABCD framework is balance – what does balance look like?

Balance is finding an existence that is mentally and emotionally stable in the critical areas of your life. Being balanced prevents disturbances to your mental health that occur with extreme and unsustainable behaviour.

We have regularly seen that in the broader context of our lives, we are balanced when we strike an equilibrium between key opposing factors. Our desires vs. reality/fate. Our experiencing self vs. our remembering self. Challenges faced vs. skills used (flow). Work vs. family life. Most of the themes covered prescribe sustainable balance that genuinely contributes to our happiness. This *golden mean* will often create a level of virtue between two distressing extremes, leaving us more content and calm.

Specifically, relating to the things we choose to do, our *values* and *goals*, by taking a balanced approach coupled with the authenticity we have developed, we can have realistic expectations of our future outcomes and approach them purposefully. We also take stock of how we are using our time to understand what we can afford to invest into our values (and make changes to increase this time). We're far more likely to reach targets when we can sustain our efforts towards them.

---

109   'Balance' – *www.merriam-webster.com* (abbreviated)
110   *Nicomachean Ethics: Books II–V: Concerning excellence of character or moral virtue* – Aristotle (c330BC)

In *Chapter 3*, before we began our exploration of these ideas, we posed some questions that we would need to answer to move closer to balance.

These questions centred around the following themes:

- Having expectations that align with your realistic capabilities.
- Enjoying the journey by balancing the *experiencing self* and *remembering self.*
- *Flow*—love being in the zone, not overwhelmed or bored.
- Managing your capability to achieve (ignoring what others expect).
- Prioritising where to expend your efforts, including significant personal development (not 100% focused on the productivity that can lead you to neglect yourself).

From the various sources analysed in *Chapter 6,* it became clear that the answers to these questions lie within:

X=Y

Knowing that some things are out of your control, your expectations and goals must only concern your thoughts and actions.

RATIONAL THINKING/UNDERSTANDING EMOTIONS

Applying reason to how you approach your time and lives without unhealthy negative emotions.

SUSTAINABILITY

Understanding that a steady approach that fits your life will provide more success, more opportunities for flow, and allow you to enjoy the journey regardless of the result.

EFFICIENCY

You must start by assessing what time you can allocate. If more time is needed, and what you are working towards is valuable enough, then you can remove unnecessary processes that don't serve you.

Exploration of these topics makes it evident that balance is a virtue. Much good advice directs us to be moderate, rational, reasonable, and calm...and many of the people we admire have a balanced air about them. Even in nature, our bodies constantly balance themselves to maintain *homeostasis,*[111] allowing the body to function correctly.

---

[111] Quite literally 'Similar' – 'Standing Still' in Latin: 'Staying the Same'

Let's explore some of the tools I have created to assess whether I am following a balanced approach. This applies both when undertaking a process towards a goal and, more generally, when balancing the multiple values in your life. After all, if you continue to address each value separately, they may clash. I truly feel these simple techniques that you can adopt for a specific goal or more generally, will vastly improve your life:

TIMEBOXING

GENERAL VALUES QUESTION

• How much of my time am I giving to my core values? Could I be doing more?

GOAL SPECIFIC QUESTION

• How much of my time am I giving to this goal? Could I be doing more?

TECHNIQUE

This technique uses ideas around sustainability, efficiency, and managing expectations. It is the first time you will see your values/goals in relation to often you work on them.

Having multiple goals you do not spend any time on is easy, yet ineffective. Here you realise that quality, not quantity will give you the life you want.

By splitting your week into sections and mapping how you spend your time, you will see that attacking one goal at full capacity doesn't leave much time for the others. Realisation of your resources helps you be more realistic about what you expect to achieve.

Alternatively, when your week is laid out in front of you, you will be able to free up time by removing tasks/commitments that no longer suit your core values.

You can apply some rational thinking to choosing your targets and enjoy your time each week.

Complete Worksheet 3 as follows (see Fig 8.4 for reference):

• **Step 1** – In pencil complete a typical week.
• **Step 2** – How many spare hours are there?
• **Step 3** – How many hours are spent advancing your values/goals?
• **Step 4** – Are you happy with this?
• **Step 5** – Can any items that don't feed your values/goals be reduced?
• **Step 6** – Re-write (in pen) how you want the week to look.
• **Step 7** – How many hours can you realistically spare for your core values/goals?

TIMEBOXING[112]

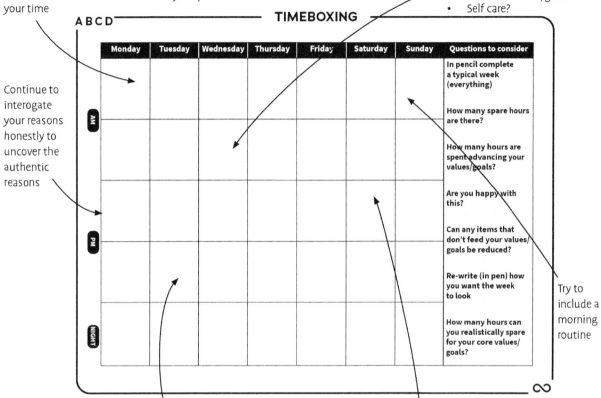

Fill in your typical week (pencil).Include everything
You want a real visualisation of how you spend
your time

Currently how much time do you spend on:
• Your core values/goals?
• Self care?

Continue to interogate your reasons honestly to uncover the authentic reasons

Try to include a morning routine

If you were honest, how could you amend this planner to make more time? Consider:
• Non-negotiables
• Negative pilot
• Reasons you do things
• Other areas of life effected

Make a commitment to prioritise your values/ goals realistically aware of exactly how much time you can realistically commit

Fig 8.4 – Timeboxing (Explained)

TIPS & PITFALLS

• Include *everything*. Wake up times, travelling between appointments, non-negotiables, TV watching time etc.
• You'll be surprised at how busy you are with the practices that are *not* moving you towards your goals.
• You are visualising how a week will look for someone with your values. If you were to uphold your values and achieve your goals, what would you do with your time?

112 Blank Worksheets for your own process can be found in Chapter 14 – *ABCD Worksheets*

- Consider reducing items that aren't necessary to make space for those that are.
- Find time for YOU. It's important to leave time to do things that will keep you content and relaxed. Dr Chatterjee tells us to 'take a holiday every day.'[113]

WHAT DOES SUCCESS LOOK LIKE?

- You will see that the time you spend on specific goals within your week is relatively short. This will allow you to manage your expectations and remind you that success won't be instant. Longer term outlook and balance is promoted.
- You can make more time for your values and goals fairly easily.
- You will find that you are able to simplify your time and make more for yourself, so you aren't burned out or wasting time unnecessarily.
- You've removing emotion from your target setting - doing fewer things *better*.

ABCD INTERACTION

- Nothing will help you prioritise what is *authentic* to you more than seeing how much of your time you have to offer it. Things you do without knowing why can be replaced with something that you value, and thoughts of filling all your spare time working on a goal can cause you to revaluate precisely how important it is.
- Setting the bar too high with unsustainable targets will cause you to be overwhelmed. Here you do the opposite, and thus you allow *consistency* of small actions that can accumulate to your intended targets.
- Visualising exactly how much time you are committing to a goal versus the total time in the week will put it into perspective. *Self-discipline* is more likely when the perception of your sacrifice is minimised. Can you say you can't spare an hour for your daughter's dance show when you spend 8 hours a week socialising?

---

113 Chatterjee, Dr R. (2022) *Happy Mind, Happy Life.*

VALUE DIALS

GENERAL VALUES QUESTION

- How will I balance the effort I give to my values to ensure I don't exceed my mental capacity and cause anxiety?

GOAL SPECIFIC QUESTION

- How does this goal interact with other important goals, and how do I balance my approach and expectations?

TECHNIQUE

As seen with the 'X=Y' graphs earlier in the book, balance isn't only between fate and desires. Humans are complex, fallible beings; therefore, you will have wants and needs on opposing ends of certain spectrums. It's one of the factors that makes you unique.

When you assess your core values and goals, you forget to acknowledge that they interact with each other. For us to have any success in any area it must balance with the rest.

It is all well and good to have grand designs for success in multiple areas, but it is likely to amount to nothing if you don't leave yourself capacity for each. If two values are deemed a priority but oppose each other, then it's unlikely you can be regimented without reducing your happiness. Equally, taking one goal with military discipline might be a non-starter if doing so prevents any progress in another.

Sustainability is vitally important to living like the person you want to be. Sustainability will not be possible without the balance of *all* the key areas of your life. Visualising these together with a simple diagram is very powerful in accepting lowered expectations, reducing internal conflict, and being happier.

Before I describe the process, I would like you to look at the following DIAL.

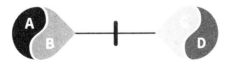

Fig 8.5 – An Example Value Dial

Throughout this book, I have discussed the framework's ABCD elements and their importance and interaction.

The authenticity and balance (AB) elements relate to finding ways of thinking and acting that allow you to be happy, positive, and flexible. This side of the framework effectively asks you to make sure that what you want is genuine, instructing you to adopt (however loosely) some philosophy of your own, and allows you to see the need to manage expectations.

The lessons on consistency and discipline (CD) teach you the importance of working hard, delaying gratification, and reframing failures. It's about getting to work to make your life how you want it to be and relishing the challenge.

I have split these two halves of the framework because they represent different sides of the same coin. In the *Value Dials* technique, this distinction is important because you will use them as a guide in your mind as to what side of the approach is prominent for a particular value or goal. If the AB side is more important, you want to be more flexible and relaxed in this area; if the CD side is prioritised, then the value/goal requires hard work and becomes non-negotiable.

As you'll see below, when you assess how your view of a certain value/goal affects other areas of your life, it is easier to picture what balance looks like and set targets and efforts appropriately.

It is a method that drastically improved my own life and gave me great perspective.

Complete Worksheet 4 as follows (see Fig 8.6 for reference):

- **For each value/goal in its own section/dial.**
- **Step 1** – Where in the dial is your current effort? (Pencil)
- **Step 2** – Moving to (AB) means? (for each other value/goal)
- **Step 3** – Moving to (CD) means? (for each other value/goal)
- **Step 4** – Move dial to balanced position in relation to life and other values/goals. (Pen)
- **Repeat for each value/goal in new section/dial.**

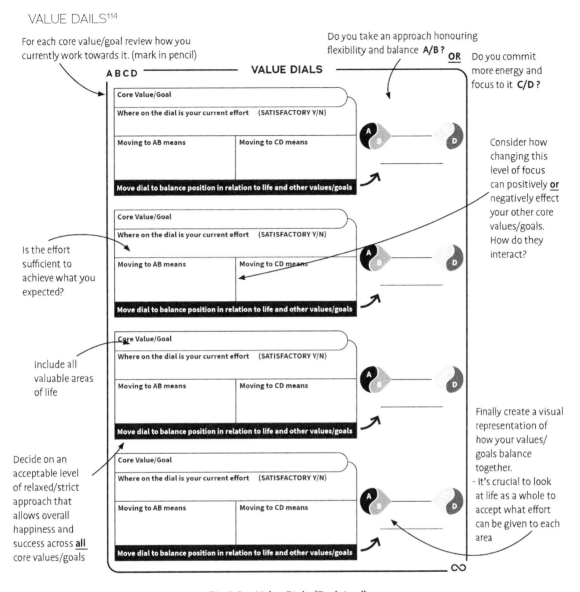

Fig 8.6 – Value Dials (Explained)

TIPS & PITFALLS

- The aim here is to visualise all your core values/goals *together*.
- Each section/dial contains one value/goal and the related answers.
- Your life isn't compartmentalised so why should your values? Seeing them lined up together will reveal limitations of how far you can commit to each.
- Write down how a more relaxed approach in one goal would benefit another, or how a more disciplined approach in one value would have negative consequences on your happiness.

- You are looking for an idea of what efforts can be given– without neglecting your enjoyment of your life as a whole.
- Your selected authentic goal may be extremely rigorous – use this as a representation of the acceptance needed across other areas of your life.
- Try including a mindset/happiness as one of the value dials. It allows you to refer to it in the context of all the other dials. For example, by being extreme across one goal, are you negatively affecting your happiness or enjoyment of life?

WHAT DOES SUCCESS LOOK LIKE?

- You will have a diagrammatic representation of how the key areas in your life interact and could be re-balanced to increase your happiness.
- This is an extension of the X=Y premise around balance. You will reduce disturbances because you can clearly see your values and align your actions with them rather than swinging between opposing, inauthentic behaviours.
- It will be apparent that extreme actions in some will not be possible if you are to enjoy others and hence your life.
- You now have an idea of the way your actions and targets should present. So, deciding how to approach these areas becomes clearer. You can show intention in your actions as you know their value to your life.
- Without setting any specific subgoals or principles that make up these goals and values, you have a quick eye reference to check if you are acting/thinking how you ought to.

ABCD INTERACTION

- This exercise is the first time you will think of your core values together. It is a real test of these values' *authenticity*, which might sound scary. Still, you are doing this process to find self-awareness, you don't have the mental capacity to attack life 100% on multiple fronts. Realisation leads to you focusing on the essentials rather than half-baked attempts across too many areas. This realisation is authenticity at its best.
- Here, you are presenting the level of approach to remain *balanced*. The idea is to prevent extreme behaviour when looking at life as multiple independent factors, rather than one journey.
- As with any method used to create balance, its use improves our chances of *consistency*. You're effectively asking yourself what the best combination is, allowing consistency instead of burning out.
- This technique also helps with *discipline* by providing motivation to stay balanced in your approach and expectations.

Pause for Thought – Please take time to make some notes:

CONSISTENCY TECHNIQUES

Consistent – adjective

'Acting or done in the same way over time, especially so as to be fair or accurate. Unchanging in nature, standard, or effect over time

(of an argument or set of ideas) Not containing any logical contradictions

Compatible or in agreement with something'[115]

'Every habit and capability is confirmed and grows in its corresponding actions, walking by walking, and running by running...therefore, if you want to do something make a habit of it, if you don't want to do that, don't, but make a habit of something else instead. The same principle is at work in our state of mind.'
– Epictetus.[116]

The third element of our ABCD framework is consistency – what constitutes consistency?

Consistency is regularly performing the small actions of our core values. Periodically acting by our highest values, we create habits that move us closer to happiness. You are what you do every day.

We have discovered that in the broader context of our lives, we are being consistent when our external actions mostly match our internal values. By creating habits through small actions, we become quietly confident and content with who we are and how we act.

More specifically, relating to the things we choose to do, our *values* and *goals*, we can outperform raw talent by being consistent in small reasonably balanced steps. All achievements, no matter how large, start with a first step; once we know what we genuinely want to attain, we can plan the course.

In *Chapter 3*, before we began our exploration of these ideas, we posed some questions that we would need to answer to generate consistency.

These questions centred around the following themes:

---

115 'Consistent' - *www.OED.com* (via Google/Oxford Languages)
116 *Discourses*, 2.18.1-5 – Epictetus (c108AD) *Discourses*, 2.18.1-5. (Translation from Holiday, R. and Hanselman, S. (2016) *The Daily Stoic*.)

- Reducing the daunting focus on the bigger picture in favour of smaller steps toward your goals.
- Choosing actions that realistically fit into your life.
- Developing experiences that can overwrite your historical story and give you confidence in your capabilities.
- Finding small daily actions that reinforce the feeling of consistency and success in your life.

From the various sources analysed in *Chapter 6*, it became clear that the answers to these questions lie within the topics we have seen:

CONSISTENCY OVER TALENT

Believing that with small regular effort, you can realise even the largest of goals.

CASE STUDIES

Confidence developed by positive examples in your life now.

SMALL NEXT STEPS

Building habits, whether toward a goal or in your behaviour, can make the journey far easier.

DAILY CONSISTENCY

Small wins can impact how you see yourself. Even a minor morning routine can centre you for the day.

Consistency is a theme shown regularly in this book. Many successful people state that their perseverance and work rate brought them to where they are. From a mental health perspective, cognitive dissonance causes anxiety, but regularly acting authentically, reduces anxiety and produces the calm to take on the world.

Let's explore the tools I have created to build consistency into my life. You may only need a slight push to track your progress in a task, or you may want to apply them across your life. Either way, I believe they will help:

PERSONAL CONSISTENCY PYRAMID

GENERAL VALUES QUESTION

- When a person has my core values - which principles do they live by?

GOAL SPECIFIC QUESTION

- To achieve my goal - what sub-goals would I need to complete?

TECHNIQUE

At this stage, you will know how much time and mental effort you can afford to give to your values/goals. By visualising how they interact with your life, you can imagine how important they are while not losing sight of other elements that make your journey enjoyable. This means you can make the work towards living these values or hitting these goals satisfying and balanced. That may be a total lifelong devotion to a project or a lighter approach to allow progress in a smaller area of your life.

Now you move to the work that is necessary to achieve this. You saw before that being a person of value is not passive. You have drilled down to find the right values and goals to focus on and made the bigger picture far less overwhelming, but you must still regularly take action to achieve anything.

Complete Worksheet 5 as follows (see Fig 8.7 for reference):

- **Step 1** – Write your core value/goal.
  My core value/goal is...
- **Step 2** – Write what point you are at currently. Your starting point.
  Where I am now...
- **Step 3** – Define some smaller principles and sub-goals that, when completed consistently are more likely to amount to your overall value/goal.
  Principles/Sub-Goals
- **Step 4** – Write how you visualise the completion of these objectives will move you toward your value/goal.
  Completing the above will get me to...
- **Repeat for each value/goal (as desired).**

PERSONAL CONSISTENCY PYRAMID[117]

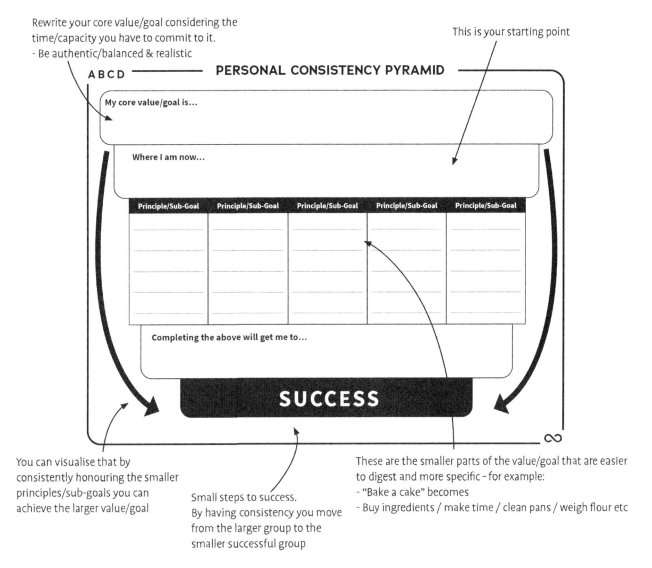

Rewrite your core value/goal considering the
time/capacity you have to commit to it.
- Be authentic/balanced & realistic

This is your starting point

PERSONAL CONSISTENCY PYRAMID

ABCD

My core value/goal is...

Where I am now...

Principle/Sub-Goal	Principle/Sub-Goal	Principle/Sub-Goal	Principle/Sub-Goal	Principle/Sub-Goal

Completing the above will get me to...

SUCCESS

∞

You can visualise that by
consistently honouring the smaller
principles/sub-goals you can
achieve the larger value/goal

Small steps to success.
By having consistency you move
from the larger group to the
smaller successful group

These are the smaller parts of the value/goal that are easier
to digest and more specific – for example:
- "Bake a cake" becomes
- Buy ingredients / make time / clean pans / weigh flour etc

Fig 8.7 – Personal Consistency Pyramid (Explained)

TIPS & PITFALLS

- The aim here is to turn a daunting value/goal into bite-sized chunks. You know the
larger target is authentic, so you don't need to focus on it daily.
- Remember that you have already seen the level of effort you can spare in your life,
so don't make these principles/sub-goals unrealistic or abundant. Don't try and do
everything at once.

117 Blank Worksheets for your own process can be found in Chapter 14 – *ABCD Worksheets*

- Make the principles/sub-goals a little more specific than your core values, if this will help you picture what is needed later.
- Try to visualise your journey from part of a larger group into a smaller, more successful group that have taken action towards what they want. You will achieve this by succeeding at these smaller goals.
- If the particular goal requires many stages, think of those you can start on now rather than ones you can start later. First things first.
- This pyramid is not set in stone (unlike real ones). You can revisit and repeat this process regularly as you complete your principles/sub-goals.

WHAT DOES SUCCESS LOOK LIKE?

- A small number of clear sub-goals/principles for each core value/goal.
- The visual representation of how by performing these consistently, you move from part of a larger group who share the value/goal to part of a smaller group who have succeeded.
- Understanding the sustainable work required to become the person you want to be without being overwhelmed by the bigger picture.
- Confidence in the process.

ABCD INTERACTION

- When you see the progress you could make at a high level in your personal consistency pyramid, it helps you picture your journey. This feeds into the *authenticity* of your chosen areas of life and will feel exciting.
- This tool directly incorporates the prior balance work as you break the value/goal into smaller goals you can *realistically* achieve. Thus, they will be easier to sustain as part of a balanced lifestyle.
- *Consistency* is far more likely when you look at granular actions within your capabilities.
- When the other areas of the framework (ABC) are being supported and nurtured with some good intention, your desire to put in the effort and remain focused grows significantly. You stop doing things you hate and can find *discipline* more readily.

VALUES AND PRINCIPLES MAPS

GENERAL VALUES QUESTION

- What *Small Next Steps* can I consistently take to be true to my principles?

GOAL SPECIFIC QUESTION

- What *Small Next Steps* do I need to regularly take to achieve my sub-goals?

TECHNIQUE

This part of the ABCD framework is where you finish determining your values and principles. Later you will see specific discipline techniques to keep you on track, but to begin your journey, you must know what the path looks like.

You're visualising your core values/goals, the principles/sub-goals that feed them, and the actions you can take. It might be the first time you have set out your actions and how they contribute to the bigger picture. For this reason, it will reduce the overwhelming nature change. Some tiny actions can lead to significant changes. You will be less scared of what is to come, providing you with the energy and empowerment to take the first step.

'Well-being is realized by small steps, but is truly no small thing.'[118]
– Zeno.

You know your values, how they interact with your life, and what time you can give to them; you know what is reasonable to aim for and still live well.

So, take some action towards making them happen.

Complete Worksheet 6 as follows (see Fig 8.8 for reference):

- **Step 1** – Write your core value/goal.
  My core value/goal is...
- **Step 2** – Write the principles/sub-goals that create progress.
  Principles/Sub-Goals
- **Step 3** – Write the actions that you will focus on short term to ensure the principles are held/sub-goals are reached.
  Actions
- **Leave Review Period Blank** (This will be chosen later)
- **Repeat for each value/goal (as desired).**

---

118 Holiday, R. and Hanselman, S. (2016) *The Daily Stoic.*

VALUES AND PRINCIPLES MAPS[119]

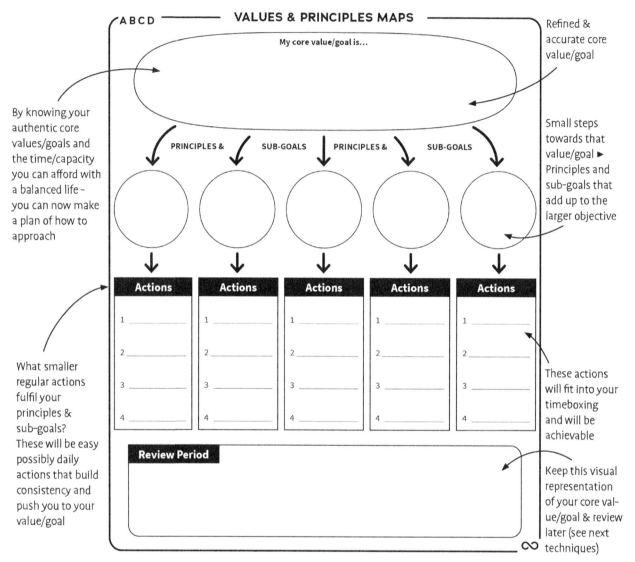

Fig 8.8 – Values and Principles Map (Explained)

TIPS & PITFALLS

- Here you bring together the previous elements of the ABCD framework. This will be the diagram that you can keep to hand to remind yourself of what small effort is needed every day to be the person you want to be.
- Reflect your known capacity from the balance techniques in your actions. Don't have too many; keep it simple.
- Make the actions reasonably specific. Actions must be prescriptive, measurable, and time sensitive. Define the action exactly and the regularity needed.
- If you want to have a morning routine with some daily wins, this could be added to any value/goal here. This also applies to the idea of *me time* or anything that allows you to be happier (including rest days, breaks, and simply doing nothing).
- Here is your time to reframe or reword the details. Though you will keep the other tools used, this map is something you can refer to time and again—get the wording right.
- Remember, rethink your approach if you find yourself writing actions for a goal that doesn't reflect your values. Don't practice what you don't want to become.
- Go over the final diagram in pen and put it in a place where you will see it regularly.

WHAT DOES SUCCESS LOOK LIKE?

- Visualisation of how small steps can lead to significant achievements.
- Having fewer things to focus on and decisions made reduces cognitive dissonance and gives a higher likelihood of peace.
- Knowing the steps that you can take *right now*. Finding them for yourself from an authentic and balanced place.
- More regular flow opportunities in your life from having challenges to face but meeting them with the required amount of effort.
- Beginning your journey.

ABCD INTERACTION

- Here are all of the ABC elements in one diagram. You can achieve consistency by keeping your goals *authentic* and your approach *balanced*. In turn, that *consistency* can lead to the most valuable accomplishments.

Pause for Thought – Please take time to make some notes:

DISCIPLINE TECHNIQUES

Self-Discipline – noun

'Self-discipline is about creating new habits of thought, action, and speech toward improving oneself and reaching institutional goals. ...True discipline is grounded in your ability to leave your comfort zone. Habit is about wanting to change, not about wanting to sweat and undergo activity. To forego or sacrifice immediate pleasure requires thought and focused discipline. ...It's about taking those small consistent steps of daily actions to build a strong set of disciplined habits that fulfil your objectives. ...Discipline is about inner and outer dimensions, discipline could be about the capacity to decide on what is right from wrong (internal consistency) and to use our skills well, properly or routine compliance and to adhere to external regulation rule compliance (external consistency).[5] 'Discipline is the thing that happens when you expend some effort (both physical and mental) to do a thing that in that moment, you don't feel like doing...'[120]

'Discipline is choosing between what you want now and what you want most.'
– Abraham Lincoln.[121]

The fourth and final element of our ABCD framework is discipline – what discipline is required of us?

Discipline is either choosing to act towards a specific goal or not taking action away from it. We aim for these choices to be made in line with our core values and not with potentially extreme behaviours that remove balance and authenticity from our lives.

We have discovered that in the broader context of our lives, that discipline need not be to miserably imbalanced levels. That is more torture than virtue and swings the course of our lives to the extreme. The discipline required is far more straightforward; we will be happier if we regularly choose actions that give us delayed gratification. This way, we can build an HFT and feel proud that our lives are balanced between what we enjoy today and what might be better tomorrow.

More specifically, relating to the things we choose to do, our *values* and *goals*. Our ambitions are genuinely what we desire, and we have chosen a balanced view of the results and efforts required, so discipline is far more accessible. Most journeys will take work, and there will

---

120 'Self-discipline' – *www.wikipedia.com*
121 US President Abraham Lincoln (c1861-1865)

be failures along the way. This isn't a passive enterprise, but the effort required will be proportionate to the time spent enjoying our lives.

In *Chapter 3*, before we began our exploration of these ideas, we posed some questions we would need to answer to determine the required level of discipline.

These questions centred around the following themes:

- Creating goals that you want to work hard at rather than failing at those imposed on you by others.
- The virtue associated with the smallest amount of regular discipline.
- The mental benefits of overcoming challenges.
- Failure and how it is often positive.

From the various sources analysed in *Chapter 6,* it became clear that the answers to these questions lie within:

BALANCED DISCIPLINE

Rather than torturous, you know that you can stick to the task at hand because it is something you respect.

CHALLENGES BRING JOY

Understanding that your body physically responds to challenges, both hormonally and mentally. You feel happier to have tested your capabilities and will find flow in these challenges.

FAILURE

It's clear from X=Y and Stoic philosophy that the world around you is almost entirely out of your control. It is obvious that you will sometime fail in your aims. Respecting that and focusing on what you can control reduces disturbances, anxiety, and gives you opportunities to learn.

We have seen that discipline is a benefit both on philosophical grounds and physiologically. There is a reason that people are elated after completing challenges, and studies show the increased happiness of those who regularly defer rewards[122]. It is vital to strike a balance so that life can be enjoyed with flexibility. Having goals and values to focus on that are not overwhelming and not inauthentic will give us the leeway required to do so.

Let's explore some of the tools I have created to maintain discipline. More than any other element of the ABCD framework, the level of discipline required is personal to you. Some

---

122 One study even mapped the lives of children who took sweets when told not too versus those who waited to receive double sweets. The delayed children were more successful throughout their lives (on average)

introspection and honesty are involved as to what is possible. Each reader is different. However, these are the tools that have helped me:

SPECIFIC AND CHALLENGING TIMELINES

GENERAL VALUES QUESTION

- Am I challenging myself enough to be the person I want to be?

GOAL SPECIFIC QUESTION

- Are my goals specific and challenging enough to provide motivation and joy from the results?

TECHNIQUE

Many of you will have heard of *SMART* goal setting - goals or objectives should be 'Specific, Measurable, Attainable, Realistic and Timely.'[123]

In *ABCD*, you are going to focus on the fundamental factors of your core values and goals that will make you more motivated.

American Psychologist Edwin A. Locke was a pioneer in the field of goal setting. His 1968 Article 'Toward a Theory of Task Motivation' sets out the features of *Goal Setting Theory* from over a decade of research:

'The basic premise of this research is that an individual's conscious ideas regulate his actions. Studies are cited demonstrating that: (1) hard goals produce a higher level of performance (output) than easy goals; (2) specific hard goals produce a higher level of output than a goal of "do your best"; and (3) behavioural intentions regulate choice behaviour.'[124]

Locke is saying that, when trying to achieve goals, it is the conscious willingness to reach them, and the intention displayed towards them that matters. A crucial factor is that the goal is specific and challenging and this is what this tool addresses.

A balance between your challenges and skills creates a sweet spot where you feel alive. Locke agrees that challenges should not be too difficult, or the motivation to achieve them reduces. Hard work is critical to your appreciation of successes and enjoyment of your journey.

---

123 Doran, Miller & Cunningham (1981) 'There's a S.M.A.R.T way to write management goals and objectives' – *Management Review*, Vol. 70, Issue 11.
124 Locke, E. A. (1968) 'Toward a theory of task motivation and incentives' –– *Organizational Behaviour and Human Performance*, Volume 3, Issue 2.

Here you will see the ABCD technique, which aims to *sharpen the saw* by enhancing your core values and goals with some much-needed specificity with which you can hold yourself accountable.

Complete Worksheet 7 as follows (see Fig 8.9 for reference):

- **Step 1** – Write your principle/sub-goal.
- **Step 2** – Define timelines that would be unrealistic.
  Easy / Impossible
- **Step 3** – Using these as a guide, what timeline would be realistic?
  Challenging
- **Step 4** – Write a review date to revisit and amend these chosen dates.
- **Repeat for each principle/sub-goal and for your core value/goal (as desired).**

SPECIFIC AND CHALLENGING TIMELINES[125]

For each principle/sub-goal define:
- A timeframe you can see easily completing
- A timeframe that would be impossible (keep it realistic not '5 seconds')

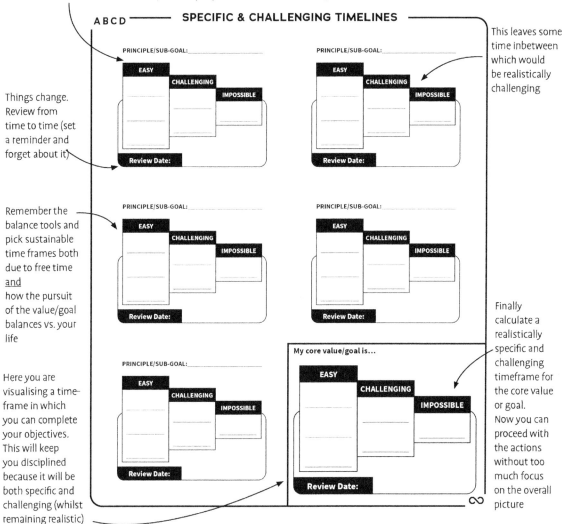

Fig 8.9 – Specific and Challenging Timelines (Explained)

TIPS & PITFALLS

- Here you will take stock of the actions you have chosen towards your principles/sub-goals. Knowing the time that you can commit, you can realistically pick timelines that will ensure you work regularly, but don't over commit.

---

125 Blank Worksheets for your own process can be found in Chapter 14 – *ABCD Worksheets*

- Make your timelines challenging to enhance the feeling of satisfaction when you achieve them.
- Be honest, realistic, and remember the time/mental capacity allocated in the balance sections of the framework.
- Set the review periods to match your case study check-ins and add them to your values and principles maps.
- Schedule reminders on your phone for checking, then enjoy a clearer mind with growing confidence.
- Focus on the *Small Next Steps* you are taking.

WHAT DOES SUCCESS LOOK LIKE?

- Enhancing the values and principles maps to have motivating timelines that increase the chances of self-discipline.
- Motivation to take one final look at the great work you have done and plan for your new journey taking the first step to success.

ABCD INTERACTION

- This tool enhances *all* the other parts of the framework improving your focus on maintaining the other ABCD elements.

CASE STUDIES

GENERAL VALUES QUESTION

- How can I ensure a realistic and positive reinforcement of my progress that keeps me learning, accountable, and enjoying my life?

GOAL SPECIFIC QUESTION

- What am I doing well? Are my chosen actions working?

TECHNIQUE

Unlike the prior ABC techniques, the way that you maintain self-discipline is a little more subjective. Motivation levels and work ethic vary from person to person, which is not necessarily a bad thing. Whatever level of effort you intend to put in, you will need to build references to your good work – particularly when humans have a habit of doing the opposite.

With that in mind and remembering that challenges are good for you (and that imbalance is generated when you are bored or overworked), you must honestly assess your progress regularly.

It is essential to assess where you are in your process. Either through daily journaling or keeping a spreadsheet of results and adherence. Different methods suit different people, but in my experience, creating case studies is a fair balance.

Case studies are small journal entries when you notice some success either in one area of focus (or in a separate area due to your efforts in this one). They act as *gratitude* for your efforts and how they pay off, encouraging further consistency.

Things are often better than you perceive.

Complete Worksheet 8 as follows (see Fig 8.10 for reference):

- **Step 1** – Write your core value/goal and date of review.
- **Step 2** – Write how progress is going and any examples of how your smaller efforts are moving you toward your larger values/goals.
  Details
- **Step 3** – Define if this is a *success* or an opportunity to *learn*.
- **Step 4** – Choose a review period to make sure you regularly consider how progress is going.

CASE STUDIES[126]

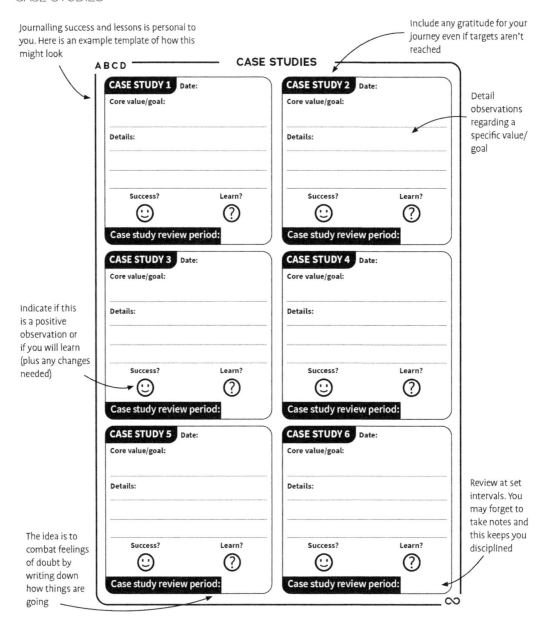

Fig 8.10 — Case Studies (Explained)

TIPS & PITFALLS

- Stay positive! There is enough negativity in the world - you're doing great!
- Don't refer automatically to previously held opinions of yourself or your life these are *new* case studies that form who you are *now*.
- Schedule reminders on your phone allowing you to forget about this and enjoy life.
- Make mental notes of when you generally feel positive and why. It can cause a paradigm shift where you look upon yourself less self-critically.
- Consistency problems create opportunities to grow. If you find that you are 'failing,' you can change the process – *you learn*. I'll cover this more in the *Failure* chapter.

WHAT DOES SUCCESS LOOK LIKE?

- Seeing examples of what you have done well along the journey, you begin to write a new authentic story for yourself in this present moment.
- If you have unexpected results, it is powerful to see that your efforts are good enough to create results you may have only dreamed of.
- Develop a healthy attitude towards yourself.
- Positive confirmation that what you are doing, is working. This allows you to be confident and relaxed.

ABCD INTERACTION

- *Authenticity*, *balance*, and *consistency* all feed into your ability to be *disciplined*. Your selection of values/goals with these factors considered makes them easier to stick to.
- This also works in reverse. As you create more case studies of successful behaviours, the actions that you have chosen will become habitual. They become an *authentic* part of who you are.

Pause for Thought – Please take time to make some notes:

SUMMARY

Congratulations!

You have worked hard to create *awareness* of, perhaps for the first time, your core values and how they fit into your life both from an efficiency and mental capacity standpoint. You've picked realistic goals and the small next steps consistent with your *values*. You can take disciplined *actions* toward your *principles* so that your core values and goals are realised while remaining happy.

Here's a summary of the *8 ABCD Techniques*:

ABCD FRAMEWORK

CORE VALUE PRIORITISATION
Consider what is important to you

WHY? WHY? WHY?
Dig deeper into the real authentic reason and amend values/goals

TIMEBOXING
Understand the time you can sustainably give

VALUE DIALS
Balance your values/goals alongside other areas of your life

PERSONAL CONSISTENCY PYRAMID
Visualise what principles/sub-goals would move
you from the start to the finish

VALUES AND PRINCIPLES MAP
Decide the small next steps that require consistency
to form your principles/sub-goals

SPECIFIC AND CHALLENGING TIMELINES
Refine the values/goals to be the right level
of challenge to drive motivation

CASE STUDIES
Regularly note positive results and take confidence
that you have what it takes to succeed

The tools are simple, but simplicity will set you up for success. Using these techniques, I have achieved some things I could never have dreamed of back in 2016, even stabilising me when the challenges faced were unprecedented.

I'd love to tell you that these were all grandiose multimillion pound, shimmering six-pack, master's degree level successes – they were not. The real victories I found were in defining authentic core values and goals that meant a lot to me and realising that my happiness in the journey towards them was as important (if not more) than the result. I reframed what I wanted and found it easier to have as part of my life with little sacrifice. All the while developing consistency that made me proud of myself for keeping promises and being who I wanted to be.

Your goals may be magnificent and enormous, and I strongly feel the techniques and lessons here can lead you to them. The ABCD framework is scalable and accessible to us all, regardless.

People deserve the tools and knowledge to make positive changes in their lives – this is my attempt to help.

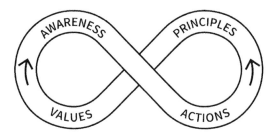

Fig 8.11 – Our Journey Through ABCD

9

THE ABCD SCHEMATIC
AND YOUR PERSONAL STATEMENT

'One Picture is Worth Ten Thousand Words.'
– Fred R. Barnard[127]

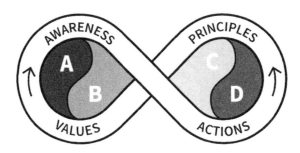

Fig 9.1 - The ABCD Schematic

VISUAL REPRESENTATION

YOU WILL BE FAMILIAR with the quote above. It is from December 1921, over a hundred years ago, yet it appears regularly through history. What would take many words to describe,[128] could be more easily summarised by a single picture.

This plays out regularly in real life. In a world with trillions of bytes of data being transferred daily, it's no surprise that we prefer to have important information neatly presented, and pictures and visualisations are often the best way to do so. From graphs and charts of statistical data points to diagrammatic instructions for flat-packed furniture – *simple is best.*

---

127 This famous quote was written in a journal promoting the use of pictures in advertising by Barnard, and is thought to originate from the Confucius quote 'Hearing something a hundred times isn't better than seeing it once'
128 Perhaps 60,000+ words across 8 chapters!

The ABCD framework is no different.

My job is to remove your chances of being overwhelmed and anxious by offering ideas to educate you and simplify your approach. An objective that won't be achieved if you had to regularly re-read or reference your copy of this book. Therefore, the lessons seen in the previous chapters are simplified into easy-to-follow techniques, then the blank worksheets in *Chapter 14*.

I can go one step further to simplify the approach – *visual representation*.

The idea of using visual representation in teaching was examined in the *International Journal of Management and Applied Research* by the University of Liverpool and Manchester Metropolitan University members.

By taking more basic data from tables or text and adjusting them into visual representations (or schematics), they found that 'Moving away from a table format towards a circular representation and using colour to highlight the inter-relationship between the two identified learning engagement patterns and learning needs makes, I feel, the framework more useful a standalone resource and guide during curriculum design and course evaluation activities.'[129]

They concluded that 'Relationships between concepts, and their contexts, can be more easily and quickly understood using diagrams rather than in textual form (Lowe, 2004). It is claimed people with normal perceptual abilities are predominantly visual (Few, 2015).'[130] In other words, if you want to get something into peoples' heads and for them to learn it, a diagram will do the job better than tables or text.

This is clear to see with brands and advertising. My family often plays a board game testing the brand knowledge of the participants, and we were shocked to see how many companies we (and our young children—before they could read) knew from just a tiny section of their brand logos.

Previously mentioned writers use the same approach to simplify complex ideas into memory - Stephen Covey has the 'The Seven Habits Paradigm,' Annie Grace uses 'Liminal Point Diagrams,' and Derren Brown displays Schopenhauer's ideas with 'The Diagonal.'

So, I felt it was a good idea to bring the ideas and lessons I have shown so far into my own *ABCD Schematic*. You will be familiar with it from the cover, and various segments appear in *Chapter 8* and on the worksheets within. I want to introduce and explain the diagram in full here to allow you to understand it and bring the image to mind when in need of inspiration in the future.[131]

129   Buckley, C. and Nerantzi, C. (2020) 'Effective Use of Visual Representation in Research and Teaching within Higher Education' – *International Journal of Management and Applied Research*, Vol.7, No.3.
130   Buckley, C. and Nerantzi, C. (2020) 'Effective Use of Visual Representation in Research and Teaching within Higher Education' – *International Journal of Management and Applied Research*, Vol.7, No.3.
131   Perhaps, like a sleeper cell assassin, upon glancing it you will be instantly reminded of all of the valuable content of this book and instantly happier!

THE ABCD SCHEMATIC

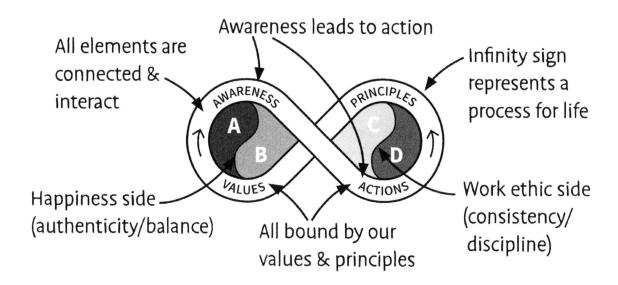

Fig 9.2 – The Components of The ABCD Schematic

PERSONAL STATEMENTS/MANTRA

Alongside the ABCD schematic is a visual representation of the lessons and techniques in this book, you may want something more personally linked to the core values/goals you have selected. Again, the purpose would be to condense all the work and thought behind your new approach and summarise it for quick reference. I have a straightforward way that may be of use.

Once you have worked through the ABCD framework, you will have identified authentic areas of your life and actions towards them. To remove the need to constantly re-read your worksheets or reiterate your intentions, you can create a simplified proxy for your hard work. I have said before that this book's real target is to reduce the stress and level of overwhelm in people's lives — not add more rules and tasks. It is not progress to reduce the stressful areas of focus, only to replace them with a textbook of complex information that must be memorised.

I showed earlier that a good approach is to spend more time *doing* things than you spend *planning* them. You are done with the planning, so you need to make the doing *easy*.

This starts with your internal dialogue as you balance your inner-critic and inner-compassionate voice:

'...meaning is attached to the names you call yourself. If you use abusive, harshly critical, or profane terminology to give utterance to your behaviours or traits, then you're heading towards emotional disturbance.

The notion that you may start to believe something if you tell yourself, it enough times, is partly true. Fortunately, you can choose what messages you give yourself and, therefore, choose how you think and feel about yourself.'[132]

Dialectic behaviour therapy (*talking* therapies) helps many people by allowing them to discuss what they are feeling. They can confide in someone compassionate that has their best interests at heart. However, no one's opinion of how you see yourself matters more than *yours*. It is critical that - how you speak to yourself, what you tell yourself, and how you refer to your actions and journey are in line with your core values. Ultimately, your speech (internal and external) is one of your behaviours, so it must match what you truly feel about yourself.

Alongside using the ABCD Schematic for the visual representation of your journey, I would recommend a short statement that sums up your core values or the guiding principles that come out of those values.

This could be a MANTRA. Originally used for spiritual reasons in India (and written in Sanskrit), a mantra can be drawn upon at a time of reflection and used to give the owner some strength in affirming their values. Positive affirmations are proven to increase self-esteem and reduce depression.

In your case, it might be less spiritual but no less effective.

'I am good enough.'

'My family is my priority.'

'Fitness enriches me.'

'I will be forged by my fires.'

If you can combine the themes of your ABCD framework process into a single sentence to summarise your intentions and guide you, it is incredibly helpful. No need to meditate or chant it in the mirror; use it when you need to, either by saying it to yourself or having it written somewhere. It may feel a little weird at first so try not to laugh at yourself too much!

I am not creative enough (and waffle way too much) to bring together a mantra for myself. If you think you might also struggle with something quite so short, then try a PERSONAL STATEMENT.

This statement, like the mantra, is to act as a reference for your hard work when you need to draw upon it. In this case though, you can allow yourself a few sentences written down

---

132 Wilson, R. and Branch, R. (2006) *Cognitive Behavioural Therapy for Dummies.*

in a meaningful place (in your journal, phone screensaver, on your desk, stuck to the fridge, tattooed on your arm.... you get the idea).

This statement or mantra will be highly personal; however, I will share the process I followed to think of my own:

- Write down some keywords that appear throughout your values and principles (goals and sub-goals).
- These will be themes and behaviours that you would like to see in yourself.
- Reread the words and pick 5-15 that feel like they hold the most meaning to you.
- Write a statement that summarises these words.
- Rewrite the statement until it feels relatable to you and suits your voice.
- Write it up and put it somewhere important.

I'll finish this chapter by sharing my own personal statement.

I have it stuck on a wall in my office to call back to on occasion; it encapsulates the words that kept arising when I created the ABCD framework and reviewed my own life. I thrive from consistency, need to take small steps in the present, have an idea of the person I want to be, and find looking back at my successes meaningful.

Apologies for the poor grammar – it's just how it came out - I hope it provides some inspiration:

'CONSISTENTLY show the INTENTION to take the SMALL NEXT STEPS towards making the GOOD BEHAVIOURS of the person you WANT TO BE, AUTOMATIC HABITS. Give the gift of SUCCESS and HAPPINESS to your future REMEMBERING SELF.'

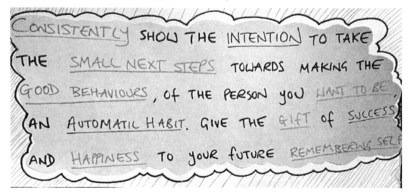

Fig 9.3 – My Personal Mantra

Pause for Thought – Please take time to make some notes:

10

PERSONAL CASE STUDY

'Knowledge without application is simply knowledge. Applying the knowledge to one's life is wisdom – and that is the ultimate virtue.'[133]
– Kasi Kaye Iliopoulos.

DEVELOPING *ABCD*

I AM QUALIFIED TO GIVE this advice and create a framework such as ABCD because I have successfully applied it to my own life. I may not be a scholar, have a million social media followers or be a celebrity. However, I have the experience of learning the contents of this book and using them first-hand. And I'm not a special case; I am an average person who has been through everyday problems and achieved fairly common goals. I'm not writing this book from the boardroom of my FTSE500 company to tell you how to be a success. I'm not riding the wave of 5 minutes of fame afforded to me because of reality TV to tempt you with the trappings of fame.

I am firmly in the target audience for this book!

As a reader, you will see similarities between your life and the personal situations I mention in this book. I can't overstate how much of a change the ideas I have covered have brought to my life. Reassessing my priorities and relinquishing some control allowed me to focus on making changes that I can honestly say have made me happy for the first time in over a *decade*.[134]

Early iterations of this book, such as the notes I made for myself in 2017, served as pre-cursors to what would eventually become *ABCD*. I was piecing together the importance of authenticity, then realising that being realistic and balanced made me feel more

---

133   Iliopoulos, K. K. (2012) *Living in Light, Love & Truth: Change Your Life Positively.*
134   Sure, I had happy periods and moments of joy in those years, but I felt like I wasn't in the zone very often.

comfortable in my skin. I would revisit and add to these ideas as I found consistency difficult or needed more discipline in what I was trying to do. Finally, the idea that these intertwined elements encapsulate so much of what I had learned made it clear that finding helpful techniques to maintain them would bring me happiness – and it did.

I have honed and developed the ABCD framework to incorporate a positive process across all areas of my life. Along the way, I had marital issues, addiction issues, overthinking, anxiety, redundancy, eating disorders, and the loss of loved ones. These events affect us all and form the landscape of human existence. Hopefully, my honesty and transparency will allow you to see similarities between my personal story and the challenges you face in your life.[135]

My life is unremarkable, and my small yet seismic successes make me more creditable than most because I have had to approach my values and goals from the same place as 99% of readers. For that reason, I have something that will help many people.

Therefore, giving a positive example of how I have used the ABCD process in practice is essential. Many of my own issues are far from resolved; we saw earlier that if you are waiting for the perfect time to start this process – it will never come – but success in some areas while still working out others is natural and will definitely happen in your journey. Don't wait for the right time to start – now is as good a time as any.

My most significant and recent example of success using the ABCD framework is here in your hands.

WRITING MY FIRST BOOK (YES, THIS ONE)

The significance of the ABCD elements became more apparent when I wrote them down. When I realised that I could be of service to many others, it felt important to at least attempt to create structure around my ideas.

However, my intention to write a book did not start there.

During a few months away from work in 2017/18, I tried to write some children's picture books. I had young children, so I read hundreds of them and thought I could do a good job. I'd regularly read for years and loved both non-fiction and fictional literature. So, I researched and planned the correct standards, language levels, and appropriate subjects for my audience and began to plan and write. This resulted in ten manuscripts that I assumed would take the global market by storm.

Publishers disagreed! However, the writing and planning process gave me such comfort that it was clear to me that I would write a book someday. It gave me purpose at a challenging

---

135 A brief sidenote on *Trauma* – this was my own journey to find solutions. Recovery is personal and the ability to function is somewhat hampered until the sufferer restores a healthy nervous system, which is dependent on the individual.

time in my life. Being unsure of a more suitable subject matter and not aware enough yet to formulate any ideas - the dream was put on hold.

Fast forward to 2021[136], and it occurred to me that if writing was authentically important in my life, I wanted to do more to honour it. I started the ABCD process and would like to share it with you below. Hopefully, you can see clearly how taking a rather large goal like 'Write a Book' is incredibly daunting. Following the ABCD process, you can reasonably prioritise and break down a more significant target into a less overwhelming journey.

You will remember the basic process of the ABCD Framework:

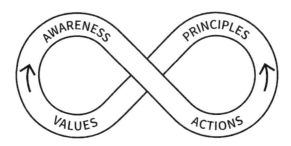

Fig 10.1

ABCD FRAMEWORK

CORE VALUE PRIORITISATION
Consider what is important to you

WHY? WHY? WHY?
Dig deeper into the real authentic reason and amend values/goals

TIMEBOXING
Understand the time you can sustainably give

VALUE DIALS
Balance your values/goals alongside other areas of your life

PERSONAL CONSISTENCY PYRAMID
Visualise what principles/sub-goals would move
you from the start to the finish

VALUES AND PRINCIPLES MAP
Decide the small next steps that require consistency
to form your principles/sub-goals

SPECIFIC AND CHALLENGING TIMELINES
Refine the values/goals to be the right level
of challenge to drive motivation

CASE STUDIES
Regularly note positive results and take confidence
that you have what it takes to succeed

Below are the ABCD worksheets that show the process I used to take some scruffy notes and a daunting goal and turn them into the book you are reading. I am incredibly grateful to be able to share them with you.[137]

---

137 I have enriched the process with some commentary as to why the stages were helpful – in your own worksheets/ notes, you can be far briefer and more personal.

CORE VALUE PRIORITISATION[138]

ABCD — **CORE VALUE PRIORITISATION**

Q1. Pick up to 10 areas of your life that are most important

1. Write a bestselling self-help book
2. Be a good father
3. Get promoted
4. Be in great physical shape
5. Travel more
6. Help my dad to sell house
7. Be well liked by everyone
8.
9.
10.

Q2. Can you control outcomes in these areas – YES/NO/PARTIAL?

1. YES / NO / **PARTIAL**
2. **YES** / NO / PARTIAL
3. YES / NO / **PARTIAL**
4. YES / NO / **PARTIAL**
5. YES / NO / **PARTIAL**
6. YES / NO / **PARTIAL**
7. YES / **NO** / PARTIAL
8. YES / NO / PARTIAL
9. YES / NO / PARTIAL
10. YES / NO / PARTIAL

Q3. If you have partial control what part can you control?

1. Writing a book
2. Upholding my values
3. Working hard
4. Making healthy choices
5. Choose destinations/save annual leave
6. Offer to help and be available
7. N/A
8.
9.
10.

Q4. In 2-3 words, how does improvement in these areas enrich your life?

1. Fulfil a life-long dream
2. Happy homelife / give children the best start
3. More money but less time
4. Look good on holiday
5. Experiences
6. Helping others
7. N/A
8.
9.
10.

Q5. Considering Q1 - Q4 – Honestly select up to 5 areas to focus on

1. Write a book
2. Be a good father
3. Work hard in my job
4.
5.

Q6. With possible Core Values/Goals in mind - Re-phrase the above as...

I am the type of person who...

1. Writes a book
2. Is a good father
3. Works hard in my job
4.
5.

Q7. Considering Q6 - Write your 'Core Values/Goals' in full

My core values/goals are...

1. To fulfil a life-long dream to write a self-help book	2. To uphold my value of being a good father	3. To do my best and work hard in my job	4.	5.

Fig 10.2 – Prioritisation!

138 Blank Worksheets for your own process can be found in Chapter 14 – *ABCD Worksheets*

HOW CORE VALUE PRIORITISATION HELPED

Refining my list of values and goals was a crucial starting point. I could clearly see that my control over many of them was only partial. Focusing on the success or sales of a future (unwritten) book was outside of my control. Instead, the purpose and enjoyment of the process that had benefitted me in 2017 became the priority.

Honestly reducing the list to areas that felt the most natural and picturing myself as holding those values further solidified their importance, leaving me with authentic core values and goals.

WHY? WHY? WHY?[139]

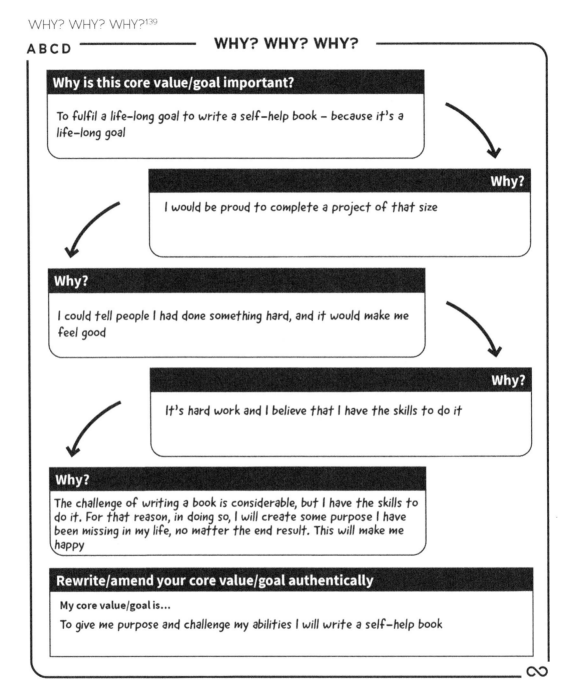

WHY? WHY? WHY?

A B C D

Why is this core value/goal important?

To fulfil a life-long goal to write a self-help book – because it's a life-long goal

Why?

I would be proud to complete a project of that size

Why?

I could tell people I had done something hard, and it would make me feel good

Why?

It's hard work and I believe that I have the skills to do it

Why?

The challenge of writing a book is considerable, but I have the skills to do it. For that reason, in doing so, I will create some purpose I have been missing in my life, no matter the end result. This will make me happy

Rewrite/amend your core value/goal authentically

My core value/goal is...

To give me purpose and challenge my abilities I will write a self–help book

Fig 10.3 – Questioning my motivations

---

139 Blank Worksheets for your own process can be found in Chapter 14 – *ABCD Worksheets*

HOW WHY? WHY? WHY? HELPED

By interrogating my reasoning, I found a more specific motivation for this goal. I discovered that I wanted to write a book because I had the knowledge to do so and combine all my reading/research in one place. Also, the fact that I wanted to do myself proud was compelling. It was clear that I lacked some self-esteem that overcoming this challenge would provide. The actual purpose of writing a book was far more personal than I had imagined.

I turned the shallow aim of writing a successful book into a more realistic and personal goal of writing an important book – primarily for my own sense of purpose, which is far more authentic than a future, uncontrollable sales figure.

TIMEBOXING[140]

Version 1 **A B C D** ———————————— **TIMEBOXING** ————

	Monday	Tuesday	Wednesday	Thursday	Friday	Saturday	Sunday	Questions to consider
AM	Wake Up @7am, Commute 8-9am, Work from 9am	Wake Up @7am, Commute 8-9am, Work from 9am	Wake Up @7am, Commute 8-9am, Work from 9am	Wake Up @7am, Commute 8-9am, Work from 9am	Wake Up @7am, Commute 8-9am, Work from 9am	Kids clubs	Relax	In pencil complete a typical week (everything) How many spare hours are there? How many hours are spent advancing your values/goals?
PM	Work till 5pm, Commute 5.30-6.30pm	Work till 5pm, Commute 5.30-6.30pm	Work till 5pm, Commute 5.30-6.30pm	Work till 5pm, Commute 5.30-6.30pm	Work till 5pm, Commute 5.30-6.30pm	Drinks with friends	Family dinner	Are you happy with this? Can any items that don't feed your values/goals be reduced?
NIGHT	Kids Clubs 7-8pm, Dinner 8-9pm, TV 9-11pm, Bed @11pm	Kids Clubs 7-8pm, Dinner 8-9pm, TV 9-11pm, Bed @11pm	Kids Clubs 7-8pm, Dinner 8-9pm, TV 9-11pm, Bed @11pm	Kids Clubs 7-8pm, Dinner 8-9pm, TV 9-11pm, Bed @11pm	Kids Clubs 7-8pm, Dinner 8-9pm, TV 9-11pm, Bed @11pm			Re-write (in pen) how you want the week to look How many hours can you realistically spare for your core values/goals?

∞

Fig 10.4a - Before

- **Step 1** – How many spare hours are there?
  Maybe a few hours Sunday AM.
- **Step 2** – How many hours are spent advancing your values/goals?
  Work and family time are covered but I am not writing at all.

---

140 Blank Worksheets for your own process can be found in Chapter 14 – *ABCD Worksheets*

- **Step 3** – Are you happy with this?
  No, I can't fit time in to write.
- **Step 4** – Can any items that don't feed your values/goals be reduced?
  - *I could go to bed at 10pm and wake up at 6am (Mon – Thu) – TV time is not benefitting me.*
  - *I could write during my commute.*
  - *If I drink less on Saturday night, I will feel fresher to write on a Sunday.*

Version 2 **A B C D** ———————————— **TIMEBOXING** ————————

	Monday	Tuesday	Wednesday	Thursday	Friday	Saturday	Sunday	Questions to consider
AM	Wake Up @ 6am, Work on Book 7–8am, Commute (Work on Book) 8–9am, Work from 9am	Wake Up @ 6am, Work on Book 7–8am, Commute (Work on Book) 8–9am, Work from 9am	Wake Up @ 6am, Work on Book 7–8am, Commute (Work on Book) 8–9am, Work from 9am	Wake Up @ 6am, Work on Book 7–8am, Commute (Work on Book) 8–9am, Work from 9am	Wake Up @ 6am, Work on Book 7–8am, Commute (Work on Book) 8–9am, Work from 9am	Kids clubs	Relax/Work on Book	In pencil complete a typical week (everything) / How many spare hours are there? / How many hours are spent advancing your values/goals?
PM	Work till 5pm, Commute 5.30–6.30pm	Work till 5pm, Commute 5.30–6.30pm	Work till 5pm, Commute 5.30–6.30pm	Work till 5pm, Commute 5.30–6.30pm	Work till 5pm, Commute 5.30–6.30pm	Drinks with friends (reduce alcohol)	Family dinner	Are you happy with this? / Can any items that don't feed your values/goals be reduced?
NIGHT	Kids Clubs 7–8pm, Dinner 8–9pm, TV 9–10pm, Bed @ 10pm	Kids Clubs 7–8pm, Dinner 8–9pm, TV 9–10pm, Bed @ 10pm	Kids Clubs 7–8pm, Dinner 8–9pm, TV 9–10pm, Bed @ 10pm	Kids Clubs 7–8pm, Dinner 8–9pm, TV 9–10pm, Bed @ 10pm	Kids Clubs 7–8pm, Dinner 8–9pm, TV 9–11pm, Bed @ 11pm			Re-write (in pen) how you want the week to look / How many hours can you realistically spare for your core values/goals?

∞

Fig 10.4b - After

- **Step 5** – How many hours can you realistically spare for your core values/goals?
  Up to 11 hours – this is actually quite a lot of time!

HOW TIMEBOXING HELPED

This stage is where I started to appreciate the size of the task and what resources I could spare. Visualising the week in this way was crucial to understanding where efforts toward my goal sat in relation to real life. Before this point, I viewed writing a book as an entirely separate enterprise and planned for much more effort than I could afford. Meaning I would 'fail' to hit the targets causing myself annoyance OR hit them and disrupt the balance of other areas in my life. Clearly, I couldn't be a full-time author from day one. This reality check allowed me to be flexible and lower my expectations. This drastically reduced the possibility of being overwhelmed.

Usefully, I saw a few hours a week wasted on activities that didn't help serve my purpose – scrolling on my phone on my commute, hungover Sundays, and watching TV late at night. These could be removed or reduced to create a realistic yet sufficient amount of time to commit to my goal.

It was easy to find this time when my week was laid out in front of me in this way and provided a dose of realism and excitement regarding the work I would need to do.

VALUE DAILS[141]

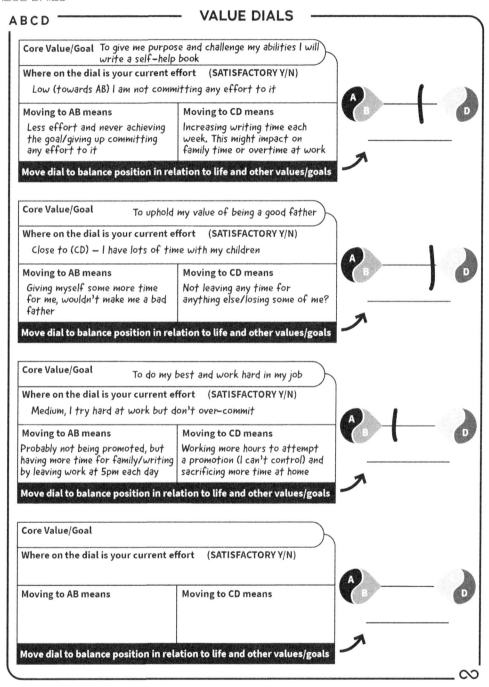

VALUE DIALS

ABCD

Core Value/Goal To give me purpose and challenge my abilities I will write a self-help book

Where on the dial is your current effort   (SATISFACTORY Y/N)

Low (towards AB) I am not committing any effort to it

Moving to AB means	Moving to CD means
Less effort and never achieving the goal/giving up committing any effort to it	Increasing writing time each week. This might impact on family time or overtime at work

Move dial to balance position in relation to life and other values/goals

Core Value/Goal   To uphold my value of being a good father

Where on the dial is your current effort   (SATISFACTORY Y/N)

Close to (CD) — I have lots of time with my children

Moving to AB means	Moving to CD means
Giving myself some more time for me, wouldn't make me a bad father	Not leaving any time for anything else/losing some of me?

Move dial to balance position in relation to life and other values/goals

Core Value/Goal   To do my best and work hard in my job

Where on the dial is your current effort   (SATISFACTORY Y/N)

Medium, I try hard at work but don't over-commit

Moving to AB means	Moving to CD means
Probably not being promoted, but having more time for family/writing by leaving work at 5pm each day	Working more hours to attempt a promotion (I can't control) and sacrificing more time at home

Move dial to balance position in relation to life and other values/goals

Core Value/Goal

Where on the dial is your current effort   (SATISFACTORY Y/N)

Moving to AB means	Moving to CD means

Move dial to balance position in relation to life and other values/goals

Fig 10.5 — Viewing my goals relating to each other

HOW VALUE DIALS HELPED

This was a priceless tool to visualise how I could balance areas of my life together. I often looked at the areas of my life in isolation, giving a myopic view. Each requiring its own focus and mental energy unrelated to others. In reality, my life has many interacting elements, and increased discipline in my goal to write a book would affect many others.

Here I saw that my initial fully committed approach to writing would impact the happy balance I had in others. Overcommitting to this project but damaging my relationship with my children for an extended period was not a decent trade. Therefore, I made concessions.

Please note that these levels can change as other areas of your life take centre stage.[142]

---

142 18 months on from this process I am currently locked in my office neglecting almost everything else to complete my final manuscript!

PERSONAL CONSISTENCY PYRAMID[143]

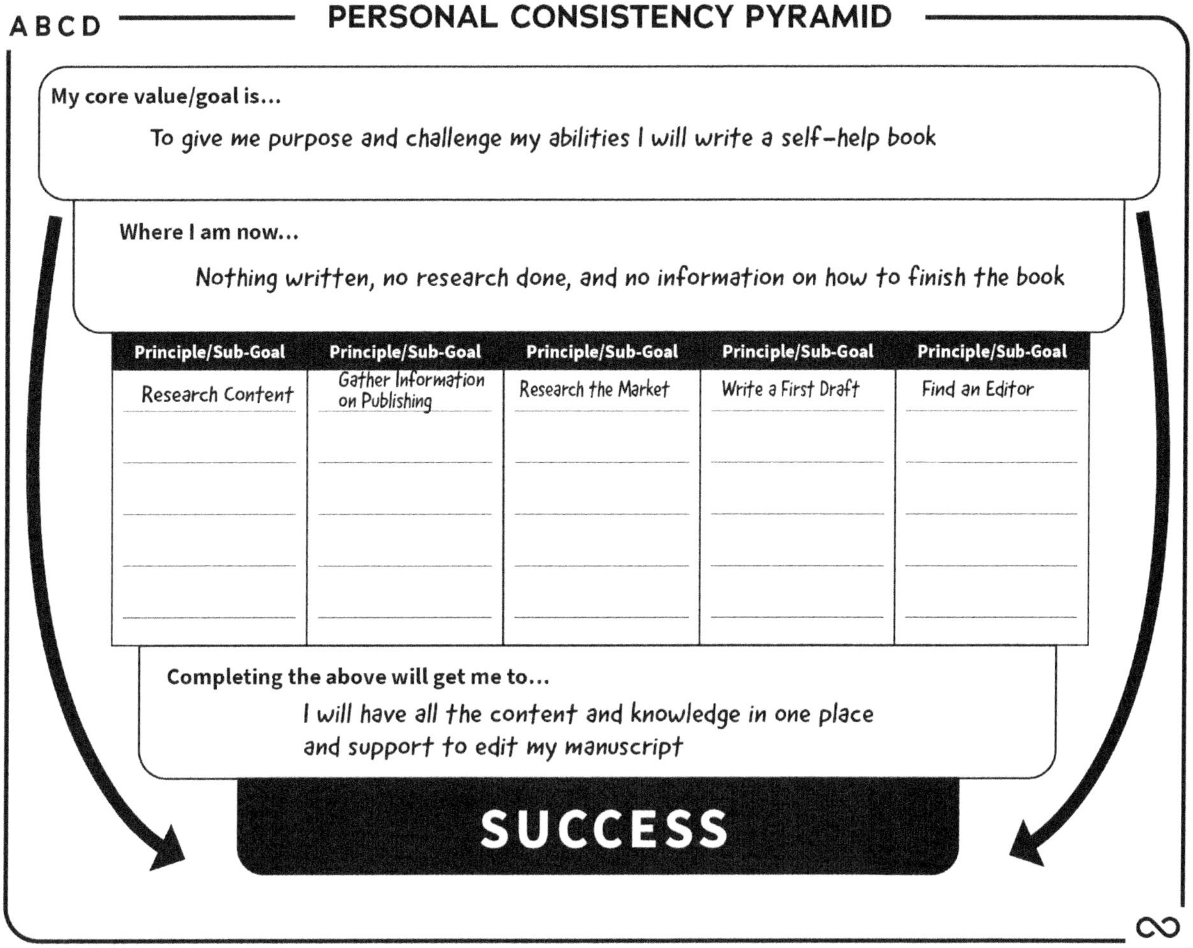

PERSONAL CONSISTENCY PYRAMID

ABCD

My core value/goal is...
To give me purpose and challenge my abilities I will write a self-help book

Where I am now...
Nothing written, no research done, and no information on how to finish the book

Principle/Sub-Goal	Principle/Sub-Goal	Principle/Sub-Goal	Principle/Sub-Goal	Principle/Sub-Goal
Research Content	Gather Information on Publishing	Research the Market	Write a First Draft	Find an Editor

Completing the above will get me to...
I will have all the content and knowledge in one place
and support to edit my manuscript

SUCCESS

Fig 10.6 – Breaking my goal into sub-goals

HOW PERSONAL CONSISTENCY PYRAMID HELPED

Viewing the smaller sub-goals through the lens of how they would transport me from a *non-author* to an *author* inspired me to continue along this path.

Purely looking at my starting position in relation to the final objective was scary. Placing far smaller, attainable sub-goals along the path as milestones, I could imagine consistently ticking off small parts of the larger target. This gave me the confidence to consistently work on the smaller jobs at hand, knowing the overall goal would follow.

VALUES AND PRINCIPLES MAPS[144]

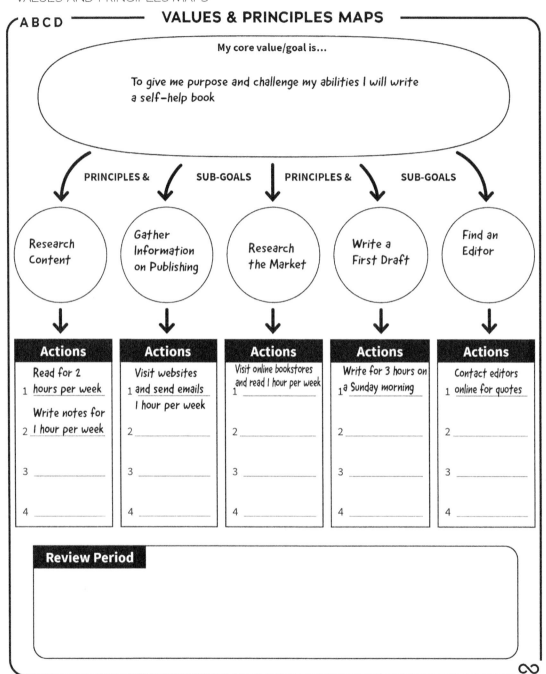

Fig 10.7- Finding the small next steps to success

HOW VALUES AND PRINCIPLES MAPS HELPED

I can let you into a secret here. This is the first part of the ABCD framework that I created. I wanted to break larger tasks into smaller areas and consistent actions. Initially, I used it to get some consistency in my diet (trust me, it took a few iterations to get it right!), but once it was refined, I used it for many areas of my life, and even my children made their own versions.

It was only later that I realised more structure was required to assess the validity of my goals and how they fit into my life. Luckily, I had already been partially doing this work, albeit haphazardly. Adding the process and clarity around the other ABCD techniques that led to here was the final part of the puzzle.

When writing this book, the smaller next steps were invaluable. Completing this book was a complex process and had many setbacks. So, it was essential to have easy small actions that I could regularly complete and some motivation to draw on periodically and keep me going, irrespective of what the result might look like in the end.

As I focused solely on writing for a few hours each week, the possibility that I might create a first draft increased automatically – with little attention paid to the idea. This took much of the pressure and anxiety I'd felt on other (far smaller) projects away.

SPECIFIC AND CHALLENGING TIMELINES[145]

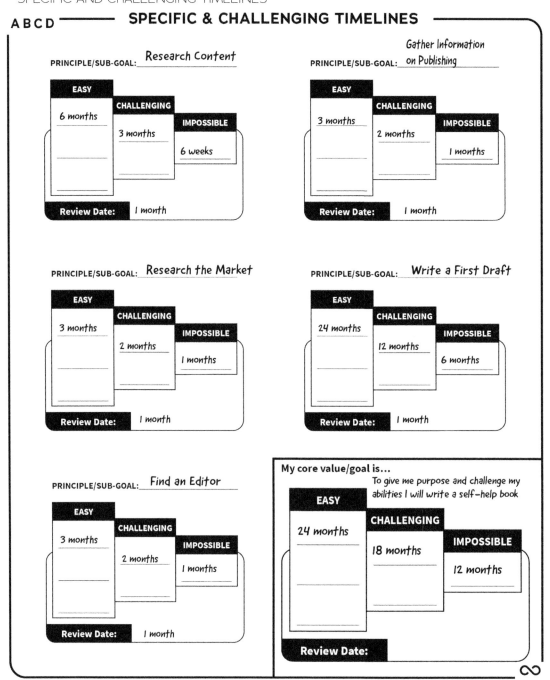

Fig 10.8 – Setting challenging timelines to feel the achievements

---

HOW SPECIFIC AND CHALLENGING TIMELINES HELPED

Ultimately, I am a lazy person. Almost everything I have ever done; I have left until deadline day. Using this technique meant I had to honestly admit to what timelines would be possible yet challenging. It pushed me to see them written down – I would need discipline if I ever wanted to complete a book whilst maintaining my enjoyable journey. Because these deadlines were now promised to me (by me), I would feel disappointed if I didn't meet them.

It's important to note that you will most likely not hit all your targets. My first draft target was July 2022, this moved to September 2022, and I finished my first draft in October 2022.

You are learning and adapting. Targets can move because life isn't stacked in your favour or known in advance. But having realistically challenging timelines will motivate you to be more disciplined.

CASE STUDIES[146]

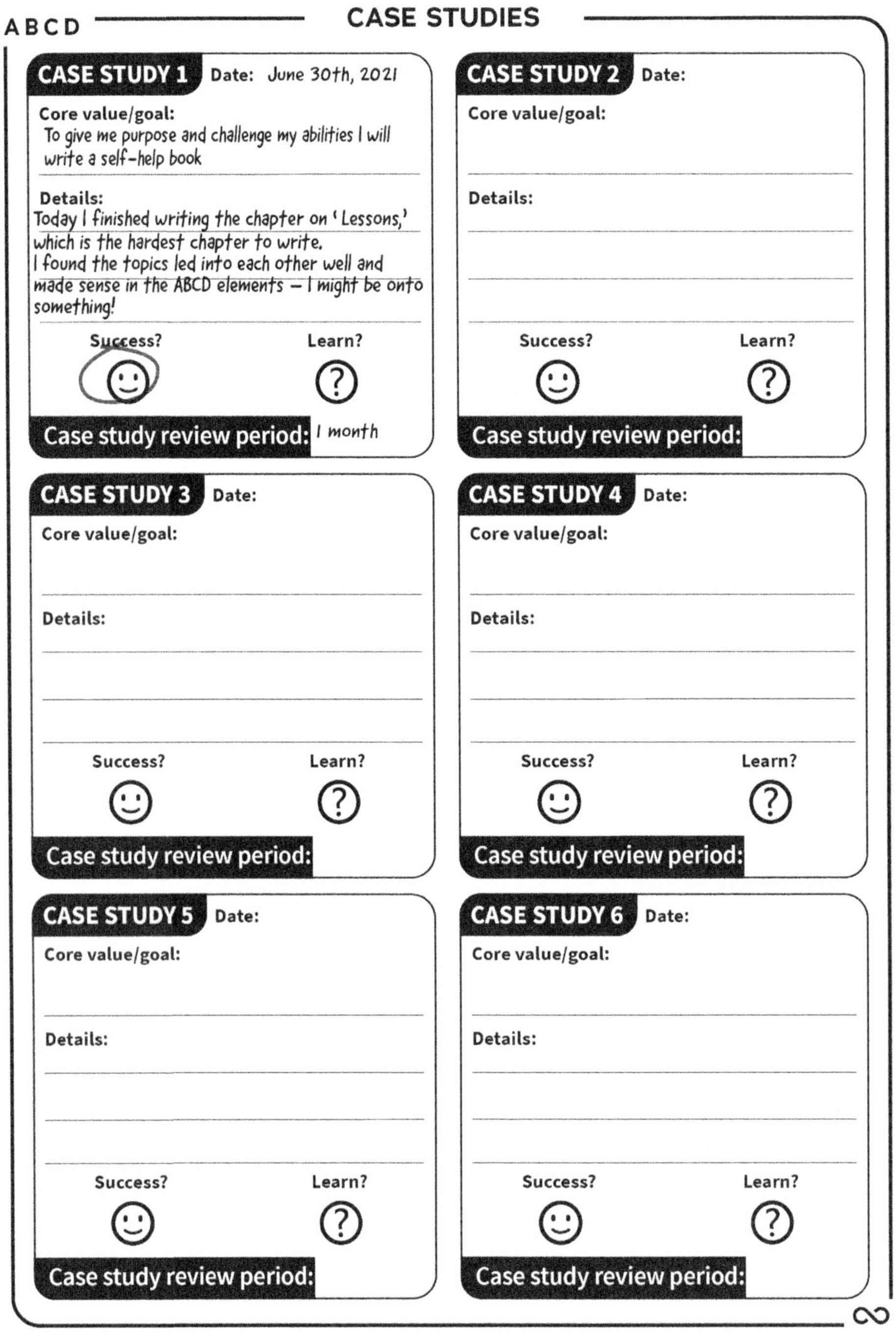
ABCD — CASE STUDIES

CASE STUDY 1 Date: June 30th, 2021
Core value/goal: To give me purpose and challenge my abilities I will write a self-help book
Details: Today I finished writing the chapter on 'Lessons,' which is the hardest chapter to write. I found the topics led into each other well and made sense in the ABCD elements – I might be onto something!
Success? Learn?
Case study review period: 1 month

CASE STUDY 2 Date:
Core value/goal:
Details:
Success? Learn?
Case study review period:

CASE STUDY 3 Date:
Core value/goal:
Details:
Success? Learn?
Case study review period:

CASE STUDY 4 Date:
Core value/goal:
Details:
Success? Learn?
Case study review period:

CASE STUDY 5 Date:
Core value/goal:
Details:
Success? Learn?
Case study review period:

CASE STUDY 6 Date:
Core value/goal:
Details:
Success? Learn?
Case study review period:

Fig 10.9 – How am I doing?

146 Blank Worksheets for your own process can be found in Chapter 14 – *ABCD Worksheets*

HOW CASE STUDIES HELPED

Finally, I took regular time to review and feel proud of my achievements—small milestones, word count targets, editing goals, etc. Life can be negative sometimes; I would often discount positives in favour of pessimism, making me feel inadequate.

Journaling case studies regularly forced me to find positives and review them. It wasn't ever very hard to find them once I looked. Confidence in my abilities and appreciation for my efforts grew exponentially each time, driving me to complete the work required to finish.

SUMMARY

Hopefully, with the help of a real-life example, I have demonstrated that with the ABCD framework, you can break a considerably large goal into more manageable tasks that can act as the small next steps toward success.

In my example, they allowed me to take the first steps toward something I could have only dreamed of.

I had always liked writing (and talking - to my wife's dismay!), but I would never dream that I could start from scratch and finish a 200-page book. Furthermore, the idea that a stranger like you, the reader, would be holding it in their hands never even entered my mind. Yet I reached this point not because I am different from anyone else. I'm not a particularly gifted writer, I don't have any experience writing a manuscript, and I can't afford to quit my job to focus on writing as a career.

I reached this point because I removed the overwhelming factors that paralysed me. I wrote for a couple of hours a week, and in being successful in this small task, I soon turned a notepad of waffle into my first book: *ABCD*.

I know the ABCD framework works because it worked for me, and the evidence is right in front of you.

You can do the same with just a little intention and work. It will change your life as it has changed mine.

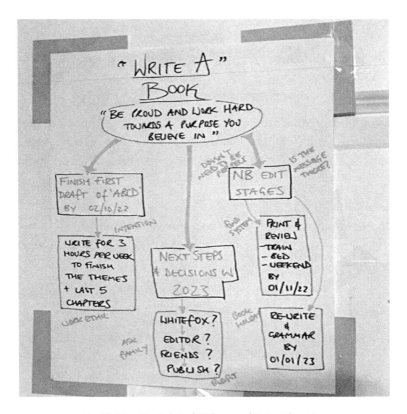

Fig 10.10 – My Original Values and Principles Map

Fig 10.11 – Researching *ABCD*

11

REFRAMING FAILURE

'I judge you unfortunate because you have never lived through misfortune. You have passed through life without an opponent – no one can ever know what you are capable of, not even you.'[147]
– Seneca.

FAILURE

Sorry to burst your bubble! It is so important that if I am going to champion the approach I have created, it is vital that you also understand that there will be difficulties along the way.

Seneca is making a point we saw in our earlier discussions about discipline and imposter syndrome. He states that we can't know what we are capable of because we have never been tested. Failure is one such test, and even when we take the considered approach that *ABCD* provides, struggles and failure are inevitable. To think that we would never come unstuck when we have seen that much of the world around us is uncontrollable would be foolish and doesn't sit with our balanced expectations of what we can achieve.

In this chapter, I will cover some topics related to failure and show why it's not as bad as you think – it provides you with the valuable opponent needed to refine your journey toward success.

REFRAMING

Do you know the person in your life who has never failed at anything? The person with a *perfect* life, *totally* in control of their destiny with no emotional difficulties, and *excellent* relationships with everyone they know? – You know the one?

---

147 Seneca. (c AD64) *On Providence.*

Can't picture anyone?

No, neither can I!

Contrary to what much of social media would have you believe, there has never been a single person who can be identified using the above questions. The first step you must take when considering this topic is to address unrealistic views on life, reframing how you see failure.

The word *failure* conjures images synonymous with losing, underachieving, embarrassment, and sometimes destitution and depression. Whether it is the team that loses the final of a competition, the grade A student who never completed their degree, or the myriad of 'fail' videos on the internet for our amusement, failure is seen as an unfavourable place to be.

Suppose it wasn't.

What if the very thing that caused you to fail, be it your inabilities or an external factor, actually redirected you onto a more fulfilling path than you could ever imagine?

Modern philosopher Ryan Holiday believes challenges present themselves for a reason and that many of the great success stories in history contain a degree of failure. In his book *The Obstacle is the Way*, he shares Marcus Aurelius' famous quote:

'The impediment to action advances action. What stands in the way becomes the way.'[148]

Then continues quite brilliantly with:

'We might not be emperors, but the world is still constantly testing us. It asks: Are you worthy? Can you get past the things that inevitably fall in your way? Will you stand up and show us what you are made of?

Plenty of people have answered this question in the affirmative. And a rarer breed still has shown that they not only have what it takes, but they thrive and rally at every such challenge. That the challenge makes them better than if they'd never faced the adversity at all.'[149]

The key word for me in this writing is '*inevitably.*' If you have made it this far in this book, you will hopefully have considered what you can control and cannot and how this factors into your judgements. You must view failure as inevitable so that it becomes more helpful and less of a surprise factor that paralyses you.

---

148 Holiday, R. (2014) *The Obstacle is the Way.*
149 Holiday, R. (2014) *The Obstacle is the Way.*

You can reframe failure in two ways:

1) FAILURE IS INEVITABLE IN YOUR LIFE

It is not embarrassing or unexpected. All you can do is your part in any area of your life, and sometimes that won't be enough because you can't control the world around you; you are a fallible (yet beautiful) human being.

2) FAILURE IS GOOD FOR YOU

Failure provides a challenge that allows you to grow and improve. Often, you learn about yourself and can make the right decisions to move forward. Either way, events in the past cannot be changed.

WHY IT IS GOOD TO FAIL

This second reframing will need further discussion for you to be convinced. Let's have a closer look at why failure is positive:

LESSONS

You already regularly learn from your mistakes. Having setbacks might sometimes feel like the end of the world, but so far in your life, you would have had many moments where things didn't go to plan - yet here you are - alive and well. In these moments, you discover the most about who you are.

GROWTH AND REDIRECTION

Stephen Covey says, 'P problems are PC opportunities.'[150] He means that when you have a problem with your production (your results/successes/accomplishments), it is always an opportunity to improve your production capacity (processes/strategy/relationships/self-care).

Any process you follow will certainly need to be amended as you go along. You can't perfect everything, and expecting to is naïve. Finding changes you can make to develop and become more effective is the benefit of having setbacks. With hindsight, you can see what could go wrong in the future and conduct what psychologist Gary Klein calls a *premortem*. You can imagine what might cause you to fail and add this to the balanced approach you decide to take.

---

150 Covey, S. R. (1989) *The 7 Habits of Highly Effective People.*

REALITY CHECKS

I once heard a lyric from a rapper named Ray Vaughan saying, 'Reality checks are how I pay for my mistakes.'[151] This clever play on words stuck with me, and I think he raises an important idea about failure. The pay-off for making mistakes/failing can often be that you better understand the reality of your situation.

You may realise that you are not capable. You may change your mind about what is important to you. You might discover that your expectations need to be lowered. You might even find you didn't have the time you thought you had to commit. These are valid reasons to rethink your approach, from amending your targets or actions to moving your 'ladder' to a different wall.

It won't feel great at the time, but your remembering self may reflect fondly on the resulting self-improvement.

FLOW

Failures help you to increase flow opportunities in two ways. Firstly, by their very nature, failures show you the point where a challenge overtakes your ability to meet it successfully. This gives you an idea of where your flow channel is, allowing you to increase your skills or reduce the challenge of a chosen task—leading you back to where flow can be found.

Secondly, suppose you fail at a task because the process was tiresome – i.e. you didn't enjoy the journey enough to sustain it. In that case, you can adjust our approach to redress the balance with something more exciting and challenging.

CASE STUDIES

The situation is not as bad as you think. After all, many people surmount considerable challenges to be very successful. More likely than a complete failure and end-of-the-world scenario is that there will be a chance to take some positives from the situation.

For instance, failure to change a habit you have had for many years shows you that you are stronger than you think. In his best-selling *Easy Way* books, addiction expert Allen Carr argues, 'There is a connection between all addictions, but the connection is not that they're signs of a lack of willpower. On the contrary, they're more likely evidence of a strong will.... It takes a strong-willed person to persist in doing something that goes against all their instincts.'[152]

These failures can give you the examples you need to encourage change. There will also be evidence in the process where things went well. For instance, you may not achieve a desired goal, but the process has improved your life.

---

151 'Ray Vaughan Freestyle' – *LA Leakers YouTube Channel* (*www.youtube.com*)
152 Carr, A. et al. (2015) *Stop Drinking Now.*

CHALLENGES ARE GOOD FOR YOU

Your mind and body respond positively to challenges:

- High frustration tolerance improves resilience in your life.
- Dopamine responses to challenges increase your baseline happiness levels.
- Testing your capabilities (overcoming imposter syndrome).
- Flow is built from meeting challenges with your best efforts.
- What doesn't kill you makes you stronger.

SOMETIMES THINGS NEED TWEAKING

Very few 'failures' require you to stop in your tracks. A slight adjustment will put you back on course:

- Reread the ABCD framework and review if you can change how you have approached the process. It's natural to adjust as you go.
- Ensure that your core values/goals are authentic. If they are, you will find a way to succeed at them and/or improve your life.
- Amend your specific and challenging timeframes to allow you the correct time.
- Review your timeboxing. You might not have the time you thought you did.
- Add motivation-based actions to your value and principle map—a weekly check-in with a friend or more regular logging.
- Leave things as they are! If you feel happier even without the desired target being reached, congratulations!

GET BACK TO IT

'Don't be afraid to fail. Be afraid to not try.'
– Michael Jordan.

Saying 'YOU CAN DO THIS' at this point is unnecessary. I firmly believe that you will have all the motivation you need when you follow the ABCD framework to define your process. Affirmations from me - a complete stranger - are not required.

The reality of the situation is that the most personal and lonely times you will experience are when you fail.

Therefore, my advice is to be honest with yourself and apply the ABCD elements to your chosen values and goals. The framework aims to reduce the chances of failing by increasing the ability to be consistent and disciplined. Another of its purposes is to be rational and realistic about why you might have failed so that you can learn.

When you have authentic core values and goals, it feels like you *have to* pursue them as they give you purpose. It will be easier to be disciplined — without this journey, you will feel hollow inside.

Matthew McConaughey tells a story when his mum described mistakes as 'Dogshit on the track.' He enriches that idea by suggesting that instead of running around the track and stepping into the mess again, you adjust your course slightly, having learned from the mistake. It's all part of the process. So...

Go easy on yourself.

'But what is philosophy? Doesn't it simply mean preparing ourselves for what may come? Don't you understand that really amounts to saying that if I would so prepare myself to endure, then let anything happen that will? Otherwise, it would be like the boxer exiting the ring because he took some punches. Actually, you can leave the boxing ring without consequence, but what advantage would come from abandoning the pursuit of wisdom? So, what should each of us say to every trial we face? That is what I've trained for, for this is my discipline!'
– Epictetus (Discourses, 3.10.6-7).[153]

You can't control what has already happened, but you can control how you react.

This is something I have learned through trial and error!

MY PERSONAL FAILURES

'The meal isn't over when I'm full. The meal is over when I hate myself.'
– Louis CK.

To ensure you don't feel like failure is ingrained in you or you are particularly unlucky, below, I'll give a few examples of my failures. Hopefully, what I have learned from them can help you put your challenges into perspective and see that you are not alone.

In some cases, I learned that something I was/wasn't doing needed changing, so I grew from these obstacles and adjusted:

---

153 Holiday, R. and Hanselman, S. (2016) *The Daily Stoic.*

CAREER

When I failed at a long-standing (and odd) target to *earn double my age* as a salary, I realised that I had no idea why I had set that target in the first place. I had blindly focused on financial gain whilst neglecting how I felt about myself and my career, working long hours, and living a life I hated.

This failure was a reality check that led to me leaving my job and retraining, which led to me finding a new sport, social group, career, work-life balance, mindset, and set of values. Only through NOT achieving what I thought I wanted could I move my ladder from the wall it was up against and find some authenticity in my own story.

HEALTH

I have been desperately trying to lose weight and be in good shape for many years. This generally involved some pretty high expectations of results alongside some harsh restrictive eating (some might say to eating disorder levels[154]).

I have set myself weight loss targets most months for the past 20 years, failing at almost every one. Most of these failures resulted from binge eating due to over-restriction. This amounts to *over two hundred* failures of the same unrealistic goal!

However, when I started to construct the ABCD framework, it became clear that my goal was not only inauthentic, but the approach needed to be more sustainable. So rather than shaming myself for eating chocolate or liking cake, I accepted who I am and made more authentic choices and balanced expectations to allow more flexibility around food.

It was frightening at first, and even with this realisation, it still took me several months of trial and error to find the right balance. I'm now at a healthy weight and have a far better relationship with food, even when eating more. This highlights the difference between repeatedly (and blindly) restarting the same goals and taking the ABCD approach to refine plans through failure.

In some cases, I needed to change my perspective a little because though I had not hit my target, I had become happier regardless:

WRITING

When I first started writing, my goal was to get published. I wrote ten children's picture books and submitted them to agents and publishers. Every submission was rejected, making me feel like a failure.

Luckily, I realised I was upset at something I couldn't control. I had done my best, and the success of the books was never as important as the process.

---

154 This is not a flippant comment I have sought therapy and programs for an eating disorder previously.

When I looked at my achievement and the feelings around it, I realised that the writing process and the required structure had made me happier than I had been for some time. I had improved my life irrespective of whether I was a published author.

MINDFULNESS

I recently set myself a target to meditate every day for a month.

After my 6th failed attempt, I realised that this 'streak' of sessions added more anxiety and pressure than the practice was helping.

I realised that I benefitted from being someone who *sometimes meditated* - no pressure and perfectly flexible. Now I meditate when I can, and I feel much better for it.

Finally, in *many* cases, I still don't know what the hell I'm doing and struggle to get all the elements of *ABCD* correct. This will happen to you too. In my case, I decided these were clearly not my core values/goals, and I let them go:

LEARNING A LANGUAGE

I've tried several times, and regardless of how I frame it and how slow I go, it's a nice idea but not a priority.

HAVING A SIX-PACK

'Visible Abs' was a goal of mine for almost two decades! It was causing me pain because I authentically didn't want to be the sort of person who trained hard enough (or ate little enough) to have them.

RUNNING A MARATHON

Every time I see the photos at the finish line, I think, 'That could be me!' - no, it couldn't - I don't like running, certainly not ten times a week.

STARTING MY OWN BUSINESS

I have had the plans ready for several business ideas in the past yet never followed through or started. You might see that as failure, though the truth is that only some are suited to entrepreneurship. So instead of comparing myself to others, I was true to myself; I realised that I have many qualities more aligned with my current profession. The added focus this brought to my career has led to several successes I wasn't expecting.

CALLING MY PARENTS WHEN I SAY I WILL

OK – so this *is* probably something I should be doing, but I'm more of a text guy!

The list could go on forever.

You can't do everything at once, and the objectives that you regularly fail at might not be for you. By applying the ABCD framework, you can prioritise and let go of the rest. You might even improve your progress in some of the more obscure areas of your life by being less overwhelmed.

Realising failure is neither uncommon nor harmful will reduce anxiety around your values and goals and allow you to be content no matter how you progress.

12

PAY IT FORWARD

'No one has ever become poor by giving.'
– Anne Frank.

HELPING OTHERS

IN THIS CHAPTER, I WILL briefly explore the idea of helping others (and seeking help). By introducing the idea of spreading the love, I'm not attempting to overload you with extra responsibility. I would however like to offer you the chance to share what you have learned. This could be as simple as setting a good example or introducing some ideas to those close to you. Helping others and the sense of connectedness that comes with it is very rewarding, so the benefit is two-fold.

Before you do reach out, be mindful of our discussions on control. You may WANT to improve the lives of others, but only they can make the changes for themselves. If the lessons resonate with them and they adopt some, then great, but if they don't, so be it. Your journey won't be affected either way.

It doesn't mean that we shouldn't regularly share experiences and wisdom that have helped us with others – if they want to listen.

ARE YOU BEING SELFISH?

You may feel like the message of this book is primarily selfish. You're focusing on yourself throughout, from the Stoic principles early in the book to your personal experiences with failure later. Yet, I believe by doing so you are being the *opposite* of selfishness, as I will explain here.

Have you ever seen someone exhausted and burnt out in many aspects of their life? Perhaps a parent of yours, a friend, or even yourself?

When people are overwhelmed or anxious, they are not useful to anyone.[155] When we struggle, we become consumed by overthinking and lack presence, and even when we take a break, we are exhausted. Furthermore, we may become agitated or snappy around those we love.

The negative effects of being overworked and stressed are abundant and you will be aware of many examples in your life and the media. It's the movie portrayal of the high-flying dad who rushes to the daughter's dance recital only to spend the whole time on his phone. It's the distracted partner thinking about if they are overeating at a restaurant instead of enjoying a date. The boss who can't educate her team because she is frantically spinning plates all day from one meeting to the next.

There's a reason that on aeroplanes, they instruct the adults to put their air masks on before they do so for their children. Because stressed and out of breath, people cannot focus well enough to ensure their child is safe.

In other words:

'Self-care is not selfish. You cannot serve from an empty vessel.'
– Eleanor Brownn.

If you ensure that you are doing well, you will have the mental bandwidth to help others. You're not so focused on a hundred goals with no clear plan. You have your strategy and priorities, and you know yourself well, providing a sense of self-confidence and capacity to help others if you choose to. Even just in setting the good example of someone who *has their shit together* will positively impact those around you. Actions speak louder than words – you'll be surprised how true that is in your own life.

Your own improved well-being has a *knock-on effect.*

People might see how well you are doing and approach you. Others might be scared to change their lives until they see the effect of your actions. For example, those who stop drinking alcohol often say that their friends will later ask them how they did it, and some will make the same change once they see someone brave enough to do it first.

Plus, those around you will greatly prefer a more level-headed and together version of you.

My wife and I saw it clearly at home. We had always had a fiery relationship. I am opinionated and talkative, and she is a lawyer used to arguing her point. This often led to

---

155 I know this from first-hand experience. It's not great surprise that the rockiest periods of my marriage have come when one or both of us is distracted, stressed or overwhelmed.

heated discussions (kind modern slang for *arguments*) about several things in our house/ life. When we had children, we wondered why they would sometimes shout for no reason, answer back, and argue. Unfortunately, they were watching us and learning these traits directly (remember Berne's PAC model).

So, we started having weekly meetings as a couple and took conversations out of the room, so the children were no longer exposed to them (plus, we improved our relationship through some other hard work).

I'd love to tell you they now don't argue and shout; they are children, after all! However, the frequency has fallen dramatically, and their calmness is noticeable. Plus, now we have some credibility when we ask them to calm down because we are more relaxed ourselves. The icing on the cake was when they also told us that we 'looked happier'...it brought tears to our eyes.

These things come full circle - helping others is excellent for us too. The benefits of contribution are reflected in much of the literature I cave cited. It was well known that the Stoics of Ancient Greece were huge contributors to their communities, teaching others and often taking up senior roles in government.

Tony Robbins says, 'The secret to living is giving, and those who experience contribution as one of their top 6 human needs know this better than anyone.'[156]

So, helping yourself before you can help others might be self-serving, but it is a vital exercise that benefits them by improving your capacity to guide and support. Ultimately, being in a better place yourself not only serves to improve your experience of life to a greater degree, but also the lives of those closest to you.

Just remember to help others for a *good* reason. If you are doing it for the plaudits, thanks, reward or to change people to how you feel they 'should' be, then you miss the whole point. People may require your help, but it is their choice and should be approached with love and generosity. It is called *self*-help for a reason.

'Be tolerant with others and strict with yourself.'
– Marcus Aurelius.

YOU DON'T HAVE TO DO THIS ALONE

Before I give a few basic ideas of how the ABCD framework can be used with others, it is worth mentioning that the need for support is not one-directional.

Though you may love for it to be the case, you will not be completely rid of all anxiety, living a life of spiritual enlightenment with no problems forever because you read this (or any) book. Life is hard sometimes; as discussed in the previous chapter, there will be inevitable obstacles. Just because within the ABCD framework, you seek to learn a more positive perspective in your life doesn't mean you must have life all figured out.

There is nothing weak about asking for support.

I strongly advocate that you use your new awareness and vulnerability from the introspective techniques in this book to reach out if you need help. The path you take will be a personal one, but the below options can prove to be beneficial in supplementing your journey:

SPEAKING TO FRIENDS AND FAMILY

People rarely talk about their feelings and struggles with others. A problem shared is a problem halved; you will be surprised how many people are glad to help.

THERAPY

I couldn't recommend therapy enough. You speak to someone professionally trained to help you understand what you want from life. I have had treatment for years, and once I found the right therapist for me, I have seen many positives in my experience.[157] It can be lifechanging, especially if you can go in with some of the lessons within *ABCD* as a base.

SEEING A DOCTOR

If you feel you might be suffering unnecessarily with something more serious, seek medical attention. Doctors are glad to hear what you are experiencing and provide guidance, and anything that you discuss is confidential.

CREATING ACCOUNTABILITY

One of the hardest things to do, even when simplified by *ABCD*, is to stay motivated. I recently created a small chat group between some like-minded people, and its purpose is to allow us to hold each other to account. We discuss our weekly/monthly goals and what we do to achieve them. The group then expects regular updates. There's nothing more motivating than needing to give evidence of progress to others, and this has been very useful for me.[158]

---

157 Not limited to taking some stressful conversations away within my relationship leaving it lighter and more fun.
158 The power of many collective programs from running clubs to group study to 12-step fellowships lies within the accountability to others.

There are many possible support avenues to explore depending on what you are going through; these are just those I found helpful. You will always be able to find a shoulder to lean on, even if it feels like you can't, so please make sure you don't keep everything all locked inside. It won't help you and certainly won't help others.

HOW CAN YOU HELP?

Here are some ideas I have tried (with varying success) to help those around me. You will know deep down which ones you could try and have many more you could think of besides. I hope these can give some inspiration for you to start benefitting your loved ones and improving the lives of not only you but your family/friends/community:

INTRODUCE ABCD TO OTHERS

This is the most obvious place to start. I'm sharing these ideas with you, and in turn, if you feel others might want to see them, then you can give them a copy of this book and see what they think.

INVOLVE OTHERS IN YOUR ABCD FRAMEWORK

If you are close enough to those concerned, including them in your process might be beneficial. This can take the form of having core values/goals involving other people's well-being. This way, you can see what is important to each other and have more awareness of those around you. Better still, if you have group goals to work towards, you can support, encourage, and hold the others in your group accountable for better chances at consistency, especially with something stressful at home like moving house, saving for a holiday etc.

CHECK-IN/MEETINGS

Family meetings are a great way to establish consistency and accountability into your life. Having some routine to discuss what is happening in everyone's lives can provide vital communication to ensure everyone is heard. Equally, my wife and I regularly do a *check in*, where we speak for three to five minutes about our day and how we feel. The other person offers no advice. They listen and understand. We found that this means we are more aware of each other's feelings and less likely to upset each other by being unaware and selfish.

LEAD BY EXAMPLE

People will likely respond best to seeing you happier and living a good life. Sometimes this is all that's needed to inspire others to make changes. So, remember, whenever you are challenged along your journey, you are doing this for yourself—but others are watching.

CHARITY

You might not have anyone close to you who (openly) needs help, yet you want to spread the word or get the buzz from contribution. Thousands of great causes and events run throughout the year for you to support, from a charity run to working with underprivileged children. It feels brilliant to give a minuscule amount back and *pay it forward*.

ADOPT A WIN/WIN MINDSET

Today's media promotes the idea that someone else must lose for you to win. The extreme ends of the political spectrum and their media make fortunes by setting people against each other. But in reality, when you win, we all win, and there is enough goodwill and happiness for us all. Particularly at home, have a mentality that it is 'one team/one dream.' Promote and encourage each other and spread positivity to support your friends and colleagues. The world can be harsh enough; don't let avoidable tension with others harm your happiness.

SHARING IDEAS WITH CHILDREN

As we saw with transactional analysis, children learn many automatic responses and the basis for their stories within the early years of their life. I only noticed the poor responses and behaviours I needed to reverse in my 30s. You don't want that same for your children, so try to work some of the lessons from *ABCD* into their lives so that some of the more reasoned responses discussed can become second nature as they grow into adults. Imagine how nice it would have been to know a bit more about yourself and have a sense of value as you were growing up!

In my case, it worked well to encourage my family to draw up their own values and principles maps and to have some collectively (see fig 12.1 and fig 12.2), we began meditating together to relax, and we drew up a family 'Fish Tank' based on the idea of a bank balance within relationships (seen earlier).

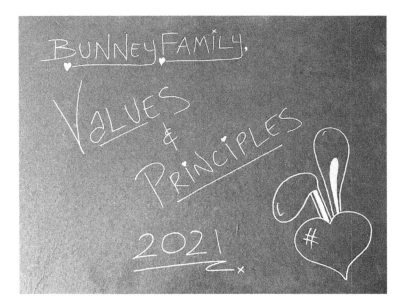

Fig 12.1 – Bunney Family Values and Principles

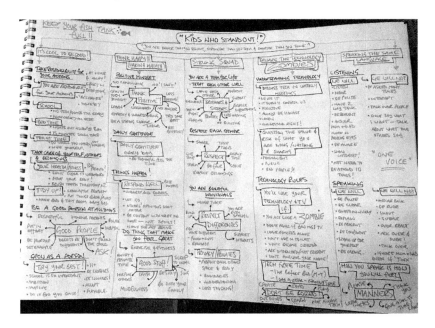

Fig 12.2 – Children's Values and Principles Map

REMEMBER-SOME PEOPLE MIGHT NOT WANT HELP

Finally, as I mentioned earlier, some people won't be receptive to your advice. This will be disappointing, but it is out of your control. Accept them for who they are and move on.

THANK YOU

Paying it forward is to react to an act of kindness or support from one person with a similar act to another. I give huge credit to those who have supported my crazy idea to write a book in my *Acknowledgements*. But I wanted to take time to thank any of you who have been kind enough to read the ABCD framework. Whether you have read an early copy to help me develop the ideas, bought a copy, or borrowed a copy from someone.

That feels like an act of kindness to me. It feels great to know that even a handful of people can share some ideas that have helped me significantly improve my life. If anyone can improve their life similarly by reading this book, that is a great way to spread these classic ideas through people's consciousness at a time when things can be challenging to say the least.

Thank you so much, and I will try to keep sharing these ideas wherever possible to help others feel a bit more content.

Pause for Thought – Please take time to make some notes:

13

CONCLUSIONS

'When we live with Authenticity, Balance, Consistency, and Discipline, we have a greater chance of being our true self. Building the vital confidence in our thoughts and actions – ABCD provides the building blocks for HAPPINESS!'[159]
– Nicholas Bunney.[160]

ITS THE END OF OUR JOURNEY – BUT NOT YOURS

Now IT'S TIME to begin your journey using the ABCD framework.

I hope the ideas within it are helpful. They have improved my life enormously, and I know my problems and desires are not a million miles from yours. Many of us are exposed to the same ideas, the same influences, and the same information as each other. We all have similar problems, similar wants, and similar needs. Crucially, this book will be helpful to so many; we all face the same challenge of balancing authentic aims with a happy existence.

By taking the journey, you have taken with me on these pages; I hope you have learned some valuable lessons. They won't all resonate with you, but I feel the process of uncovering these points in the given order is powerful and robust. By looking at your happiness and the problems you face before learning what some experts believe, you add structure and a narrative of critical, flexible, and compassionate thinking to your storyline.

Suppose you can harness the power of honest review, taking back authorship of your own story, which past exposures and a deluge of information have obscured. You will start to feel some extraordinary benefits.

Some straightforward techniques have been included to act as guides, not prescriptions, of how you might conduct this review. They aim to amalgamate the key lessons within each

---

[159] Bunney, N. J. (2023) *ABCD: Finding Happiness through Awareness, Values, Principles and Actions*
[160] Sorry – I've always wanted to have my work cited so this could be the only chance I get!

ABCD element and help you bring some of this wisdom to your own life. As many have experienced, including me, by having this level of awareness and intention, even forgetting the possible successes for a moment, you will be living a better life. Stop treating living as a *noun* and start seeing it as a *verb*.

Take an active role in managing your life.

Of course, many of you are perfectly happy with how your life is going and will be expecting to see significant results from this process.

The case for you experiencing success by using *ABCD* is strong. Of course, only you can make the changes that lead to your achievements. However, if you believe in what you do because it is authentic, you enjoy your life outside of your core goals because you understand the balance between them and your life; you see far greater consistency due to this sustainable approach. Thus, your chance of discipline is elevated because you will turn up regularly.

This is the best way to approach any ambition. Many of the most successful people who have ever lived became successful because they loved what they were doing and worked hard at it. This is only possible when you apply the teachings that you have discovered in the ABCD framework.

This way, you will avoid burnout and overwhelm by enjoying every day and knowing what is important to you deep down –even in your failures; you are happy with your efforts.

In place of anxiety about outcomes is a quiet confidence that your best is *always* good enough.

With this confidence comes an unexpected space within. The congested and anxious mindset you once found is gone. In its place, a sense of calm and added bandwidth can be used to focus more effectively on your core values and goals and helping others. A better partner, parent, friend, colleague, and mentor. Those around you will be happier due to the simple efforts encouraged in this book. My relationships and connection with others changed unrecognisably once I better understood myself and focused my attention correctly.

I am *happier* due to *ABCD,* and it will do the same for you.

So don't wait for *yet*, or perfection; life is too short – it must be enjoyed today. Good luck.

IT'S THE BEGINNING OF YOUR JOURNEY

Nicholas Bunney

14

ABCD WORKSHEETS

'The ability to simplify means to eliminate the unnecessary so that the necessary may speak.'
– Hans Hoffmann.

I AGREE WITH THE ABOVE quote from German-American artist Hans Hoffmann. Life is complicated, and there is so much to take in. I began this book by speaking about how overwhelming life is and how we are overexposed to the point of inaction; choices and information paralyse us. Simplicity is crucial.

So here, I summarise the techniques that make up the ABCD framework and provide blank worksheets for you to use in your own review:

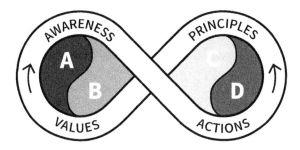

Fig 14.1

ABCD FRAMEWORK

CORE VALUE PRIORITISATION
Consider what is important to you

WHY? WHY? WHY?
Dig deeper into the real authentic reason and amend values/goals

TIMEBOXING
Understand the time you can sustainably give

VALUE DIALS
Balance your values/goals alongside other areas of your life

PERSONAL CONSISTENCY PYRAMID
Visualise what principles/sub-goals would move
you from the start to the finish

VALUES AND PRINCIPLES MAP
Decide the small next steps that require consistency
to form your principles/sub-goals

SPECIFIC AND CHALLENGING TIMELINES
Refine the values/goals to be the right level
of challenge to drive motivation

CASE STUDIES
Regularly note positive results and take confidence
that you have what it takes to succeed

ABCD ——————— **CORE VALUE PRIORITISATION** ———————

Q1. Pick up to 10 areas of your life that are most important

1._____   6._____
2._____   7._____
3._____   8._____
4._____   9._____
5._____   10._____

Q2. Can you control outcomes in these areas – YES/NO/PARTIAL?

1. **YES / NO / PARTIAL**   5. **YES / NO / PARTIAL**   8. **YES / NO / PARTIAL**
2. **YES / NO / PARTIAL**   6. **YES / NO / PARTIAL**   9. **YES / NO / PARTIAL**
3. **YES / NO / PARTIAL**   7. **YES / NO / PARTIAL**   10. **YES / NO / PARTIAL**
4. **YES / NO / PARTIAL**

Q3. If you have partial control what part can you control?

1._____   5._____   8._____
2._____   6._____   9._____
3._____   7._____   10._____
4._____

Q4. In 2-3 words, how does improvement in these areas enrich your life?

1._____   5._____   8._____
2._____   6._____   9._____
3._____   7._____   10._____
4._____

Q5. Considering Q1 - Q4 – Honestly select up to 5 areas to focus on

1._____   3._____   5._____
2._____   4._____

Q6. With possible Core Values/Goals in mind - Re-phrase the above as...

I am the type of person who...

1._____   3._____   5._____
2._____   4._____

Q7. Considering Q6 - Write your 'Core Values/Goals' in full

My core values/goals are...

1.	2.	3.	4.	5.

Fig 14.2 – Core Value Prioritisation

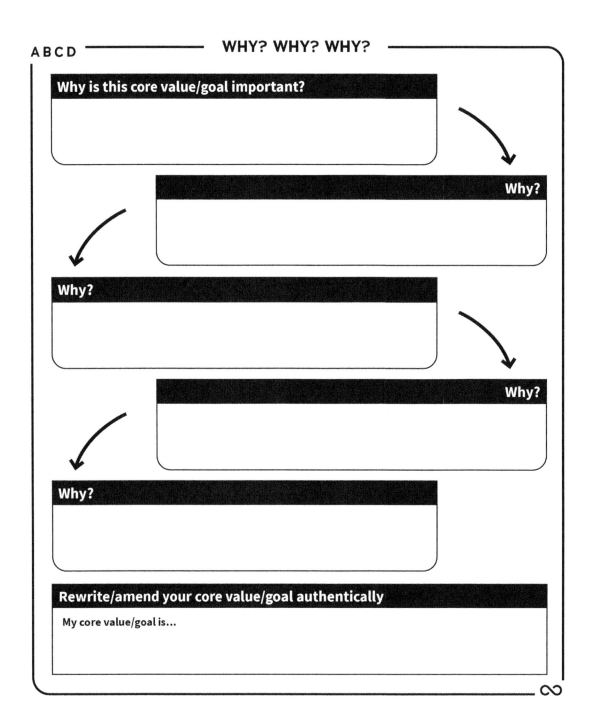

Fig 14.3 – Why? Why? Why?

TIMEBOXING

ABCD

Questions to consider	Sunday	Saturday	Friday	Thursday	Wednesday	Tuesday	Monday
In pencil complete a typical week (everything)							
How many spare hours are there?							
How many hours are spent advancing your values/goals?							
Are you happy with this?							
Can any items that don't feed your values/goals be reduced?							
Re-write (in pen) how you want the week to look							
How many hours can you realistically spare for your core values/goals?							

AM   PM   NIGHT

8

Fig 14.4 — Timeboxing

A B C D ———————————— VALUE DIALS ——————

Core Value/Goal	
Where on the dial is your current effort (SATISFACTORY Y/N)	
Moving to AB means	Moving to CD means
Move dial to balance position in relation to life and other values/goals	

Core Value/Goal	
Where on the dial is your current effort (SATISFACTORY Y/N)	
Moving to AB means	Moving to CD means
Move dial to balance position in relation to life and other values/goals	

Core Value/Goal	
Where on the dial is your current effort (SATISFACTORY Y/N)	
Moving to AB means	Moving to CD means
Move dial to balance position in relation to life and other values/goals	

Core Value/Goal	
Where on the dial is your current effort (SATISFACTORY Y/N)	
Moving to AB means	Moving to CD means
Move dial to balance position in relation to life and other values/goals	

Fig 14.5 – Value Dials

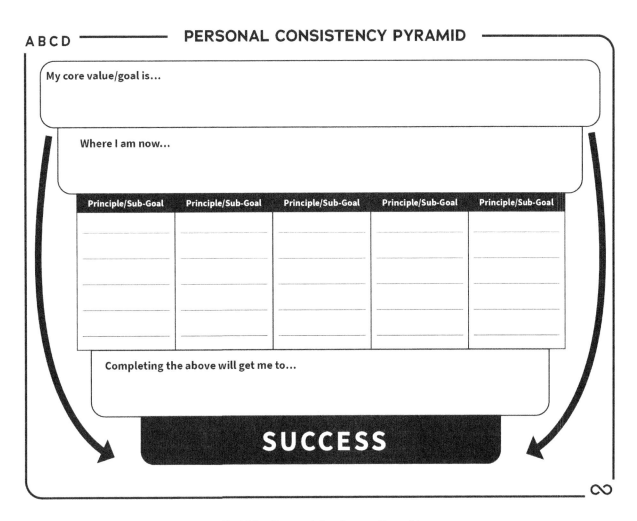

Fig 14.6 – Personal Consistency Pyramid

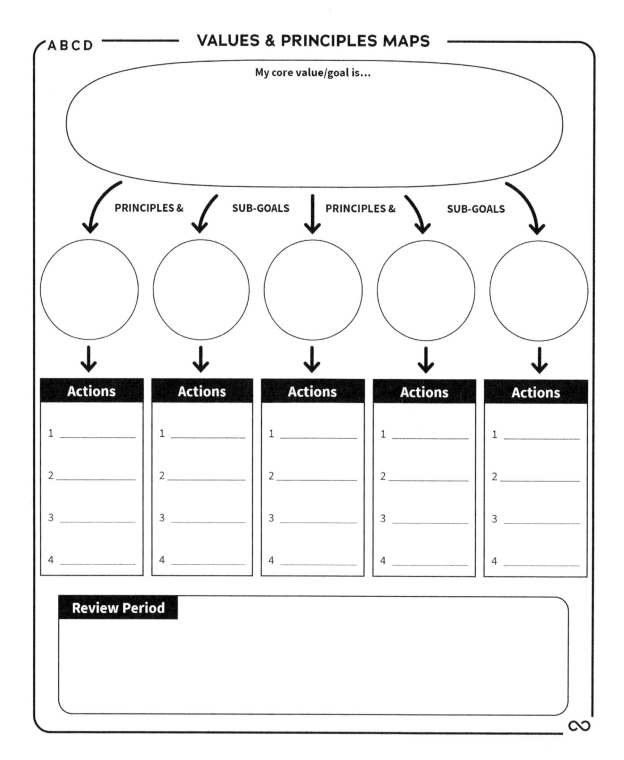

Fig 14.7 – Values and Principles Map

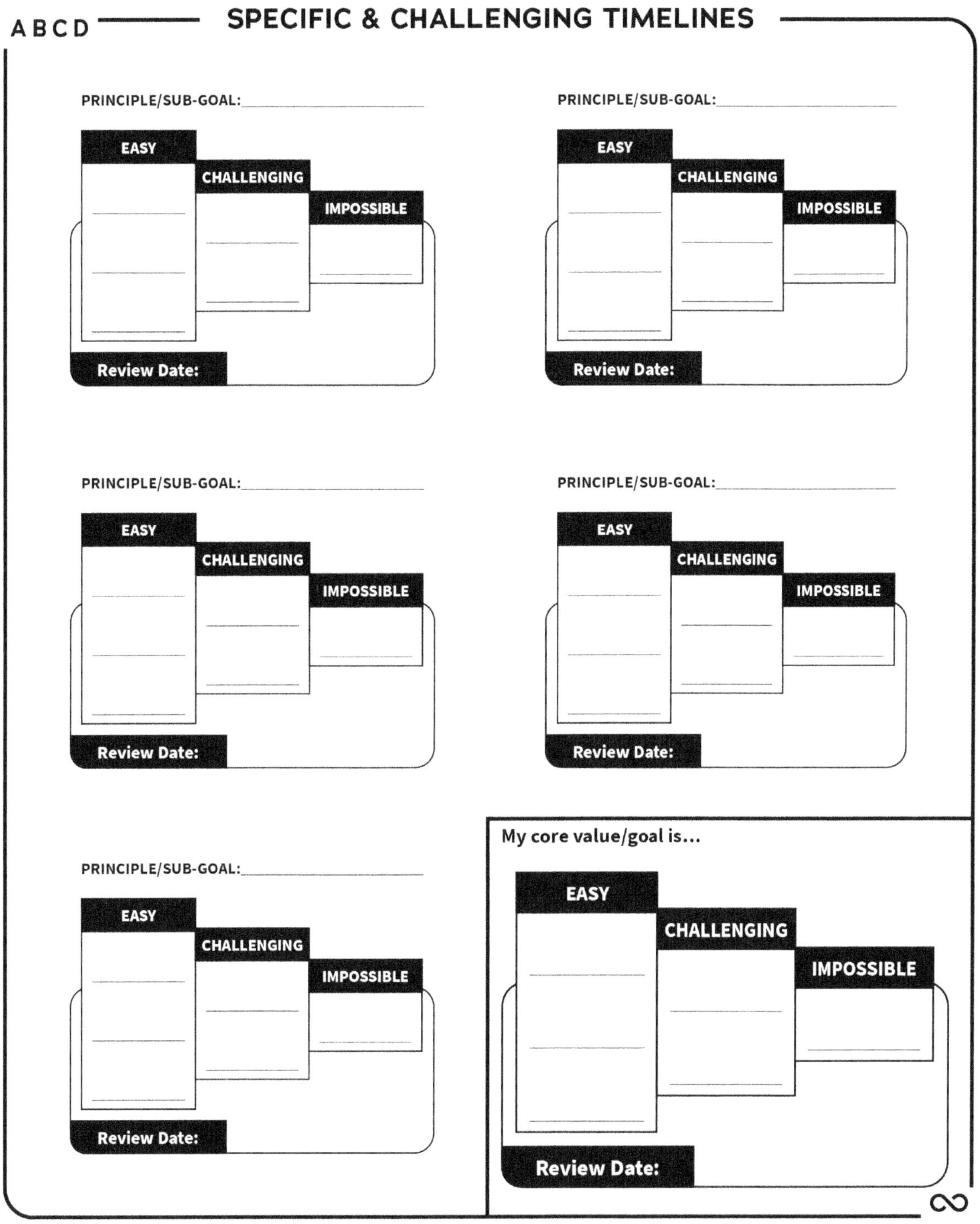

A B C D ——— SPECIFIC & CHALLENGING TIMELINES ———

PRINCIPLE/SUB-GOAL:_____

EASY
CHALLENGING
IMPOSSIBLE

Review Date:

PRINCIPLE/SUB-GOAL:_____

EASY
CHALLENGING
IMPOSSIBLE

Review Date:

PRINCIPLE/SUB-GOAL:_____

EASY
CHALLENGING
IMPOSSIBLE

Review Date:

PRINCIPLE/SUB-GOAL:_____

EASY
CHALLENGING
IMPOSSIBLE

Review Date:

PRINCIPLE/SUB-GOAL:_____

EASY
CHALLENGING
IMPOSSIBLE

Review Date:

My core value/goal is...

EASY
CHALLENGING
IMPOSSIBLE

Review Date:

Fig 14.8 – Specific and Challenging Timelines

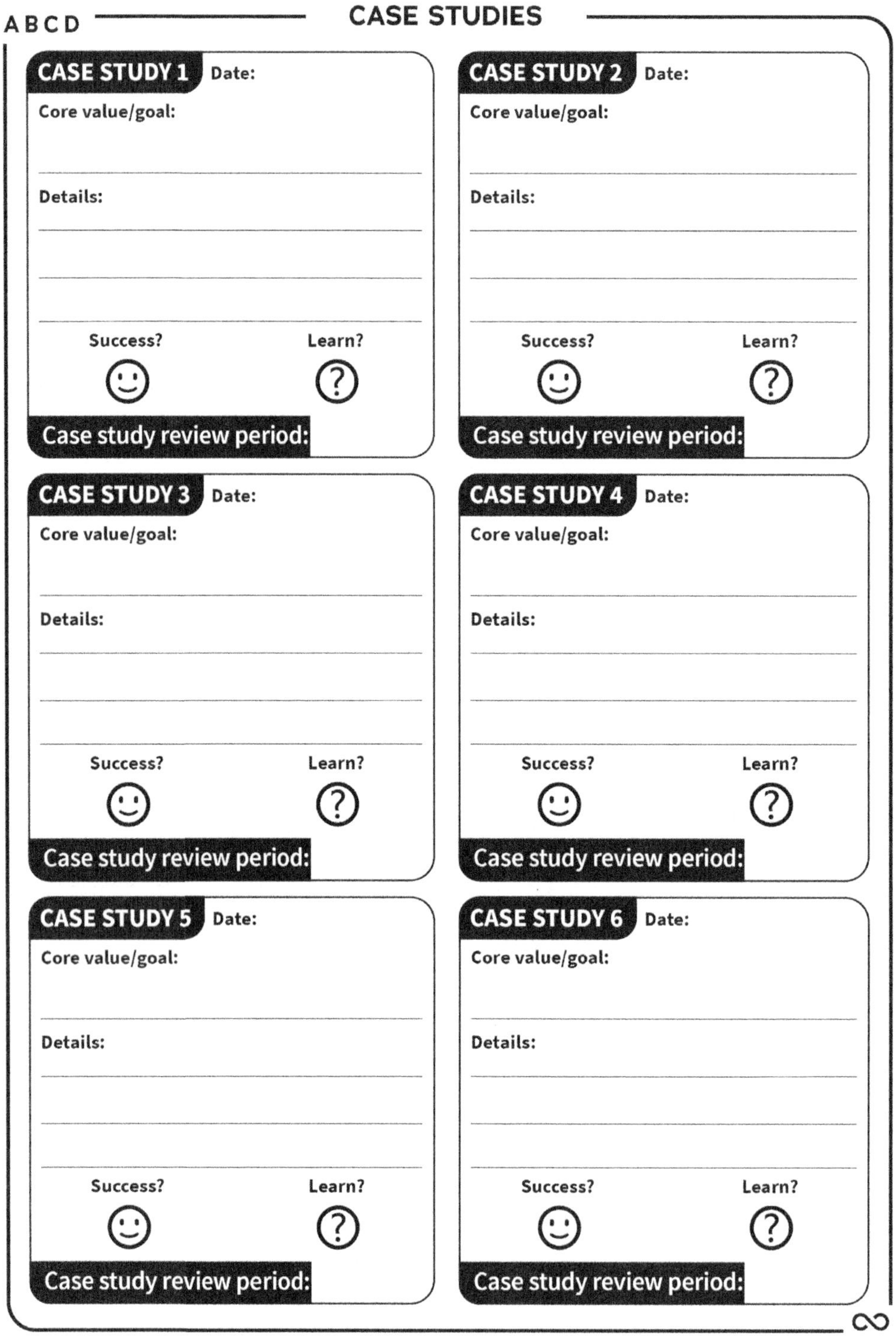

A B C D ———————— CASE STUDIES ————————

CASE STUDY 1 Date:

Core value/goal:

_____

Details:

_____
_____
_____

Success?   Learn?
🙂   ⍰

Case study review period:

CASE STUDY 2 Date:

Core value/goal:

_____

Details:

_____
_____
_____

Success?   Learn?
🙂   ⍰

Case study review period:

CASE STUDY 3 Date:

Core value/goal:

_____

Details:

_____
_____
_____

Success?   Learn?
🙂   ⍰

Case study review period:

CASE STUDY 4 Date:

Core value/goal:

_____

Details:

_____
_____
_____

Success?   Learn?
🙂   ⍰

Case study review period:

CASE STUDY 5 Date:

Core value/goal:

_____

Details:

_____
_____
_____

Success?   Learn?
🙂   ⍰

Case study review period:

CASE STUDY 6 Date:

Core value/goal:

_____

Details:

_____
_____
_____

Success?   Learn?
🙂   ⍰

Case study review period:

Fig 14.9 – Case Studies

Pause for Thought – Please take time to make some notes:

REFERENCES

BOOKS CITED

Aristotle. (c330BC) *Nicomachean Ethics: Books II–V: Concerning excellence of character or moral virtue.*

Brown, B. (2018) *The Gifts of Imperfection: Let Go of Who You Think You're Supposed to Be and Embrace Who You Are.*

Brown, D. (2016) *Happy: Why more or less everything is absolutely fine.*

Carr, A. et al. (2015) *Stop Drinking Now.*

Chatterjee, Dr R. (2022) *Happy Mind, Happy Life.*

Covey, S. R. (1989) *The 7 Habits of Highly Effective People.*

Cox, C. (1922) *Listen To This.*

Csikszentmihalyi, M. (2002) *Flow – The classic work on how to achieve happiness.*

Descartes, R. (1637) *Discourse on the Method of Rightly Conducting One's Reason and of Seeking Truth in the Sciences.*

Dryden, W. (1994) *10 Steps to Positive Living.*

Durkheim, E. (1897) *Le suicide: Etude de sociologie.*

Easter, M. (2021) *The Comfort Crisis: Embrace Discomfort to Reclaim Your Wild, Happy, Healthy Self.*

Epictetus. (c108AD) *Discourses.*

Epictetus. (c125 CE) *Enchiridion of Epictetus.*

Gladwell, M. (2008) *Outliers: The Story of Success.*

Grace, A. (2018) *This Naked Mind: Control Alcohol.*

Hammond, M. (2006) *The Meditations of Marcus Aurelius.*

Holiday, R. (2014) *The Obstacle is the Way.*

Holiday, R. and Hanselman, S. (2016) *The Daily Stoic.*

Iliopoulos, K. K. (2012) *Living in Light, Love & Truth: Change Your Life Positively.*

Kahneman, D. (2011) *Thinking, Fast and Slow.*

McRaven, W. H. (2017) *Make Your Bed: Little Things That Can Change Your Life...And Maybe the World.*

Machlup, F. (1962) *The Production and Distribution of Knowledge in the United States.*

McConaughey, M. (2020) *Greenlights.*

Nelson, P (1977) *There's a Hole in My Sidewalk: The Romance of Self-Discovery.*

Sacks, O. (2012) *Hallucinations.*

Schopenhauer, A. (1851) *Councils and Maxims.*

Seligman, Dr M. (2012) *PERMA.*

Seneca. (c AD64) *On Providence.*

Shakespeare, W. (c1599-1601) *The Tragedy of Hamlet, Prince of Denmark.*

Wilson, R. and Branch, R. (2006) *Cognitive Behavioural Therapy for Dummies.*

Zahn, T. (2013) *Star Wars: Scoundrels.*

ARTICLES AND STUDIES CITED

Berne, E. (1957 and 1958) 'Ego states in psychotherapy' and 'Transactional analysis: Anew and effective method of group therapy' – *American Journal of Psychotherapy,* 11(2) and 12(4).

Buckley, C. and Nerantzi, C. (2020) 'Effective Use of Visual Representation in Research and Teaching within Higher Education' – *International Journal of Management and Applied Research*, Vol.7, No.3.

Doran, Miller & Cunningham (1981) 'There's a S.M.A.R.T way to write management goals and objectives' – *Management Review*, Vol. 70, Issue 11.

Erikson, E. (1959) 'Identity and the Life Cycle' – *Psychological Issues,* Vol 1, No.1.

Griffiths, M. D., Demetrovics, Z. et al. (2016) 'Problematic social media use: Results from a large-scale nationally representative adolescent sample' - *PLoS ONE,* Vol 12(1), Article e0169839.

Huang, S. and Jin, L. and Zhang, Y. (2017) 'Step by Step: Sub-Goals as a Source of Motivation' –– *Organizational Behaviour and Human Decision Processes,* July 2017, Vol. 141, Pages 1-15

Grossman, I. and Kross, E. – (2014) 'Exploring Solomon's Paradox: Self Distancing Eliminates the Self-Other Asymmetry in Wise Reasoning About Close Relationships in Younger and Older Adults' – *Psychological Science,* Vol.25, Issue 8.

Jagannath, A. et al. (2017) 'The genetics of circadian rhythms, sleep and health' –– *Human Molecular Genetics*, Volume 26, Issue R2, 01.

Locke, E. A. (1968) 'Toward a theory of task motivation and incentives' –– *Organizational Behaviour and Human Performance*, Volume 3, Issue 2.

Maslow, A. H. (1943) 'A Theory of Human Motivation' - *Psychological Review*, 50, 370-396.

Ortiz-Ospina, E. and Giattino, C. and Roser, M. (2020) 'Time Use' – www.ourworld-indata.org

'Are You Addicted to Social Media?' – *www.leehealth.org*

'Dr. Anna Lembke: Pain, Pleasure, and the addictive chase for Dopamine' – *www.finding-mastery.net*

'How Much Data is Created Every Day in 2022' - *https://techjury.net/blog/how-much-data-is-created-every-day/#gref*

O'Neil, A. (2022) 'Life Expectancy (from birth) in the United Kingdom from 1765 to 2020' –- *https://www.statista.com/*

'National Life Tables – life expectancy in the UK: 2018 to 2020' – *www.ons.gov.uk*

Friscia, A. (2021) 'Opinion commentary – Social Media connects us to one another, creates reality disconnect' – *www.theslateonline.com*

'Research and development expenditure of leading internet companies from 2014 to 2021' – *www.statista.com*

'Sleep Survey' – *Chemist 4 U* (carried out by One Poll 2018) - *https://www.chemist-4-u.com/sleep-study/*

'Suicide rate in the United Kingdom (UK) from 2000 to 2020' – *www.statista.com*

'UK: daily hours spend on mobile 2019-2021' – *www.statista.com*

'UK's internet use surges to record levels' - *https://www.ofcom.org.uk/*

'Why You Are The Way You Are' – *www.tonyrobbins.com*

'You Now Have a Shorter Attention Span Than a Goldfish' – *www.time.com*

MEDIA CITED

Chasing Excellence Podcast with Ben Bergeron.

Farnam Street – Learning Community - *https://fs.blog/*

Freeze the Fear – BBC1 (April-May 2022).

I AM (movie) – (2010).

LA Leakers YouTube Channel (*www.youtube.com*)

Modern Wisdom Podcast.

TED Talk – 'Why we do the things we do' – Tony Robbins (2006).

The Social Dilemma – Netflix (2020).

'University of Pennsylvania Commencement Address' – Denzel Washington (2011).

OTHERS CITED

www.wikipedia.org (of course!)

Various quotes (from various sources) that I found helpful, funny, and inspiring – I hope they were of use to you too.

ACKNOWLEDGEMENTS

It has been a lifelong ambition to write a book. It was a pleasure to be able to do so, and I've thoroughly enjoyed all the conversations I've had with anyone who would care to listen. But the process is long and often frustrating – it wouldn't be possible without the support and love of the following people.

Firstly, I would like to thank Candice for all your support for the last five years and beyond. I have been selfish at times and continually distracted while editing this book. Thanks for taking the wheel so I could feel safe enough to pursue my dream. Your tireless striving to give your best to our family never ceases to amaze me. I genuinely hope you know that you're doing a fantastic job – I promise to tell you more.

Secondly, to all those who helped me along the way with the support and encouragement I needed. My family for letting me waffle at them about my ideas; Maxi and Sisi for telling people I am an author before I was ready to think of myself as such; my friends for not taking the piss too much out of Nik, the 'Author;' Candice, Mum, Dad, Mem, Milan, Michelle, and Frankee (in spirit at least!) for being my first readers – your feedback was invaluable and helped me so much; Nick Earl – without the work we have done together – I couldn't have translated my thoughts onto the page.

Special thanks also go to Sasha Boyce, my editor, for overcoming anxiety-inducing technical issues to provide me with precious editorial review, line editing, and proofreading. Having studied English and spoken it for 40 years, I was shocked to discover how little I knew about writing it.

Finally, to Wayne Kehoe, my brilliant designer. What I learned from you within two weeks of us meeting was invaluable to publishing this book. Your knowledge has been priceless. Not to mention that you took a quite confusing 200-page scrawl and turned it into something I am so proud of.

Thank you all so very much.

Printed in Great Britain
by Amazon

24511230R00139